JEFFERSON AND THE EMBARGO

JEFFERSON
AND THE EMBARGO

BY

LOUIS MARTIN SEARS

OCTAGON BOOKS

A DIVISION OF FARRAR, STRAUS AND GIROUX

New York   1978

OCTAGON BOOKS
A DIVISION OF FARRAR, STRAUS & GIROUX, INC.
19 Union Square West
New York, N.Y. 10003

LIBRARY OF CONGRESS CATALOG CARD NUMBER: 66-28377
ISBN: 0-374-97220-6

Manufactured by Braun-Brumfield, Inc.
Ann Arbor, Michigan
Printed in the United States of America

TO THE MEMORY OF

LOUISE HAWLEY MARTIN

WHOSE BEAUTIFUL LIFE OF DEVOTION TO DUTY
WAS AN INSPIRATION TO ALL WHO KNEW HER
THIS BOOK IS DEDICATED WITH THE
COMPLETE AFFECTION OF
HER GRANDSON

PREFACE

Some years ago, the author prepared for the Chicago Literary Club a study of Jefferson as a pacifist. In the course of his work, he became so interested in the philosophy of Jefferson that he set himself the larger task of indicating the practical working out of the pacific theories which Jefferson so inspiringly enunciated. This carried him through Jefferson's contribution to the foreign policy of Washington and the theories of international law which governed his own administration, to a review of the embargo as the practical culmination of Jeffersonian pacifism, and led him to certain conclusions, which, while not revolutionary in their character, seem to indicate a somewhat different Jefferson from the model so ably set by Henry Adams.

First, it would seem that in urging the embargo Jefferson was pursuing not a hasty opportunism, but rather the logic of his entire philosophy of life. Secondly, the exigencies of the situation revealed Jefferson as an administrator of a high order, a phase of Jefferson's ability which has been generally slighted, perhaps from an instinctive assumption that philosophers and practical men do not inhabit the same body.

A fresh examination of the Jefferson Papers, especially of the letters to Jefferson, reveals a more generous support for the embargo than it has been customary to represent, and shows, besides, in certain localities a remarkable prosperity, fostered by the opportunity of a closed market, and inviting the investment of capital formerly tied up in shipping. In its aggressive aspect, the embargo must be judged by its material and moral effect upon Great Britain and France. And the present study suggests with respect to Great Britain what the elaborate examination by Dr. Frank

Edgar Melvin of "Napoleon's Continental System" confirms for France, that the actual pressure was severe, and came far nearer to producing the desired result than the enemies of Jefferson, or even his friends, perceived. Like many a more martial conflict, this warfare of self-denial brought success much nearer to the vanquished than was comfortable for the victors.

To the members of the staff of the Division of Manuscripts in the Library of Congress, as well as to Dr. C. O. Paullin of the Carnegie Institution in Washington, I desire to express my thanks for many courtesies in the prosecution of my researches. To the editors of The *American Political Science Review, The Quarterly Journal of Economics, The South Atlantic Quarterly,* and the *American Historical Association, Annual Reports,* are due my grateful acknowledgment of their kind permission to reprint chapters and parts of chapters which originally appeared under their auspices. Chapter II, *Jefferson and the Law of Nations,* appeared originally in the *American Political Science Review* for August, 1919, and has subsequently been translated into Spanish for *Inter-America.* Chapter VII, *The Middle States and the Embargo,* appeared in part under that title in the *South Atlantic Quarterly* for April, 1922. Other portions of this chapter may be found in the *Quarterly Journal of Economics,* February, 1921, under notes on *Philadelphia and the Embargo of 1808.* Some of this same material is covered also in the *Annual Report of the American Historical Association* for 1920, under the same caption as above. Chapter VIII, *The South and the Embargo,* appeared originally in the *South Atlantic Quarterly* for July, 1921. Chapter X, *British Industry and the American Embargo* first appeared in the *Quarterly Journal of Economics* of November, 1919.

I take this opportunity to express my gratitude for helpful criticism to Professor William E. Dodd of the University of Chicago, whose learning has been an inspiration and whose friendship an encouragement for many years. To Professors Andrew Cunningham McLaughlin and Conyers Read, I am also much indebted for a reading of the manuscript, and for numerous suggestions of value to the work in its earlier form as a doctoral dissertation at the University of Chicago. Professor William K. Boyd, and William T. Laprade, of Duke University, and Professor Arthur H. Hirsch, of Ohio Wesleyan University, have placed me under deep obligation by their further and careful examination of the manuscript and by their helpful suggestions toward its progress through the press.

Also, I wish to call attention to the excellent monograph on "The American Embargo 1807-1809," by Walter Wilson Jennings, Ph.D., in the "University of Iowa Studies in the Social Sciences."

I cannot conclude these words of preface without tribute to the letters of Jefferson. They are more than masterpieces of epistolary art. They are source material for what Mr. Gamaliel Bradford calls psychography. They are the delineation of a great soul, whose struggles for the welfare of mankind should never cease to interest the humanity he sought to serve.

L. M. S.

CONTENTS

JEFFERSON AND THE EMBARGO

CHAPTER I

THE UNDERLYING POINT OF VIEW

When Thomas Jefferson, in December, 1807, gave executive approval to the embargo on American ships and goods, he carried theory into practice and put to the test perhaps the most perfect substitute for war up to that time devised. There was abundant provocation for war itself. The European belligerents, Great Britain and France, locked in a death grapple for world power, recognized no neutral right they felt bound to respect, and the bankrupt diplomacy of each spurned with utter fatuity a good will which should have been invaluable. What between the tightening blockade by Great Britain on the one hand and the impotent but exasperating retaliations of Napoleon on the other, America, as the chief of neutral carriers, either must fight the mistress of the seas and the foremost of land tyrants in a triangular combination, or else she must submit to outrages intolerable for a sovereign state, however modest its position in the world concert. To Jefferson the former course appeared quixotic; the latter, unthinkable. The alternative was to stay at home and preserve our flag from the insults it was certain to meet on the high seas or in French ports. In the nature of a compromise measure, the embargo contained features common to both war and submission. An embargo, to be satisfactory, had not merely to safeguard our own shipping; it had also to awaken European consumers to the folly of their governments in cutting them off from needed supplies. In this sense the embargo was coercive, a close kinsman to the blockade as a form of actual warfare. In another sense the embargo was submissive, a twin brother to surrender, for it was idle to imagine that those rights were defended whose possessor dared not even assert them. But, as the world was situated in 1807, this intermediate position seemed to its sponsor his country's only outlet from a sea of difficulties. It was the matured policy of a lifelong hatred for war. One cannot understand Jefferson's initiation of the embargo and his subsequent relation to its enforcement without examining his point of view as it ripened into pacifism. For the embargo was the practical outcome of a philosophy long maturing. It was the projection into foreign affairs of the peace ideals of a democracy, the contribution to international polity of one of the world's greatest democrats.

The clew to Jefferson's sentiments on war and peace alike is his democracy, his confidence in the innate virtue and intelligence of mankind and its potentiality for self-government. He believed in the power of self-government and education to uplift the common man and waged a lifelong warfare with the strait-jacket ideal designed to enthrall and exploit him. But the very intensity of his democratic conviction proclaimed Jefferson a thinker rather than a man of action, a philosopher and theorist rather than an executive. And if the embargo appears more plausible in theory than successful in practice, it merely shares the characteristics of its sponsor. To understand the measure, one must needs know the man. Only as his democracy and his pacifism are revealed can we explain the embargo as their outcome.

Jefferson's early reputation in Virginia rested upon public spirit and reform policies rather than upon proved capacity for leadership. His contribution to the Revolution was the Declaration of Independence, not his rather helpless career as war governor of the State. The Federal Union employed him to best advantage as the messenger of liberty to its friends beyond the sea. His principal service after his return was to organize democratic opposition to the privileged orders in eastern cities into a political victory in 1800, which saved the Union from western secession. Executive detail interested him little, and his presidency was distinguished rather by a grasp of future needs and restraint under provocation than by brilliancy of administration. In retirement, he was the Sage of Monticello, an oracle, but chiefly a spectator, devoting his last strength to the cause of education, the foundation stone in his scheme of democracy. But among the interests of his long and varied career, the cause of peace held permanent place.

The truth of this appears in the midst of the Revolution. Although one does not look to Thomas Jefferson for a military history of the American Revolution, yet his references to its operation are surprisingly few. He understood that final success would depend largely upon sea power, and, in the absence of this element of victory, as early as July, 1774, when the Boston Port Bill was agitating the colonies, he advocated a non-importation agreement against all goods subject to British entry duties.[1] Again, when the Continental currency commenced to depreciate, partly for lack of a foreign market, Jefferson favored either free trade, supported by alliance with a strong naval power,[2] or else complete non-importation.[3] In this recommendation of non-importation, Jefferson was already promulgating the great pacific formula of his presidential term, while naval power, though anathema to his ideals, was, ironically enough, to claim him as its father.

Of interest, in the light of the recent disposition to attribute French intervention after Saratoga to the fear that Great Britain and America were about to conclude a peace

[1] *The Works of Thomas Jefferson.* Federal Edition, II. 42-44. "Resolutions of Albemarle County."

[2] *Ibid.,* II. 307. See also III. 249, Jefferson to DeLaLuzerne on the utility of sea power.

[3] *Ibid.,* II. 307. See also II. 491, 502, which foreshadow his later embargo policy.

and wage joint war upon the French West Indies,[4] is a letter from Jefferson to Franklin intimating such a possibility unless Franklin exerted himself to prevent it.[5] Franklin did his part, and France intervened, but two years later (1779) Jefferson was so weary of war, though as yet its fury had not touched Virginia, that he preferred "a ten years' war sometime hence" to one unnecessary moment of the present.[6]

Bitterly as he detested the war, upon occasion he could commend to Washington the honorable conduct of the foe.[7] Nor was he indifferent to British prisoners in detention camps. His appeal to Governor Henry not to sacrifice the comfort and happiness of prisoners to petty whims of economy—a shaft at his excellency's principal vice—was in keeping with a plan to encourage Hessian settlements within the state. Toward this end, during his own term as governor, he proclaimed a grant of two cows and exemption from taxes and militia duty to such Hessians and other foreigners as would abandon the British cause and take up land in Virginia. This consideration for enemy mercenaries is evidence of Jefferson's broad humanity.

Indeed, fair treatment to the enemy was parcel of the humanitarianism which Jefferson accounted the dignity of civilized warfare. He congratulated himself in the early days of the war that the refinements of civilization were ameliorating the lot of prisoners, "so that an enemy is an object of vengeance, in arms and in the field only."[8] But war proved less an exchange of knightly courtesies than he had anticipated, and British atrocities soon led him to justify American retaliation as the sole means of stopping the

[4] C. H. Van Tyne, "Influences which Determined the French Government to Make the Treaty with America, 1778," *American Historical Review*, XXI. No. 3. April, 1916.
[5] *The Works of Thomas Jefferson*, II. 307.
[6] *Ibid.*, II. 375.
[7] *Ibid.*, III. 84.
[8] *Ibid.*, II. 145-146.

progress of human butchery.[9] In his rôle of casuist, Jefferson represented a twentieth-century type. But it was, in truth, difficult to preserve generous ideals against an enemy like Tarleton, and, in his term as governor, Jefferson was compelled to threaten retaliation against prisoners and to justify his case by depositions from Virginia captives, whose tales of horror influenced their hearer to an analysis of British civilization which would edify its most irreconcilable opponents of today:

> The present war having so long cut off all communication with Great Britain, we are not able to make a fair estimate of the state of science in that country. The spirit in which she wages war, is the only sample before our eyes, and that does not seem the legitimate offspring either of science or of civilization. The sun of her glory is fast descending to the horizon. Her Philosophy has crossed the channel, her freedom the Atlantic, and herself seems passing to that awful dissolution whose issue is not given human foresight to scan.[10]

In his executive capacity, Jefferson came into intimate contact with military discouragements[11] through his nominal command of the militia. He found it a poor tool, yet all his life he remained an advocate of voluntary in preference to professional military service. That the militia of the Revolution was a poor reliance appeared to Jefferson no justification for the curse of standing armies, and no excuse to the citizen for the evasion of his highest duty. His solution was to improve the existing system.

It was in character that an individualist and democrat should shun excess of military discipline, so that one is not surprised to find that Jefferson's "Draft of a Bill for Providing against Invasions and Insurrections" provided no heavier military punishment than degrading, cashiering, drumming out of the army, and whipping not to exceed

[9] *The Works of Thomas Jefferson,* II. 147.
[10] *Ibid.,* III. 461.
[11] *Ibid.,* II. 487.

twenty lashes, even for the most serious offences.[12]   Yet even these rules were more rigorous than Virginians were disciplined to obey,[13] and, at a critical juncture in 1781, Jefferson was under the humiliating necessity of admitting to La Fayette that it was not in his power "to do any thing more than to represent to the General Assembly that unless they can provide more effectually for the Execution of the Laws it will be vain to call on Militia."[14]

The service was, in truth, no object lesson in efficiency. Jefferson complained that it was easy to evade, expensive to the public, distressing and disgusting to individuals,[15] and not reliable for long campaigns or for use in distant counties.[16]   Militiamen were too proud to work on the fortifications[17] but not ashamed to steal the arms and ammunition which the state had provided.[18]

The whole militia system threatened to collapse before a British device for disarming entire regions under temporary occupation by placing the inhabitants under parole.   This general parole afforded a favorite evasion of military duty to pusillanimous Colonists, who even courted the oath as a conscientious excuse for shirking their duty to the state. Jefferson combatted the evil in a circular letter to the county lieutenants, urging all whose consciences forbade their taking up arms to take refuge behind the British lines.[19]   If, however, any chose to break parole and to aid their countrymen, Jefferson made it clear that he would not send them back to the British.[20]   He took the proper ground of Americanism

[12] *The Works of Thomas Jefferson,* II. 301. V. S. A. May 10, 1777.
[13] *Ibid.,* III. 214.
[14] *Ibid.,* III. 280.
[15] *Ibid.,* III. 192.
[16] *Ibid.,* III. 200.
[17] *Ibid.,* III. 277.
[18] *Ibid.,* III. 231.
[19] *Ibid.,* III. 145.
[20] *Ibid.,* III. 152.

and common sense, that "He is a bad citizen who can enter-
tain a doubt whether the Law will justify him in saving his
country or who will scruple to risk himself in support of the
spirit of a Law where unavoidable Accidents have prevented
a literal compliance with it."[21]

Notwithstanding the tribulations of unpreparedness, Jefferson was not easily discouraged by his countrymen, even
if at times he was compelled to reduce his expectations of
their immediate achievements. He refused to sacrifice the
ideals of his life to momentary exigencies, and, in 1779,
while the war was pressing on, he found time for the more
congenial task of drafting "A Bill for the Amending of the
Constitution of the College of William and Mary," in which
he recited the great need of a training school for "the
future guardians of the rights and liberties of their country."[22]

It was no part of Jefferson's plan, one is assured, to subject those liberties to military despotism. An old complaint
against George III was his quartering of British troops in
America without consent.[23] The constitutions which Jefferson proposed for Virginia in 1776[24] and in 1783[25]
guarded against executive tyranny by intrusting military
prerogative to the legislative branch. A decidedly acrimonious letter from Jefferson to Steuben[26] complains of a self-
important quartermaster to whom "We did not think it
proper to resign ourselves and our Country implicity—but
thought we had some right of judgment left to us," while
one of the most spirited passages in the *Notes on Virginia*[27]
protests against the infamy of even the suggestion to betray

[21] *The Works of Thomas Jefferson*, III. 147.
[22] *Ibid.*, II. 432.
[23] *Ibid.*, II. 86.
[24] *Ibid.*, II. 171.
[25] *Ibid.*, IV. 147-166.
[26] *Ibid.*, III. 212, 213.
[27] *Ibid.*, IV. 34.

the cause of liberty throughout the world by summoning a dictator to the rescue of a free people. "What clause in our constitution," demands Jefferson, "has substituted that of Rome, by way of residuary provision, for all cases not otherwise provided for?"[28]

Peculiarly congenial to such a spirit as Jefferson's, therefore, must have been the task of drawing up rules of etiquette for Washington's Farewell to Congress upon surrendering his military commission. Great as were the General's merits, he must subordinate himself to civil law. In the brief formula of Jefferson, "When the General rises to make his address, and also when he retires, he is to bow to Congress, which they are to return by uncovering without bowing."[29]

As was to be expected, Jefferson welcomed peace in a hearty spirit of conciliation[30] and was solicitous that it exist among as well as within the states.[31] But the real significance of the Revolution for Jefferson's later pacificism lies in a philosophical residuum best defined in a celebrated passage from the *Notes on Virginia* (1782). Though he asserts that the military resources of Virginia and of the Federation are considerable, he deprecates their employment against any European power, England not excepted, preferring that American energies be devoted to the development of a continent. He is a prose Hamlet pitting in argument the increment of production against the false arithmetic of war. And, although he advocates an open door and perfect freedom for necessary commerce, he would cheerfully abandon the ocean altogether for the sake of a universal agriculture. Nevertheless, since America had already chosen the path of commerce, in which occasional wars would be inevitable,

[28] *The Works of Thomas Jefferson,* IV. 36.
[29] *Ibid.,* IV. 202.
[30] *Ibid.,* IV. 184.
[31] *Ibid.*

preparedness was a duty. Without provoking war, America should resist its shocks. Here the sea, even as it invited war, offered its own security. Land armies would be useless for offence, inadequate for defence. Security depended upon sea power, but not upon naval supremacy. In Jefferson's words :

To aim at such a navy as the greater nations of Europe possess, would be a foolish and wicked waste of the energies of our country-men. It would be to pull on our own heads that load of military expense which makes the European labourer go supperless to bed, and moistens his bread with the sweat of his brows. It will be enough if we enable ourselves to prevent insults from those nations of Europe which are weak on the sea, because circumstances exist, which render even the stronger ones weak as to us.[32]

Naval powers of the first rank could not risk their entire forces in distant waters. America would be her own base of supplies, from which detached territories might readily be seized. Moreover, present resources equal to equipping annually a navy of eighteen hundred guns at a cost of $2,304,000 could be counted upon to double every twenty years, as the country grew in wealth and population. In brief, Jefferson had already molded the ideals and policies of his post-Revolutionary career. An ideal pacifism under-lay a pragmatism and opportunism by no means blind to the continental and even international rôle which America might yet be called to play.

Jefferson was himself to be an empire builder in the great destiny awaiting his country. The interval between the Revolution and his own presidency was for him an indispensable apprenticeship in statecraft. His mission to France and the portfolio of state under Washington, though they necessarily destroyed some illusions of international comity, introduced the needful leaven to convert a Virginia farmer into a patriotic cosmopolitan. If the note of idealism

[32] *The Works of Thomas Jefferson*, IV. 100-102.

seems less pronounced in these years of the new tutelage, the breadth of interest widens as the philosopher of democracy accommodates his theory to the exigencies of an unregenerate world.

In naught was the conflict sharper than between his views of an ideal agricultural state and the needs of an aggressive, commercial people. In this Jefferson made a virtue of necessity. Discarding Chinese exclusiveness as admirable but not practicable, and condemning even free trade as unattainable,[33] though all the world would be the gainer from a free exercise of this "natural right,"[34] Jefferson was concerned to secure commercial treaties favorable to the new nation, even at the bayonet point of a protective tariff.[35]

Closely allied with this strong commercial policy was a scheme for internal improvements, linking the West with the Potomac in order to break the New York and Philadelphia monopoly of trans-Alleghany trade.[36] The cause lay near to his heart, and in 1784 he was urging George Washington to devote to it the years of his retirement. Thus, in the tariff and internal improvements, Jefferson, though by no means the apologist of protection, and though unequivocally opposed to Federal activity where state resources were sufficient, was in some sense anticipating the "American Plan" of a later statesman.

But if he sacrificed something to principle in the field of commercial intercourse, he could inveigh against undemocratic manifestations at home with the full approval of his conscience. The Order of the Cincinnati was his particular detestation. He condemned it as contrary to the Federation, unconstitutional in several states, and foreign to the

[33] *The Works of Thomas Jefferson,* IV. 469.
[34] *Ibid.,* IV. 445; VI. 64.
[35] *Ibid.,* IV. 469-470.
[36] *Ibid.,* IV. 267.

spirit of them all.[37]   He feared its concentration of power
and honor as a menace to the government itself, not only
through its own patronage in the development of a military
aristocracy, but through the corrupt agency of European
powers as well.   He beheld in the Order the seed of a division between the civil and the military authority.[38]   Even its
social and eleemosynary features found no favor with Jefferson.   He foresaw dissensions at its meetings[39] and professed to lament the spirit of dependence which its treasury would ingraft in succeeding generations of loungers and
snobs, "too proud to work, and drawing out a miserable
existence by eating on that surplus of other men's labour
which is the sacred fund of the helpless poor."[40]   The horrible
object lesson of the French aristocracy, among whom Jefferson moved as the minister from his country, rendered him
almost a fanatic in demanding the total extinction of the
Order as the only hope for the republic.[41]

Jefferson's residence at Paris cost the democratic elements in the Constitutional Convention a powerful champion.
But his interpretation to Frenchmen of American political
trends was of value to both countries,[42] while his correspondence with American leaders permitted a silent presentation
of his own views upon the greatest political achievement of
his time.   His admiration for this achievement was great
but not unqualified.   The mildness of the old Congress in
coercing the several states warranted the strengthening of
the Federal arm.[43] But the absence of a bill of rights[44] boded
ill for liberty, particularly in the failure to provide against

[37] *The Works of Thomas Jefferson,* IV. 325.
[38] *Ibid.,* IV. 347.
[39] *Ibid.,* IV. 323-329.
[40] *Ibid.,* V. 59.
[41] *Ibid.,* V. 221-223.
[42] *Ibid.,* V. 16 ff.
[43] *Ibid.,* V. 319.
[44] *Ibid.,* V. 385.

standing armies and suspension of habeas corpus. Notwithstanding these imperfections, already subject to popular censure,[45] he paid tribute to the Constitution as a triumph of
reason over passion, which unhappily the world was too far
oppressed to imitate.[46]

His mission to France brought Jefferson into early touch
with the Algerine question, a sore spot of European diplomacy, and converted him, free trader and pacifist though he
was, into the altogether surprising rôle of a propagandist of
sea power. Yet acceptance of commerce as a legitimate field
of American endeavor inevitably dictated an acquiescence in
naval power as its indispensable concomitant, and the Algerine nuisance merely focused the issue. "Can we begin it
[a navy] on a more honorable occasion," Jefferson repeatedly
asks, "or with a weaker foe?"[47]   Nearer to the scenes of insult than his countrymen at home, he tells us that his facul-
ties were "absolutely suspended between indignation and impotence,"[48] and he assured his American correspondent, with
characteristic scope of vision, that "The motives pleading
for war rather than tribute are numerous and honorable,
those opposing them are mean and short sighted."[49] He held
that power could alone insure the maintenance of peace,[50]
and in its absence he advised Americans to keep out of the
Mediterranean.[51]   Until the United States should be strong
enough for independent action, he recommended a league
with other nations for a perpetual cruise against the Algerines, eight months out of twelve.[52] And he advised Washington to sound Spain for a possible subsidy in return for

[45] The Works of Thomas Jefferson, V. 426.
[46] Ibid., V. 423.
[47] Ibid., IV. 376-377, 390-391, 398.
[48] Ibid., IV. 392.
[49] Ibid., IV. 398. To James Monroe. Paris. February, 1785.
[50] Ibid., V. 106-107. Paris. May 10. 1786.
[51] Ibid., V. 345-346. September 25, 1787.
[52] Ibid., VI. 86. New York. July 4, 1790.

fighting her battle against the pirates.[53] Nor did he relinquish
this idea of a subsidized cruise,[54] even though Congress
preferred to toy with a $40,000 ransom for American cap-
tives.[55]

So pronounced a stand against the Algerines wrought its
logical reflex in a general belligerency of spirit quite out of
plumb with Jefferson's prevailing temper.   In 1788 he was
predicting the Great War so soon to burst over Europe,[56]
and, in sundry aphorisms on the perils of a "want of respectability in the national character,"[57] he warned the nation to
hold itself in readiness for rich plums ripe for the shaking.
A strong front could demand as the price of our neutrality
the opening of much territory then closed to American shippers.[58]

But no prospects of national aggrandizement could
swerve Jefferson from his hostility to standing armies.   He
rejoiced that the new Constitution had muzzled the dog of
war "by transferring the power of letting him loose from the
executive to the Legislative body, from those who are
to spend to those who are to pay."[59]   In 1792 he opposed
increasing the regular army to five thousand men, holding
that fifteen hundred woodsmen would easily end the Indian
war.[60]   And he looked upon the encouragement which Indian uprisings afforded to the war party as their chief inconvenience.[61]

Quite otherwise with sea power, the national specific
against insult,[62] particularly useful against nations with

[53] *The Works of Thomas Jefferson*, VI. 397.
[54] *Ibid.*, VI. 439-440.   March 18, 1792.
[55] *Ibid.*, VI. 473.   April 10, 1792.
[56] *Ibid.*, V. 398-399.
[57] *Ibid.*, V. 79.
[58] *Ibid.*, V. 438.
[59] *Ibid.* VI., 11.
[60] *Ibid.*, VI. 407.
[61] *Ibid.*, VI. 243.
[62] *Ibid.*, IV. 450-51.

stakes in the West Indies.[63] He welcomed (1785) a packet service between Havre and New York as the nucleus of a navy,[64] and deprecated (1788) the failure of Congress to secure Paul Jones for a rear admiral, in order that he might gain experience for that time "when we shall be more populous than the whole British dominions and able to fight them ship to ship,"[65]—a delectable prospect pending solely upon the success of the land office in first ridding us of debt,[66] and not to be compromised by premature forfeiture of legalized piracy in the fitting out of privateers.[67]

Adjusting naval expenditures to the income from land sales was characteristically Jeffersonian. He abhorred national debts,[68] and regarded the license to pile them up as a prime cause of war. The best safeguard against such accumulations of debt seemed to him a limit upon their legal existence. He held that no generation should be permitted to bind its successor by obligations in the incurring of which the latter was not consulted. And he believed that the world's peace would be immeasureably advanced if all loans expired at the end of the nineteen years during which any one generation remained dominant.[69]

On the other hand, it is not surprising that this economic point of view should have led Jefferson to a smug complacency over those world disasters which might profit the United States as a neutral. His moralizings, in 1790, on the prospective war between England and Spain are the calculations of a shop-keeper with a sharp ear for trade. Humanity is subordinated to lucre in dicta like the following: "I

[63] *The Works of Thomas Jefferson*, IV. 451, 400.
[64] *Ibid.*, IV. 435.
[65] *Ibid.*, V. 403.
[66] *Ibid.*, IV. 451.
[67] *Ibid.*, VI. 439.
[68] *Ibid.*, V. 348.
[69] *Ibid.*, VI. 8.

hope peace and profit will be our share."[70]   "Our object is
to feed and theirs to fight. If we are not forced by England,
we shall have a gainful time of it."[71]   "If there be war,
France will probably take part in it.   This we cannot help,
and therefore we must console ourselves with the good price
of wheat which it will bring us."[72]   "Since it is so decreed
by fate, we have only to pray their souldiers may eat a great
deal."[73]

But cynical cash balances are no measure for the many-
sided Jefferson.   Side by side with petty calculations of national loss and gain,[74] he is capable of arguing for observ-
ance of treaty obligations, even when contrary to immediate interests,[75] "under a conviction that . . . stipula-
tions by Treaty are irrevocable but by joint consent, let a
change of circumstances render them ever so burthensome."[76]
He rejoices that the treaty with Prussia sets a precedent for
fair dealing among the nations.[77] Nor does he exclude even
the Indians from the number of those entitled to honorable
treatment.[78] On the contrary, he would exert the power of
government to restrain greedy land grabbers from forcing
America into war merely to serve their own wicked purposes.[79]

The military arm should be wielded not in behalf of
speculators in Indian lands, but only for high national ends.
Of these latter, one appeared very early in the Western
question.   Even as the Louisiana Purchase was to strain the
Jeffersonian theory of strict interpretation, so the long train

[70] *The Works of Thomas Jefferson,* VI. 84.
[71] *Ibid.,* VI. 89.
[72] *Ibid.,* VI. 106.
[73] *Ibid.,* VI. 145, 108.
[74] *Ibid.,* V. 101-102.
[75] *Ibid.,* VI. 40.
[76] *Ibid.,* VI. 184.
[77] *Ibid.,* V. 184.
[78] *Ibid.,* VI. 302, *passim.*
[79] *Ibid.,* VI. 224, 455.

of preliminary negotiation taxed whatever of pacifism survived in Jefferson the diplomat and cabinet minister. Already, in 1790, the imminence of war between Spain and
England brought the Louisiana question into the limelight.
Our growing West needed a Mississippi port and outlet.
This, Jefferson set himself the task of securing. Yet his
policy was distinctly that of waiting watchfully. Western
allegiance to the new republic hinged ultimately upon our
control of New Orleans,[80] but, in attaining this goal, temperament and necessity alike urged Jefferson to caution.
In controversies between Spain and Great Britain, he in-
stinctively chose neutrality[81] as the wisest course, so long at
least as the belligerents kept their treaty obligations,[82] from
a perception that American strength would count more
effectively in swaying the balance of power than if used on
one side or the other. He would even submit to the passage
of foreign troops across American territory[83] rather than,
by refusal, provoke insults and war, which we were not prepared to resist. In the critical posture of European affairs,
he believed that American interests might be conserved
without the costs and dangers of war.[84]

More immediately threatening than a western problem,
quite certain in the final event to yield to diplomatic negotiation, was the question of American rights at sea, an element on which our independence of England was as yet far
from being acknowledged. What Jefferson counted a natural right was by no means easy to uphold, and the British
decision, in 1791, to restrict American trade to vessels built
in the United States, put a decided crimp in those profits
which a European war would naturally hold out for any

[80] *The Works of Thomas Jefferson,* VI. 116.
[81] *Ibid.,* VI. 142.
[82] *Ibid.,* VI. 123. New York, August 12, 1790.
[83] *Ibid.,* VI. 142, 144.
[84] *Ibid.,* VI. 444, March 18, 1792.

neutral nation prepared for sudden accessions to its shipping. As Washington's prime minister, Jefferson was already confronting the great foreign problem of his own administration.

Professional duty required Jefferson to make diplomatic representations against British seizure of American sailors off the African coast.[85] But his interest was far keener in the blockade of France projected in 1793, which threatened to exclude our goods from much of continental Europe. Such a contingency presented, according to Jefferson, a *casus belli*, and he took the constitutional ground that, even as the executive could not in a positive sense declare war, so, in a negative sense, it should not compel peace by a failure to summon the legislature for deliberation upon the issues involved.[86] Yet he trusted that the sovereign legislature, when duly assembled, would seize the golden opportunity of teaching humanity the lesson of an appeal, not to the sword, but to enlightened self-interest by a retaliation in kind, which should exclude European goods and vessels from our own ports.[87]

A blockade of continental Europe presaged disaster to neutral commerce in direct violation of one of Jefferson's favorite concepts, that of a law of nature which guaranteed to nations at peace the rights of uninterrupted intercourse.[88] Even regulations of contraband chafed this militant free trader, who asserted that "in the present improved state of the arts when every country has such ample means of procuring arms within and without itself, the regulations of contraband answer no other end than to draw other nations into the war."[89] His chief consolation was that the treaty

[85] *The Works of Thomas Jefferson*, VII. 157, October 12, 1792.
[86] *Ibid.*, VII. 250. March, 1793.
[87] *Ibid.*
[88] *Ibid.*, VII. 314-315, 386, 387, May 7, 1793.
[89] *Ibid.*, VII. 314-315. May 7, 1793.

with Prussia already recognized the futility of contraband and thereby erected a new milestone in international relations.[90]

He perceived the gains which might be ours as the great neutral carrying nation and protested against any British discrimination respecting foreign-built vessels flying our flag,[91] especially since it was no part of our intention to allow foreigners to participate in the war profits through ownership of our shipping shares. The troubled state of the times induced him to comment upon the Lusitania case more than a century before its occurrence. He asked:

Can it be necessary to say that a merchant vessel is not a privateer? That tho' she has arms to defend herself in time of war, in the course of her regular commerce, this no more makes her a privateer, than a husbandman following his plough, in time of war, with a knife or pistol in his pocket, is thereby made a soldier? The occupation of a privateer is attack and plunder, that of a merchant-vessel is commerce & self preservation.[92]

He particularly condemned the British definition of grain as contraband, and held that British action in restricting our grain market made us unneutral by disenabling us from dealing equally with both belligerents.[93] He was wholly out of sympathy with Great Britain's attempt to starve an enemy nation[94] at our expense. All in all, the times furnished new arguments, not only for naval preparedness, but also for a protective tariff and non-intercourse.[95] "It is not to the moderation and justice of others," Jefferson regretfully concedes, "we are to trust for fair and equal access to market with our productions, or for our due share in the transportation of them; but to our own means of independence, and the firm will to use them."[96]

[90] *The Works of Thomas Jefferson*, VII, 314-315.
[91] *Ibid.*, VII. 386-387. June 13, 1793.
[92] *Ibid.*, VII. 494. August 16, 1793.
[93] *Ibid.*, VIII 24-31. September 7, 1793.
[94] *Ibid.*, VII. 28. September 7, 1793.
[95] *Ibid.*, VIII. 114-118. December 16, 1793.
[96] *Ibid.*, VIII. 117.

It is evident that, in 1793, Jefferson was not the leading pacifist in President Washington's cabinet. And a four years' trial of the Hamiltonian policy of truckling to Great Britain justified his complacent reflections on what might have been had America only followed his advice in a strong assertion of neutral rights. "A little time will unfold these things, and show which class of opinions would have been most friendly to the firmness of our government, and to the interests of those for whom it was made."[97] Quite a contrast, this, to his more characteristic wish that we give it all up,—commerce, and the carrying trade, even a diplomatic establishment—and live by agriculture alone.[98]

His militant neutrality and advanced definition of contraband point to Jefferson as an original thinker and a pathfinder in pacifism. His philosophy of a national morality is equally creditable. "For a nation as a society forms a moral person," declares Jefferson, "and every member of it is personally responsible for his society."[99] He believed that true reformation of this body politic was attainable only by persuasion, not at all by force.[100] A practical expression of this code of ethics is Jefferson's contribution to the fourth annual message of Washington. "The interests of a nation, when well understood," affirms the secretary of state, "will be found to coincide with their moral duties."[101] This doctrine was well in harmony with its expounder's belief in peace as the true law of nature,[102] though he was obliged to make exception of man, whose boasted civilization merely enabled him "to pursue the principle of *bellum omnium in omnia* on a larger scale, and in place of the little contests of

[97] *The Works of Thomas Jefferson,* VIII. 277. January 22, 1797.
[98] *Ibid.,* IX. 65-66. April 22, 1799.
[99] *Ibid.,* VII. 84-5. 1792.
[100] *Ibid.,* VII. 122. To Thomas Paine, June 19, 1792.
[101] *Ibid.,* VII. 160-161. October 15, 1793.
[102] *Ibid.,* VII. 400. To Genêt, June 17, 1793.

tribe against tribe."[103] Peace being thus the true law of nature and of nations, Jefferson set a high value upon personal
cordiality among diplomats as a means to its attainment.[104]

To preserve the friendship of republican France, which
felt itself ill used at our neutrality in its war against allied
Europe,[105] and at the same time to convince the American
people that their honor was safe from British aggression,
constituted a perplexing problem to Washington's advisers.
But on one point Jefferson was adamant, namely, his determination to uphold the right of individual citizens to manufacture and to export munitions.[106]   In his mind this was no
violation of neutrality, and his attitude is the more convincing because he objected to allowing France to fit out privateers in the United States, since her enemies were forbidden
to do it by treaty.[107]   Such nicely balanced neutrality was not
calculated to curry favor with the Republican party, now
assuming form under his own leadership.   On the other
hand, he was loath to proceed to extremities against certain
violators of neutrality at Charleston merely to please the
British ministry.[108]   Further to placate French sentiment, he
advocated prompt interest and loan payments to the *de facto*
government at Paris.[109]

The interval of Jefferson's retirement from the cabinet
of Washington enabled him to consolidate Republican persons and principles for the electoral campaign of 1796, but
called forth little that was new in his pacifism.   Free from
the irritations of office, he was at liberty to indulge his own

[103] *The Works of Thomas Jefferson,* VIII. 264.   January 1, 1797.
[104] *Ibid.,* VII. 202.   January 1, 1793.   VII. 449.   July 14, 1793.   See
also VIII. 281.   February 9, 1797.
[105] *Ibid.,* VII. 302.
[106] *Ibid.,* VII. 326.   See also VIII. 84-85.
[107] *Ibid.,* VII. 333.   Opinion on the *Little Sarah.*   May 16, 1793.   See
also VII. 440, 485.
[108] *Ibid.,* VII. 357.
[109] *Ibid.,* VII. 371.

philosophy, which craved for peace, with honor to be sure,[110] but a peace not to be sacrificed to the issues of war until the policy of non-intercourse should have been weighed and found wanting.[111] A peace such as the Jay Treaty offered to purchase by the sacrifice of western interests seemed to him no settlement at all, but only an invitation to future aggression.[112]

Whatever perils darkened his country's future, the election of 1796 summoned Jefferson to take his share in facing them. His ancient friendship for the new chief magistrate encouraged him to hope for a peaceful course, and wise measures.[113] He trusted Adams to recover lost ground by putting more backbone into foreign relations than Washington had used.[114] But the President soon adopted an anti-French attitude by no means agreeable to Jefferson;[115] and the more strongly pro-British became the government's policy, the more actively pacific were the Vice-President's sentiments. To his old friend, Elbridge Gerry, he went so far as to write:

> Peace is undoubtedly at present the first object of our nation. Interest & honor are also national considerations. But interest, duly weighed, is in favor of peace even at the expence of spoliations past & future; & honor cannot now be an object. The insults & injuries committed on us by both the belligerent parties, from the beginning of 1793 to this day, & still continuing, cannot now be wiped off by engaging in war with one of them.[116]

So pragmatical a pronouncement is inconsistent with hypersensitiveness to the opinion of other nations whose "kicks & cuffs prove their contempt."[117] But this with him is rare.

[110] *The Works of Thomas Jefferson*, VIII. 145.   April 25, 1794.
[111] *Ibid.*, VIII. 147-8.   May 1, 1794.
[112] *Ibid.*, VIII. 221.   March 2, 1796.
[113] *Ibid.*, VIII. 260.   December 28, 1796.
[114] *Ibid.*, VIII. 293.
[115] *Ibid.*, VIII. 300, 305.
[116] *Ibid.*, VIII. 313.   June 21, 1797.
[117] *Ibid.*, VIII. 318.

His norm is a serene originality, mindful of America's mission to pioneer in many things.

Once convinced that Adams was bent on war with France, he condemned a system which permitted the executive to press matters so far as to commit the nation to war against its will.[118] For a brief period in 1798 he regarded the war as imminent.[119] But, with prophetic insight, he concluded that France would harass us by annoying decrees rather than by war,[120] while our part was to bear the yoke a little longer,[121] to avert wars as far as possible by limiting the borrowing power of government,[122] and at the same time to prepare ourselves by a trained militia,[123] . . . a program not devoid of those inconsistencies which have so enchanted the critics of Jefferson. A nominal peace was, however, maintained, the credit for which Jefferson was disposed to assign to the moderation rather than to the necessities of France.[124] To whomsoever it was due, Jefferson was permitted to enter upon his own administration in a time of peace. His inaugural outlined an intention to continue peaceful relations with all nations, entangling alliances with none, and he recommended the militia as the best reliance for a nation at peace.[125] A more intimate communication of this period to Thomas Paine disclaims "implicating ourselves with the powers of Europe, even in support of principles which we mean to pursue,"[126] while such coercion as was needful to preserve our more immediate interests, he be-

[118] *The Works of Thomas Jefferson*, VIII. 387.
[119] *Ibid.*, VIII. 392, 395.
[120] *Ibid.*, VIII. 408.
[121] *Ibid.*, VIII. 417.
[122] *Ibid.*, VIII. 481. Nov. 26, 1798.
[123] *Ibid.*, IX. 18. January 26, 1799.
[124] *Ibid.*, IX. 55-63.
[125] *Ibid.*, IX. 198.
[126] *Ibid.*, IX. 212-213, 219; X. 27, 298-301.

lieved we possessed in our commerce,[127] which would induce foreign nations in their own interest to be accommodating.

He had scarcely taken office when the western question entered upon a new phase in the prospective cession of Louisiana by Spain to France.[128] He felt that French occupation of our western boundary would impose an impossible strain upon the traditional friendship of the two nations,[129] since "There is on the globe one single spot, the possessor of which is our natural and habitual enemy. It is New Orleans."[130] With such views, it was inevitable that he should seek a *rapprochement* with Great Britain,[131] and, in the summer of 1802, he expressed delight at the "various manifestations of just and friendly disposition toward us"[132] on the part of the British government.

Jefferson's correspondence with Monroe,[133] Livingston,[134] and Du Pont de Nemours[135] indicates the Louisiana Purchase as the supreme practical outgrowth of his pacifism. He felt that Louisiana was certain to be ours whenever France became sufficiently entangled in Europe to make it worth our while to occupy the country, but he preferred to work out manifest destiny by peaceful means. "It secures us," he rejoices, "the course of a peaceful nation."[136]

In the light of Jefferson's earlier patronage of the navy, and encouragement of the militia, one would expect a large development of both arms during his administration. Repeated admonitions in his annual messages to Congress[137]

---

[127] *The Works of Thomas Jefferson,* IX, 220.
[128] *Ibid.,* IX. 263.
[129] *Ibid.,* IX. 357.
[130] *Ibid.,* IX. 364. See also X. 20 n.
[131] *Ibid.,* IX. 365.
[132] *Ibid.,* IX. 386.
[133] *Ibid.,* IX. 419.
[134] *Ibid.,* IX. 442.
[135] *Ibid.,* IX. 437-438.
[136] *Ibid.,* X. 28.
[137] *Ibid.,* IX. 337, 413.

attest the permanence of his interest in the militia. But the
navy counts for less than one might anticipate, possibly because the seaports and big-navy men were in the Federalist
camp. He preferred gun-boats to frigates[138]and resented
Federalist obstruction to his plan for the economical defence
of the country. Yet his heart could thrill at naval feats in
Algerine waters, which he trusted would prove to the world
that American patience was due, not to a lack of courage,
but to "a conscientious desire to direct the energies of our nation to the multiplication of the human race and not to its
destruction."[139]

Peace and economy reënforced each other in Jefferson's
program. A tax on stock shares in order to levy "a sensible portion of the expences of a war on those who are so
anxious to engage us in it,"[140] met his approval before election, and, after it, he asserted that "Peace is our most important interest, and a recovery from debt."[141] To the political economist, Thomas Cooper, he enunciated the doctrine
that, "If we can prevent the government from wasting the
labors of the people, under the pretence of taking care of
them, they must become happy. Their finances are now
under such a course of application as nothing could derange
but war or federalism."[142] He believed that sound finances
could be readily adjusted to emergencies, and that in peace
times loans and internal taxes were a mistake,[143] a conviction which the common people seem to have shared.[144] The
National Bank he despised on political as well as economic
principles, fearing its disloyalty in periods of crisis.[145]

[138] *The Works of Thomas Jefferson*, X. 41, 124.
[139] *Ibid.*, IX. 332.
[140] *Ibid.*, IX. 112.
[141] *Ibid.*, IX. 309.
[142] *Ibid.*, IX. 403.
[143] *Ibid.*, IX. 412.
[144] *Ibid.*, IX. 445.
[145] *Ibid.*, X. 57-58.

Having preserved peace with the Indians by just deal-ings,[146] and having won it from the pirates by the glorious exploits of a navy on which he proposed to economize, Jefferson might view the Napoleonic wars with a virtuous aloofness. From his comfortable vantage, he exclaims, "Tremendous times in Europe! How mighty this battle of lions & Tygers! With what sensations should the common herd of cattle look on it? With no partialities, certainly. If they can so far worry one another as to destroy their power of tyrannizing, the one over the earth, the other over the waters, the world may perhaps enjoy peace, till they recruit again."[147] His own impulse is to succor the unfortu-nate while administering the means of annoyance to none.[148] Indeed, he is too keen a statesman to desire any one power to rule supreme. Against England he bears no malice; neither against France. "We consider each," he adds, "as a necessary instrument to hold in check the disposi-tion of the other to tyrannize over other nations."[149] In the closing message of his first administration, he congratu-lates the country and, by inference, himself that "from the governments of the belligerent powers especially we continue to receive those friendly manifestations which are justly due to an honest neutrality."[150] Not until his second term was Jefferson to drain in its full bitterness the cup of neutrality violated.

The position of a neutral, then as now, was intolerable. Friction over Florida,[151] uncertainty concerning the Louis-iana boundary, and a fear that French intentions were hostile,[152] inclined Jefferson in the summer of 1805 to an

[146] *The Works of Thomas Jefferson,* IX. 407, 410.
[147] *Ibid.,* X. 32.
[148] *Ibid.,* X. 42, October 17, 1803.
[149] *Ibid.,* X. 67-68.
[150] *Ibid.,* X. 112.
[151] *Ibid.,* X. 140.
[152] *Ibid.,* X. 171.

alliance with Great Britain.[153]   But the continued insolence
of British war vessels off our coast[154] soon led him to change
tack and to reassert the proposition that "we will remain
uprightly neutral in fact, tho' leaning in belief to the opinion
that an English ascendancy on the ocean is safer for us
than that of France."[155]   He esteemed the death of Mr.
Fox an additional blow to any British-American entente,
for, as he wrote Monroe, "His sound judgment saw that
political interest could never be separated in the long run
from moral right, & his frank & great mind would have
made a short business of a just treaty with you."[156]

Any lingering dreams of overtures to Great Britain were
rudely shattered by the *Chesapeake* outrage, which the
President's own proclamation sufficiently describes:

> And at length a deed, transcending all we have suffered, brings
> the public sensibility to a serious crisis, and forbearance to a
> necessary pause. A frigate of the U S. trusting to a state of peace
> and leaving her harbor on a distant service, has been surprised and
> attacked by a British vessel of superior force, one of a squadron
> then lying in our waters to cover the transaction, & has been disabled
> from service with the loss of a number of men killed & wounded.
> This enormity was not only without provocation or justifiable cause;
> but was committed with the avowed purpose of taking by force from
> a ship of war of the U S. a part of her crew: and that no circum-
> stance might be wanting to make its character, the commander was
> apprised that the seamen thus forcibly . . . were native citizens
> of the U S.[157]

Here, if ever, was a test of national self-control, and
Jefferson met it.   He considered it no part of his duty to
commit Congress to a declaration of war in preference to
nonintercourse or other measures.[158]   He granted full time
for Great Britain to disavow the act[159] and at once set

[153] *The Works of Thomas Jefferson*, X. 168, 171, 172.
[154] *Ibid.*, X. 188.
[155] *Ibid.*, X. 263-264.
[156] *Ibid.*, X. 296-7.
[157] *Ibid.*, X. 441-444.
[158] *Ibid.*, X. 433.
[159] *Ibid.*, X. 451.

about recalling our merchantmen at sea for a mobilizing of resources.[160]   Yet his own wrath was deeply stirred, and he approved the war spirit which swept the country in a unanimity long unknown.   "Now," he exults, ". . . they have touched a chord which vibrates in every heart.   Now then is the time to settle the old and the new."[161]   With war in prospect, he felt it a good time to bring our Spanish troubles to an end, and he outlined a plan not unworthy of the Ostend Manifesto.   While one force was seizing Florida, another should engage Mexico, and Cuba should be annexed;[162] rather an imperial program for a pacifist, but Jefferson had suffered much disillusionment.

The outcome, however, was not war but the embargo. An entire generation had passed away since the Declaration of July 4.   Meanwhile, for Jefferson youth had departed and experience had arrived.   The embargo was the ripened policy of a thinker who had inspired independence, but who had shuddered at the horrors of her birth.   It coincided with a calm estimate of Britain, the old time enemy, and a cool comprehension of France, the quondam ally. It combined impartiality with economy and suited the inclinations of a statesman who was too much of a farmer to love commerce, yet could not afford to despise it. It agreed with the personal qualms of a patriot who had found one war quite enough, while it safe-guarded America from the world's primal curse.   Such were the considerations leading Jefferson to the grand experiment in pacifism which promised so much and achieved so little.

And now, when the world is gasping in horror at the struggle so recently ended and praying for guidance to avoid future outbreaks, whatever pertains to former experiments toward world peace acquires an interest more than academic.

[160] *The Works of Thomas Jefferson,* X. 456.
[161] *Ibid.,* X. 471.
[162] *Ibid.,* X. 476-477.

All the circumstances attending the embargo—its causes, operation at home and abroad, and final repeal—take on a fresh significance just now, when the true meaning of the freedom of the seas demands an answer and when the rights of neutrals seek a fresh definition and a more effective sanction. In the rising day of a new democracy, humanity may still learn many lessons from the greatest of democrats. And of all the lessons of his career, that which cost Jefferson most in preliminary education, in anxiety, and, later, in chagrin, was the embargo. The following pages endeavor to shed some light upon Jefferson's experience with his cherished scheme. First, however, let us glance at the embargo of Jefferson with reference to prevailing conceptions of the law of nations. For the embargo of 1808 was the product of a two-fold evolution. It grew, as we have just seen, out of the natural pacifism of Jefferson himself. Other roots tapped the sequences of earlier American history. Still others linked with the progressive effort of Europe and America to classify and ameliorate international relations. The embargo, thus viewed, is a part of Jefferson's concept of international law.

The results of the measure as gleaned from a one year's trial under circumstances most adverse, are scarcely the index of its wisdom. Jefferson had fair reason to anticipate not only the saving of American ships and goods, which did come about; but he was also legitimately entitled to count on European developments, either responsive to the embargo or independent of it, which should vindicate his judgment and his concessions to peace. For Jefferson, in 1807, was no youthful enthusiast, but a statesman of ripe experience. It is true that he owes his undying fame to no other quality more than to the abiding permanence of an idealism which, in most men, dies with youth. But the preceding summary of his point of view reveals a rather curious blending of the practical, sometimes almost of the cynical, with the idealistic, and accounts for the matter-of-fact and even pedestrian application which Jefferson was to give to what in theory was novel and humanitarian.

Though it is doubtful whether idealism played a very conscious part in Jefferson's first determination to experiment with the embargo—it lay at hand, a ready weapon forged in the armory of a long experience in asserting national dignity in the face of insults and injuries beyond our physical power to repel—on its theoretical side, it appeared to be a consistent application, or possibly extension, of principles derived by Jefferson from his studies in the law of nations.   For the embargo should be considered as part of a progressive effort in Europe and America to classify and ameliorate international relations.   The embargo, thus viewed, is a part of Jefferson's concept of international law, and as such it leads into a fruitful aspect of Jefferson's thinking.   An inquiry, therefore, as to the position of the embargo and its author in the general field of international law may properly precede any examination of the measure itself, its causes, its operation at home and abroad, and its final repeal.

CHAPTER II

JEFFERSON AND THE LAW OF NATIONS

The embargo upon commerce which Congress, at the suggestion of President Jefferson, decreed in 1807 was more than an experiment in practical politics. It was a test on a magnificent scale of a theory of international law long maturing in the President's mind, and the fitting contribution of a new nation to a body of doctrine which owed its revival, if not its inception, to the need of curbing the international anarchy which accompanied the rise of modern states. The law of nations was a new development. Less than two centuries had passed since Grotius put forth the pioneer work *De jure belli ac pacis* (1625). The interval between the publication of this book and the issuance of the embargo decree was, in fact, the classical period in international law. The labors of Leibnitz, Wolff, Vattel, and Bynkershoek built up a system popular, not only with doctrinaires and philosophers, but even with enlightened despots in their more subjective moments. By the close of the eighteenth century, the law of nations had acquired as much prestige as it could ever hope to secure without the support of its own guns and navies. It was the highest political expression of an age which believed in the perfectibility of human relations through sheer intellect. If its dicta sometimes failed to govern the actions of courts and cabinets, its infringement was not a matter of indifference.

International law since Grotius has in reality known two great eras and is now entering upon a third. The first culminated between 1758 and ,the French Revolution, when for an entire generation Vattel's *Le Droit des gens, ou principes de la loi naturelle appliqués à la conduite et aux*

affaires des nations et des souverains enjoyed a vogue which
has been accorded to but few of the world's books.[1] The
Napoleonic Wars overthrew this older law of nations along
with the nations it represented. It was amid the débris
and ruins of this international law that Jefferson inaugurated his embargo. A second stage of development marked
the century between the Congress of Vienna and the meeting of the Hague Conference in 1907. This was essentially
a period of disillusionment. The age of reason had succumbed to the unreason of much that was human, and
visions of immediate perfection paled and faded before the
Darwinian view of imperceptible evolution. International
law, then, as the expression of a pragmatic and skeptical
world, contented itself with as efficient a system of balance
of power as it could devise and endeavored at two world
gatherings to place a limit upon the military use of the tools
which modern industrialism had created. In the tragedy
of the World War the international law of Gladstone, Bis-
marck, Nicholas II, and Bryan was swept away as utterly
as the older system of the "fathers."

From this larger synthesis of the law of nations, it is
of interest to examine more particularly Jefferson's acquaint-
ance with the authorities upon the subject[2] and his concep-
tion of his own relation to the law. Jefferson had all his
life been a student of political theory, and the authors to
whom he refers from time to time and a perusal of whom
he recommends to his friends constitute a gallery of the

[1] For an interesting study of Vattel, see Charles G. Fenwick, "The
Authority of Vattel" in *The American Political Science Review*, VII
(1913), 395-410. An article by Thomas Willing Balch in the *Pennsylvania Law Review* for 1916 also treats of Jefferson's interest in the law
of nations.

[2] Among others he cites: *The Writings of James Madison* (Hunt
ed.), II. 43, Madison to Thomas Jefferson, March 16, 1784, "The tracts
of Bynkershoek, which you mention"; *The Works of Thomas Jefferson*
(Federal ed., 1904-05), IV. 29, Puffendorf; IV. 248, Bynkershoek;
VI. 63, Adam Smith; also Montesquieu, Locke, Burke, De Lolme,
Hume, Molloy, Beccaria, and Vattel.

political scientists of his period. The underlying concept of eighteenth century political thought was the theory of compact. Like most of his contemporaries, Jefferson accepted the contract theory as it had developed in England through Hooker and Milton in theology, Hobbes and Locke in politics,[3] and as it had been popularized in France through Montesquieu and Rousseau. His own "Declaration of Independence" embodied the finest statement in English of the theory.

Up to 1776, Jefferson had been thinking of the theory in a somewhat limited aspect as an explanation for the origin of individual societies and governments. But the exigencies of practical administration which faced him as secretary of state and later as chief executive called his attention to a phase of the general theory not frequently emphasized. The customary explanation of compact presupposed a state of nature out of which man emerged into organized society by means of a formal and specific agreement.[4] On all points not covered by this agreement, he was still regarded as in the original state of nature. The significance of this for the law of nations was that the state of nature was one of peace.[5] No Nietzschean school of thought had as yet arisen to glorify war as the natural state of man. To eighteenth century thinkers war was the abnormal and the unnatural; and the state of nature which governed both

[3] For an epitome of the place of the theory of contract in American thought, see L. M. Sears, "The Puritan and his Anglican Allegiance" in *Bibliotheca Sacra,* October, 1917.

[4] *M. de Vattel* (Carnegie Institution, 1916), Introduction by A. de Lapradelle, p. xviii: "Dans l'école de droit de la nature et des gens, à laquelle appartient Vattel, le contrat joue un grand rôle. De même qu'il est à la base de l'Etat, dans le droit public interne, sous le nom de pacte social, il est encore à la base du droit international public, sous le nom de traité. Par le pacte, l'Etat se forme. Par le traité il s'assure les droits nécessaires à son développement."

[5] See J. S. Reeves, "The influence of the Law of Nature upon International Law in the United States," etc., in *American Journal of International Law,* III (1909), 559. See also *The Works of Thomas Jefferson,* VII. 400.

individuals and nations, except as modified by special laws and treaties, was a state of peace. Vattel furnished the text;[6] Washington and his advisers, the sermon. The neutrality which the United States pursued in 1793 was a definite advance in international law, based upon the fundamental pacifism of the state of nature idea included in the theory of compact.[7]

Neutrality was, in fact, dictated by plain necessity, but Jefferson found authority for it among the lawyers, and it was pleasant to indulge in what Genêt termed the "aphorisms" of Vattel.[8] This same neutrality continued under Adams, in spite of the near approach to war in 1798, and it remained the fixed policy of Jefferson's own term. It bore a golden harvest in the carrying trade of a warring world, for, until the decrees and orders of the chief contestants closed the seas to our shipping, neutrality paid financially as well as morally. But the increasing rigor of the belligerents after 1805 forced the issue anew, and the decision to maintain neutrality rested, it must be confessed, more upon the practical impossibility of attacking both offenders than upon any theory that our own state of nature was peaceful. Most of Jefferson's allusions to Vattel and other authorities

[6] *M. de Vattel* (Carnegie Institution, 1916), Introduction by A. de Lapradelle, p. xxiv: "Vattel, le premier, déclare que l'impartialité n'est pas obtenue par l'égalité des secours, mais par l'absence de secours. 'Ne point donner de secours, quand on n'y est pas obligé; ne fournir librement ni troupes, ni armes, ni munitions, ni rien de ce qui sert directement à la guerre . . . ne point donner de secours et non pas en donner également:' telle est sa formule," etc. See also *ibid.,* p. xxxvi.

[7] See J. J. Burlamaqui, *The Principles of Natural Law* (5th ed., Dublin, 1791), p. 164: " . . . let us observe that the natural state of nations, in respect to each other, is that of society and peace." *M. de Vattel* (Carnegie Institution), Introduction by A. de Lapradelle, p. xxiii: "Machiavel donnait aux princes le conseil d'épouser les querelles les uns des autres, en vue de partager, avec le vainqueur, les dépouilles du vaincu. Diplomate de l'école de Jean-Jacques, Vattel, au contraire, les engage à rester spectateurs. Pour la première fois le nom de *neutralité* pénètre dans un traité de droit des gens."

[8] *The Works of Thomas Jefferson,* VII. 485, Jefferson to Gouverneur Morris, August 16, 1793.

are to be found in the correspondence of 1793. Another ten years of conflict taught the futility of appeals to text-books against the might which Napoleon and Canning both mistook for right. By nature a theorist, inexorable destiny made of Jefferson a realist. Yet devotion to ideals is, after all, his salient characteristic. And his utterances upon the law of nations and its framers possess a unique interest for a world which is once more called upon to formulate not only its practice, but its theory as well. If the following pages seem to concern many matters besides the embargo, the latter may still be kept in mind as the practical outcome of much theorizing.

Frequently his allusions are only incidental. For example, the right of an assembly to determine its own quorum reminds him of Puffendorf.[9] Again he says of Bynkershoek's works: "There are about a fourth part of them which you would like to have. They are the following tracts. *Questiones juris publici—de lege Rhodeâ—de dominio maris—du Juge conopetent des Ambassadeurs,* for this last if not the rest has been translated into French with notes by Barbeyrae."[10] More important, because of their subject, are his observations on *The Wealth of Nations*:

> In political economy, I think Smith's *wealth of nations* the best book extant, in the science of government Montesquieu's *spirit of laws* is generally recommended. It contains indeed a great number of political truths; but also an equal number of heresies: so that the reader must be constantly on his guard. . . . Locke's little book on government is perfect as far as it goes. Descending from theory to practice there is no better book than the *Federalist.* Burgh's *Political disquisitions* are good also, especially after reading De Lolme. Several of Hume's political essays are good. There are some excellent books of Theory written by Turgot & the economists of France. For parliamentary knowledge, the *Lex parliamentaria* is the best book.[11]

[9] *The Works of Thomas Jefferson*, IV. 29.
[10] *Ibid.,* IV. 248.
[11] *Ibid.,* VI. 63, Jefferson to Thomas Mann Randolph, May 30, 1790.

Several of the above named works were regarded by Jefferson as indispensable to the training of a lawyer. And a chart of readings, recommended to his young cousin for daily study between the hours of twelve and two, includes Molloy, *De jure maritimo;* Locke, *On Government;* Montesquieu, *Spirit of Law;* Smith, *Wealth of Nations;* Beccaria; Kaim, *Moral Essays;* and Vattel, *Law of Nations.*[12]

But the law of nations meant to Jefferson far more than an elegant supplement to a legal education. It was a reality in diplomacy, ready to function upon any issue. In 1792, that issue was Spain. During the Revolution, Spain had encroached upon Georgia. But the peace treaty failed to recognize her gains, and she was obligated to return them to Georgia. So far as the treaty applied, this might be to Georgia direct, or, on the theory that British sovereignty still held when the attacks were made, restitution might be made to Britain first, for transfer to the United States. In support of direct dealings between Spain and the United States, Jefferson enlisted the doctrine of natural right, we being the real proprietors of the places seized; and, to support natural right, he appealed to Vattel.[13] The case was simple. If Britain was the real proprietor, it was certain that she had never ceded her rights to Spain. On the contrary, her relinquishment had been to the United States. If America was the original and lawful proprietor, the situation was absurd, for America and Spain were allies at the very time the seizures occurred. Common sense alone would uphold the American contention, but Jefferson called in a battery of legal support. "See," he urges, "on this subject, Grotius, 1. 3. c. 6, §26. Puffendorf, 1. 8, c. 17, §23. Vattel, l. 3, §197, 198."[14]

[12] *Ibid.,* VI. 72, Jefferson to John Garland Jefferson, June 11, 1790. For a comment on Beccaria, see *ibid.,* I. 71.

[13] *American State Papers,* Foreign Relations, I. 252, March 18, 1792. See Vattel, I. 3, p. 122.

[14] *American State Papers,* Foreign Relations, I. 252, March 18, 1792.

The law of nations was equally serviceable for American rights to navigation on the Mississippi. "What sentiment," demands Jefferson, "is written in deeper characters than that the ocean is free to all men, and their rivers to all their inhabitants?"[15] Obstructions to river navigation had always been acts of force, and, if recognized, were matters of treaty and not of natural right. Even exclusive control of the lower waters of a river gave its owners no dispensation from the general law. And, in the case in question, Spain held on both sides of the Mississippi so narrow a zone "that it may in fact be considered as a strait of the sea."[16] On this point, as in the case of the Georgia claims, the authorities are duly cited: "See Grot. 1. 2. c. 2 §11, 12, 13, c. 3. §7, 8, 12. Puffendorf, 1. 3. c. 3. §3, 4, 5, 6. Wolff's. Inst. §310, 311, 312. Vattel, 1. 1. §292, 1. 2. §123 to 139."[17]

The right of navigation being granted, that of mooring vessels to the shore and even of landing if necessary was the inevitable corollary. Lest there be any doubt of this simple truth, Jefferson calls to witness "Grot. 1. 2. c. 2. §15. Puffend. 1. 3. c. 3. §8. Vattel, 1. 2. §129."[18] If these were not convincing, there was the further arsenal of Roman law. The Romans placed river navigation on the basis of natural right—"(flumina publica sunt, hoc est populi Romani, Inst. 2 t. 1. §2)"[19]—and derived an incidental right to the use of the shores "(Ibid., §1, 3, 4, 5)"[20] This shore privilege was automatically extended in emergency to the beaching of a damaged ship when simply mooring it would prove unsafe. Here Jefferson quotes at length from "Inst. 1. 2. t. 1. §4."[21] It thus appears that all the lawyers, both

[15] *American State Papers*, Foreign Relations, I. 253.
[16] *Ibid.*, p. 254.
[17] *Ibid.*, p. 254.
[18] *Ibid.*, p. 254.
[19] *Ibid.*, p. 254.
[20] *Ibid.*, p. 254.
[21] *Ibid.*, p. 254, March 22, 1792.

ancient and modern, upheld American rights upon the Mississippi. Is it surprising that the case was finally won?

Meanwhile even more urgent difficulties with Great Britain pressed for solution. The Peace of Paris was violated by both parties. Great Britain still held the western forts;[22] America still owed the royalist debts. In supporting the American position, Jefferson took for his major premise the validity of the *status quo* as defined at the time of the peace-signing.[23] He next pointed out that the treaty became binding only when it was published to the country at large.[24] At the moment when the treaty was so proclaimed, much British property was by the fortune of war in American hands. The claim to permanent ownership of these confiscations would hold in law, save for the custom grown quite general in Europe of returning to individuals their private property.[25] America would have been glad to observe this courtesy had the war been of a normal character, but such was far from the case. Our resources were too exhausted to permit of mere amenities. Moreover, Great Britain had placed us as rebels beyond the pale of international law. "She would not admit our title even to the *strict rights* of ordinary war; she cannot then claim its *liberalities;* yet the confiscations of property were by no means universal, and that of debts still less so."[26]

Even granting the righteousness of certain British claims, reason and law were one in cautioning delay in their payment.[27] In Jefferson's own formula: "Time and con-

---

[22] For a recommendation of commercial retaliation on this account, see *The Works of Thomas Jefferson,* I. 210.

[23] *American State Papers,* Foreign Relations, I. 201, May 29, 1792, citing "Vattel, 1.4. s. 21," and "Wolf, 1222."

[24] *American State Papers,* Foreign Relations, I. 201, quoting "Vattel, 1. 4. s. 24" and s. 25; "Wolf, s. 1229."

[25] *American State Papers,* Foreign Relations, I. 201-202, May 29, 1792, quoting Bynkershoek "Quest. Jur. Pub. I. 1. c. 7."

[26] *American State Papers, Foreign Relations,* I. 202, May 29, 1792.

[27] *Ibid.,* pp. 208-209, citing "Vattel, 1. 4. s. 51" and "Bynkershoek, 1. 2. c. 10." See also Bynkershoek, 1. 1. c. 7.

sideration are favorable to the right cause—precipitation to the wrong one."[28] And as for interest, that was preposterous, even according to British precedents.[29] Where both debtor and creditor lost, the court would not double the loss of one to save that of the other. In both natural and municipal law, in questions "de damno evitando melior est conditio possidentis."[30] All the more so where the creditor inflicted the damage.[31]

Turning to British delinquencies, Jefferson quotes the treaty pledge to retire *"with all convenient speed,"*[32] and conjures up Vattel to show that this really meant "as soon as possible."[33] In his reply, the British minister disclaimed any authority to surrender the posts, and the conference was barren as respects its chief objective.

Nevertheless, one truly constructive development grew out of the diplomatic interchange as to debts and forts. Hammond expressed the regret that Great Britain and the United States had no buffer state between. He feared trouble from rival army posts on either side the Canadian border. Thereupon Jefferson suggested that both sides restrict their forces to a minimum to be agreed upon. And the friction of wits between Jefferson and Hammond then generated a thought spark of more value to humanity than many a treaty of peace. Seizing Jefferson's idea of a limitation of armaments, Hammond went the further step of urging the abolition of all military posts in favor of trading stations. Jefferson hailed the suggestion. "I told him," he records, "that the idea of having no military post

[28] *American State Papers,* Foreign Relations, I. 211, Section 45.

[29] *Ibid.,* I. 213. He quotes here Lord Mansfield, "Dougl. 753," and 376.

[30] *American State Papers,* Foreign Relations, I. 213. See also *The Works of Thomas Jefferson,* VII. 84-85.

[31] See in this connection *American State Papers,* Foreign Relations, I. 214, citing "Wolf, s. 229" and s. 1224, and "Grotius, l. 3. c. 20, s. 22."

[32] *American State Papers,* Foreign Relations, I. 206, May 29, 1792.

[33] *Ibid.,* I. 206, citing "Vattel, l. 4. c. 26."

on either side was new to me, that it had never been mentioned among the members of the Executive.   That therefore I could only speak for myself & say that, *prima facie,*
it accorded well with two favorite ideas of mine of leaving
commerce free, & never keeping an unnecessary souldier,
but when he spoke of having no military post on either side
there might be difficulty in fixing the distance of the nearest
posts."[34]   A great war was to intervene before the unforti-
fied Canadian boundary became a fact.   But Jefferson and
Hammond both deserve credit for the germ of a real pacifism and of international good-neighborliness.   Less heeded
than the grand climaxes in his life, this conversation of
Jefferson with Hammond is memorable for its genesis of a
great idea.   It marked him as a trail-blazer in international
law.

While Washington and his cabinet were struggling with
these American issues, the war cloud in Europe was threatening to engulf all the neutrals.[35]   The death grapple between England and France, which lasted with one brief
intermission from 1793 to 1815, raised from the first grave
questions of international law and the rights of neutrals,
and called from our own state department important declarations of principle.   When Great Britain first threatened her
paper blockade, Jefferson assured Pinckney, the American
minister at London, that such an infringement of neutral
rights was past belief.[36]   The law of nations was too in-
grained in civilized practice, as witness the recent American
treaty with Prussia which went even so far as to deny the
existence of contraband, "for, in truth, in the present improved State of the arts when every country has such ample

[34] *The Works of Thomas Jefferson,* I. 227, Anas Papers, 1792.

[35] It had really been looming since 1787, even before the French Revolution began, and Jefferson had then predicted our eventual neutrality
(see *The Works of Thomas Jefferson,* I. 114) and attempted to demonstrate its advantages to both belligerents.

[36] *The Works of Thomas Jefferson,* VII. 314, May 7, 1793.

means of procuring arms within and without itself, the regulations of contraband answer no other end than to draw
other nations into the war.   However, as nations have not
given sanction to this improvement, we claim it, at present,
with Prussia alone."[37]

Such a view of contraband was not likely to countenance
the British objection to shipments of arms for French
account, and Jefferson vigorously asserted the right of our
citizens to a traffic in munitions, a right in which they were
amply sustained by the law of nations, which simply designated munitions as contraband if the enemy could capture
them.[38]   What was true of cargoes was equally true of their
vessels.   The law of nations insured their right to pass
unharmed, "and no one has a right to ask where a vessel
was built, but where is she owned?"[39]   To assert this right
was all the more essential, as our increasing commerce demanded additional cargo space, and shipping once purchased
enjoyed the protection in some cases of specific treaties; in
others, of the general law of nations.[40]

Questions of navigation, contraband, blockade, and
seizure were of course fundamental.   Upon their solution
depended the ability of America to remain outside the general conflagration.   But even more annoying, for the moment, were the demands of the French agents on American
soil.   These parvenus in diplomacy outraged all the canons
of the old régime by their insolent demands, to yield which
would be suicidal, to refuse, churlish.   The balance between
gratitude and self-interest was, indeed, hard to preserve, and
the law of nations was in demand as a prop for a neutrality
more sensible than romantic.

[37] *The Works of Thomas Jefferson*, VII. 314-315, May 7, 1793.
[38] *Ibid.*, VII. 326, May 15, 1793. See also *ibid.*, pp. 84-85; also *American State Papers*, Foreign Relations, I. 147, 188, November 30, 1793.
[39] *The Works of Thomas Jefferson*, VII. 386-387, Jefferson to Gouverneur Morris, our Minister at Paris, June 13, 1793.
[40] *Ibid.*, VII. 416, Jefferson to James Monroe, June 28, 1793.

The most offensive of these French representatives, the Girondist Genêt, although he violated all the laws of hospitality by his conduct at Charleston and Philadelphia, contrived to place the American government on the defensive. Jefferson explained to him our point of view with an almost loving patience, finding ample vindication for neutrality in the pages of Vattel and Wolff. He quoted at length from Vattel:[41]

'Tant qu'un peuple neutre veut jouir surement de cet etat, il doit montrer en toutes choses une exacte impartialité entre ceux qui se font la guerre. Car s'il favorise l'un au prejudice de l'autre, il ne pourra pas se plaindre, quand celui-ci le traitera comme adherent et associé de son ennemi. Sa neutralité seroit une neutralité frauduleuse, dont personne ne veut etre la dupe. Voyons donc en quoi consiste cette impartialité qu'un peuple neutre doit garder.

'Elle se rapporte uniquement à la guerre, et comprend deux choses. 1, Ne point donner de secours quand on n'y est pas obligé; ne fournir librement ni troupes ni armes, ni munitions, ni rien de ce qui sert directement à la guerre. Je dis *ne point donner de secours et* non pas *en donner egalement;* car il seroit absurde qu'un etat secourut en meme tems deux ennemis. Et puis il seroit impossible de le faire avec egalité, les mêmes choses, le même nombre de troupes, la meme quantité d'armes de munitions, &c. fournies en des circonstances differentes; ne forment plus de secours equivalens, &c.'

If the neutral power may not, consistent with its neutrality, furnish men to either party, for their aid in war, as little can either enroll them in the neutral territory, by the law of nations. Wolf, s. 1774 says, 'Puisque le droit de lever des soldats est un droit de majesté qui ne peut etre violé par une nation étrangere, il n'est pas permis de lever des soldats sur le territoire d'autrui sans le consentement du maitre du territoire.' And Vattel, before cited, 1.3, s. 15, 'Le droit de lever des soldats appartenant uniquement à la nation ou au souverain, personne ne peut en enroller en pays étranger sans la permission du souverain. Ceux qui entreprenent d'engager des soldats en pays étranger sans la permission du souverain et en general quiconque debauche les sujets d'autrui, viole un des droits les plus sacrés du prince et de la nation. C'est le crime qu'on appele *plaigiat* ou vol d'homme. Il n'est aucun etat policé qui ne le punise très sévérement.'

. . . The testimony of these and other writers on the law and usage of nations, with your own just reflections on them, will

[41] *American State Papers*, Foreign Relations, I. 154-155, Jefferson to Genêt, June 17, 1793, quoting "Vattel, 1. 3. s. 104."

satisfy you that the United States, in prohibiting all the belligerent Powers from equipping, arming, and manning vessels of war in their ports, have exercised a right and a duty, with justice and with great moderation.

Jefferson continued this discourse on the law of nations by recalling to his unwilling pupil, Genêt, the principle that friendly goods in the vessel of an enemy are free, while enemy goods in the vessel of a friend are prize. Exceptions to this rule did occur, it was true, and it was the effort of the United States to convert the exception into the rule and establish the principle that free ships make free goods.[42] But this was in each case a matter for special treaty, and where such a treaty had not been concluded, the general law of nations still prevailed. Unhappily, we had no such treaty with England, Spain, Portugal, and Austria. And if, for the time being, this might seem to operate against France, by exposing her goods if found in our ships to seizure by the said powers, there was at any rate the compensation of gaining our goods whenever they were found in the vessels of these same enemies of France. America herself, as Jefferson explained, was the real loser by the principle she was seeking to make popular, and she would continue to lose as long as its acceptance was only partial. The advantages would appear only when the principle that free ships make free goods should become the universal law of nations. Then, indeed, our position as a friendly neutral would vastly improve through exemption from search. "To this condition we are endeavoring to advance, but as it depends on the will of other nations, as well as our own, we can only obtain it when they shall be ready to concur."[43]

[42] See *The Works of Thomas Jefferson*, I. 96, for an early mention of this principle.

[43] *American State Papers*, Foreign Relations, I. 166-167, Jefferson to Genêt, July 24, 1793. For the same idea, see *ibid.*, I. 170, Jefferson to Gouverneur Morris, August 16, 1793.

The neutrality which Jefferson was so zealously explaining to Genêt involved an equal care in upholding our rights against Great Britain.[44] Jefferson particularly objected to the British naval orders of June 8, 1793, designed to cut off American grain from enemy countries. He insisted that grain was not contraband and that for America to submit would be an unneutral act, tantamount to war upon France. "[Great Britain] may, indeed, feel the desire of starving an enemy nation; but she can have no right of doing it at our loss, nor of making us the instrument of it."[45] He further made it clear to Hammond that we were within our rights in according to France certain special courtesies, such as admission of her prizes and privateers into our ports and even of her regular line-of-battle ships in face of emergencies, such as storms, pirates, and enemies;[46] though, for ordinary cruising on our coast beyond the three-mile limit,[47] England possessed equal rights with France and all other nations.[48]

Jefferson's own bias was frankly French throughout the cabinet crises which Genêt precipitated.[49] So far as American interest would permit, he remained true to his Gallophile sentiments. Even when the irritation over Genêt was at its height, he did not lose sight of those French interests which the conduct of a scatter-brained minister had so gravely jeopardized. To steer a firm yet just course

[44] *Ibid.,* p. 170, on neutrality. See also *The Works of Thomas Jefferson,* VII. 302, 309, 387, 415.

[45] *The Works of Thomas Jefferson,* VIII. 28, Jefferson to Thomas Pinckney, September 7, 1793. Also *American State Papers,* Foreign Relations, I. 239. Also H. E. Egerton, *British Foreign Policy in Europe to the End of the 19th Century,* pp. 374-375. Lord Grenville, on his side, relied on Vattel to prove England's right to this corn seizure, *American State Papers,* Foreign Relations, I. 241, July 5, 1793.

[46] *American State Papers,* Foreign Relations, I. 176, September 9, 1793. Also *The Works of Thomas Jefferson,* I. 271, 273, 289-290.

[47] *American State Papers,* Foreign Relations, I. 183, November 8, 1793.

[48] *Ibid.,* I. 176.

[49] *The Works of Thomas Jefferson,* I. 259, 271-273, 326-328, etc.

was not easy. To deal with the "Reds" of 1793 was as embarrassing as might be. A statesman engaged in treaty making with the Bolsheviki can appreciate the difficulties involved. Aside from tolerating the vagaries of a one-time friend, America might not ignore the effect upon home pólitics of crowning Genêt as a martyr. If for this reason only, the state department was fortunate to be under the guidance of a devotee of international law and a friend of France.

Jefferson left the cabinet on January 1, 1794, while the final disposition of Genêt was still pending. But he had already accomplished much. He had been firm but not uncompromising over the surrender of the posts and British relations on the border. His Mississippi policy was shaped by the necessity of maintaining peace with Spain without casting off the West from the older states. His friendship for France had withstood the vexations of an inexperienced and irresponsible government. Is it too much to attribute this steadfastness to the influence of a general body of principles incorporated in the law of nations? Certainly Jefferson was conscious of their authority.

An underlying concept of a genuine international law, possessing a moral if not a physical sanction, thus appears as part of Jefferson's thought. He was, however, too good a lawyer and too experienced a statesman to regard this as a completed revelation from on high, and he himself made valuable contributions to both theory and practice. One of these was his insistence upon the principle that free ships make free goods. To this, reference has already been made.[50] A second, and this is of especial interest today, was no less than a plea for a league of nations. He urged it for the first time in 1786, while he was our minister at Paris; and, although the idea was not acted upon in his

[50] But see also *The Works of Thomas Jefferson*, I. 390.

lifetime, he never wholly abandoned it. The common objective of the league, as proposed by Jefferson, was joint action against the Barbary Pirates.[51] All the powers with a stake in the Mediterranean commerce were asked to place a quota of ships under the direction of an international body sitting at Paris. Coöperative effort under unified command would make short shrift of the pirates. But the project fell through; partly because it was in advance of the time, partly because the government of the Confederation was not strong enough to bind America herself to a share in the compact.

A vital element of Jefferson's scheme of international law was his work on behalf of neutrals. His ideas concerning freedom of the seas and contraband succumbed before a great European war. The only rights of neutrals were those maintained by force. But force might be active or passive. The former was war, and a neutral at war ceased to be neutral. But there is a power in passive resistance which many tyrants have learned to respect. And Jefferson determined to turn that power to account in shaping American foreign policy in the difficult years from 1805 to 1809. His solution was the embargo.

The embargo of 1807 was not a sudden expedient. Jefferson had worked it out in detail more than thirty years before. The resolution of Albemarle County, put forth in July, 1774, was the work of his pen.[52] It declared for

[51] *Ibid.*, I. 100-103. See also *American State Papers,* Foreign Relations, I. 104-105, report of Thomas Jefferson on the Mediterranean Trade, January 3, 1791. Also *ibid.*, p. 134, March 7, 1792. Also *The Works of Thomas Jefferson*, IX. 265, June 11, 1801.

[52] The resolution of Albemarle County should be remembered with the Mecklenburg Declaration of Independence as one of a series of economic and political protests developing all along the western frontier from Pennsylvania to the Carolinas. Taken together, these indicate a sectional self-consciousness which marked the west as united, not only as against the Mother Country but also as against tide-water counties and the older East. Shut off from a European market, the West might contemplate with more serenity than commercial centers on the coast the workings of an embargo.

a very real embargo, proposing "an immediate stop to all imports from *Great Britain,* (cotton, osnabrigs, striped duffil, medicines, gun-powder, lead, books and printed papers, the necessary tools and implements for the handicraft arts and manufactures excepted, for a limited term) and to all exports thereto, after the first day of *October,* which shall be in the year of our Lord, 1775; and immediately to discontinue all commercial intercourse with every part of the *British* Empire which shall not in like manner break off their commerce with *Great Britain.*"[53]

The report on commerce, prepared while Jefferson was secretary of state, is less definite as to an embargo but does advocate reprisal against European powers guilty of discriminating against our trade. The suggested remedy was a system of "Counter prohibitions, duties, and regulations."[54]

In 1794, after Jefferson had withdrawn from the cabinet, he again pronounced in favor of commercial retaliation as an efficient substitute for war. The misfortune of war was that it injured the punisher quite as much as the punished. "I love, therefore, mr. Clarke's proposition of cutting off all communication with the nation which has conducted itself so atrociously."[55] The objection that this might bring on war anyway, he countered by saying that, if it came, we should meet it; if it did not come, the experiment would have paid. A certain reasonableness would at least mark its attempt, inasmuch as the best hope of obtaining justice from the British government lay in bringing pressure upon it from the British people, and "this can never be excited but by distressing their commerce."[56]

[53] *The Works of Thomas Jefferson,* II. 43-44.
[54] *The Writings of George Washington* (Ford ed.), XII. 414, note.
[55] *The Works of Thomas Jefferson,* VIII. 147-148, Jefferson to Tenche Coxe, May 1, 1794.
[56] *Ibid.,* VIII. 150, Jefferson to George Washington, May 14, 1794.

As vice-president, Jefferson was more the critic than the statesman. He clung to the view that war was useless, particularly that which so nearly came in 1798, and although his references to commerce are not especially numerous, he restated his belief in commerce as the most efficient instrument for compelling justice. In this, his attitude was that of "I told you so." Thus he declares:

> If the commercial regulations had been adopted which our legislature were at one time proposing, we should at this moment have been standing on such an eminence of safety & respect as ages can never recover. But having wandered from that, our object should now be to get back, with as little loss as possible, & when peace shall be restored to the world, endeavor so to form our *commercial* regulations as that justice from other nations shall be their mechanical result.[57]

He predicted that as soon as Great Britain and France should have adjusted their difficulties, they would both combine to exclude America from the ocean "by such peaceable means as are in their power."[58] And, in moments of dejection, he seems to have thought it useless to resist. "What a glorious exchange would it be could we persuade our navigating fellow citizens to embark their capital in the internal commerce of our country, exclude foreigners from that & let them take the carrying trade in exchange: abolish the diplomatic establishments & never suffer an armed vessel of any nation to enter our ports."[59] But this need not be taken seriously. It is a leap into the Utopia, which Jefferson in his calmer moods seeks to attain by more practicable means.

As President, in his first months of office, Jefferson defined the policy which he adhered to for eight years. He insisted that freedom of the seas must be restored, but

[57] *Ibid.,* VIII. 293, Jefferson to Thomas Pinckney, May 29, 1797.
[58] *Ibid.,* VIII. 374, Jefferson to James Madison, February 22, 1798.
[59] *Ibid.,* IX. 65-66, Jefferson to Edmund Pendleton, April 22, 1799. For similar pessimism, see *ibid.,* VIII. 286-287, May 13, 1797; also *ibid.,* IX. 95, January 18, 1800.

opposed taking up arms for the purpose.[60]   He reiterated
his definition of contraband, as everything or nothing, and
extended it to commerce.   Either all commerce with belligerents was lawful, or none was.[61]   Again, neutrals must be
maintained in their rights; yet we were in no condition
for a war on their behalf,[62] and "those peaceable coercions
which are in the power of every nation if undertaken in concert & in time of peace, are more likely to produce the
desired effect."[63]   Already, in these early utterances, one
might perceive a reminiscence of the league of nations idea
of 1786, a recognition that international law actually counted
little in times of stress, and a forecast of that embargo which
was eventually to be put into operation.

On the general subject of commerce, he continued to
uphold the principle that free ships make free goods,[64]
though he recognized that the principle would never count
for much until Great Britain yielded her assent.   And this
she would never volunteer, nor could she be forced to it.[65]

Notwithstanding the incorrigibility of England in her
abuse of sea power, Jefferson was too far-seeing to wish
her destruction.   Great Britain had herself to thank for
the world's indifference to her fate.[66]   But it would be a
mistake to wish either Britain or France eliminated from
the balance of power.[67]   Now and then one might even
find points to emulate in British practice, as, for example,

[60] *The Works of Thomas Jefferson*, IX. 219, Jefferson to Dr. George
Logan, March 21, 1801.
    [61] *Ibid.*, IX. 299, Jefferson to Robert R. Livingston, September 9, 1801.
    [62] *Ibid.*, IX. 300-301.
    [63] *Ibid.*, IX. 300.
    [64] See John Taylor, *Curtius, A Defence of the Measures of the Ad-
ministration of Thomas Jefferson*, 1804, pp. 111-118.
    [65] *The Works of Thomas Jefferson*, X. 27, Jefferson to James Madi-
son, Secretary of State, July 31, 1803.
    [66] *Ibid.*, X. 67, Jefferson to James Monroe, January 8, 1804, and p. 77,
Jefferson to James Madison, April 23, 1804.
    [67] *Ibid.*, X. 67.   He preferred England to France, though, after all:
ibid., p. 263-264, May 4, 1806.

that of conveying prizes to the nearest neutral port, a procedure "so much for the interest of all weak nations that we ought to strengthen it by our example."[68]

Other interpolations in the law of nations were less to be desired, and Jefferson in his fifth annual message condemned them as "founded neither in justice, nor the usage or acknowledgment of nations."[69] He never lost sight of America's interest in the law of nations and remained convinced that commerce was our best weapon for its defense, a weapon whose virtues should not be forfeited by acts of belligerency, whose chief usefulness was, in fact, "to encourage others to declare & guarantee neutral rights, by excluding all intercourse with any nation which infringes them."[70]

Jefferson thought he beheld a kindred spirit in the Emperor Alexander, and a letter on the subject of neutral rights addressed in 1806 by the chief of democrats to the Tsar of all the Russias is of great interest. Jefferson entreated Alexander to throw all the weight of his influence in favor of "a correct definition of the rights of neutrals on the high seas," and suggested that excluding offenders against neutral rights from all commerce with other nations would provide an appropriate sanction, efficient, and at the same time preferable to war.[71]

The possibility of peace which had prompted this letter to Alexander did not materialize. Instead, the war entered upon a deadlier phase, and the British blockade of Napoleon intensified the demand for ships and stimulated the impressment of American sailors to man them. Impressment, as a crying abuse, complicated the already numerous infractions of international law which America must endure or pre-

---

[68] *The Works of Thomas Jefferson,* X. 118, Jefferson to James Madison, November 18, 1804.

[69] *Ibid.,* X. 188, December 3, 1805.

[70] *Ibid.,* X. 247-248, Jefferson to Thomas Paine, March 25, 1806.

[71] *Ibid.,* X. 250, Jefferson to Alexander First, April 19, 1806.

vent.[72] Negotiations with Great Britain had been proceeding for some time with slight result, and, in March, 1807, Jefferson warned Monroe, who was in London with Pinkney, that no treaty with Great Britain which failed to take cognizance of the impressment question could possibly be -ratified.[73] On the other hand, he had slight faith that an agreement would be reached. In the event of failure, there was the old weapon of embargo, forged in 1774 and never fully tested.[74]

The embargo, nevertheless, almost missed being tested at all, for the affair of the *Chesapeake* in the summer of 1807 nearly precipitated the war which the embargo was planned to avoid.[75] Sentiment in America ran very high over the insult of halting and searching our warship, and Jefferson himself shared the enthusiasm of the hour.[76] Cooler counsels prevailed, however,[77] and the worst violation of international law to which America had submitted since the ratification of the Constitution passed off with a tardy apology from Great Britain. During the excitement, our shipping had been recalled,[78] and this circumstance rendered the embargo easier of enforcement when it was finally decided upon in December, 1807.

To generalize concerning Jefferson and international law : his position is excellent. Acquainted with the leading thought and thinkers of the eighteenth century, he based his early concept of international law on the theory of compact and the recognition of a state of nature wherein man

[72] *The Works of Thomas Jefferson,* I. 406-407, February 2, 1807. For an earlier statement on impressments, see *American State Papers,* Foreign Relations, I. 131, February 7, 1792.

[73] *The Works of Thomas Jefferson,* X. 375, Jefferson to James Monroe, March 21, 1807.

[74] *Ibid.,* X. 381, Jefferson to James Bowdoin, April 2, 1807.

[75] *Ibid.,* I. 410-419.

[76] *Ibid.,* X. 466, 471.

[77] *Ibid.,* I. 427 ; *ibid.,* X. 433, 456, 458.

[78] *Ibid.,* I. 421-422, advantages of keeping shipping near home.

was primarily in a condition of peace. These pacific theories remained with him in active politics, and he early (1774) declared for an embargo, a principle to which he adhered as a substitute for war until opportunity arose to put it to the test.

In his busy years in the state department, he witnessed the initial stages of a world conflict which spelled the negation and downfall of the international law of the eighteenth century. He himself appealed to the authorities in this older law and found in them a support for the neutrality which Washington pursued in 1793 and later. But this contribution of Grotius, Wolff, Vattel, and others to the actual politics of a rising nation was in a sense the "twilight" of the classical school of international law.

Its appeal henceforth was chiefly academic, and men turned from the ruins of the old to reconstitute a new law of nations. In the latter undertaking, Jefferson was no mean figure. Amid the wealth of his ideas on a multiplicity of topics one may glean a general system of international law, in which the rights of neutrals, their freedom of commerce, the principle that free ships make free goods, and the denial of any contraband, constitute the body; while the spirit gleams forth in aspirations for a league of nations, in reluctance to see even enemies perish, and in hopes for a future of coöperative effort.

Finally, the same fundamental pacifism which led him to welcome a frontier unguarded by troops, impelled him to clutch at any device offering the least promise as a substitute for war. Here the embargo stands out as Jefferson's grand experiment in pacifism. That it failed, for reasons which concern its operation rather than its philosophy, was a tragedy. Jefferson and his embargo did not complete a working scheme of international law. On the other hand, neither can be ignored in any study which attempts to show the struggle which man has made to lift himself above the brute.

Up to this point, our study has been the background of thought and experience which led Jefferson to the embargo as a practical solution for the crisis of 1807. In some measure, the preceding pages have analyzed Jefferson as a thinker. But thought bore fruit in action. It is with Jefferson as a doer and administrator that we are next concerned. How did he reach the final decision? What annoyances and compensations vexed or soothed the most difficult years of his life? And what judgment should posterity render upon his "Grand Design" and its administration? Questions of this sort can be answered only by a study of the embargo and Jefferson in action.

CHAPTER III

THE ADOPTION OF THE EMBARGO TO APRIL 30, 1808

The affair of the *Chesapeake* and the consequent near
approach to war demonstrated to the most confirmed of
optimists the need of more aggressive action. An embargo
early suggested itself as the most available weapon short of
actual war. The possibilities which it involved were matter
of earnest discussion throughout the summer and autumn of
1807, and the final decision was not reached until conflicting
viewpoints had been weighed. One of the most roseate
views was advanced by J. Barnes, an American stationed at
Leghorn, Italy, who predicted, in the event of an embargo,
the speedy collapse of the British Empire. His letter to
Jefferson is of especial significance as one of the factors
contributing to the latter's confidence in the aggressive rather
than the merely defensive possibilities of an embargo:

> In fine, we have only to *Shut* our ports & *remain firm*—the
> *People* of *England* would *do* the *rest*—for British manufacturers
> being precluded from the Continent of Europe almost entirely, their
> chief resource is the U. S. consequently about 150,000 Manufac-
> turers being thrown out of Bread would *rise* in Mass and *compel*
> the Minister to open our Ports at *any price,* or they would Massacre
> him—The disposition of the People of England I well know; having
> been about four years in that Island.[1]

A sentiment equally favorable to an embargo was expressed to Jefferson by his boyhood friend, John Page, who
wrote from Richmond on July 12, 1807, that he had heard
repeated arguments:

> that an immediate embargo is necessary, because before the usual
> meeting of Congress all the british Ships &c will have left us, & even
> our own Vessels, & Sailors, who will be impressed or detained in

[1] Jefferson Papers, Library of Congress.

British Ports throughout their Empire: & that their Ships of War
& Privateers without further notice will sweep our vessels which
may be at Sea, from the Surface of the Seas; that an immediate
stop to all intercourse with Britain is indispensibly necessary, to
retrieve our lost honor, & to bring the mad King to his senses; &
that that measure alone would be of more consequence than any
naval and military preparations we can ever make. . . . I con-
fess that when I recollect the hatred which G.3d bears to you, & our
Country & his low Cunning, abominable perfidy, & execrable practice
of issuing secret Instructions, through Channels of Communication
unknown to his ostensible Ministers, by which means he began & by
which alone he *did begin & carry on* his former War with the *U.S.*,
I am nearly of the same opinion, & fear that you will lose by delay
as it is evidently certain that *he* is bent on a war with the *U.S.*, rely-
ing on the support of the federal partizans, avowed Tories, his own
Subjects here, &.*Burr's Choice Spirits,* & I suppose Insurrections
of Slaves in the Southern States; and foolishly believing, that he
had conquered Napoleon, & had added Turkey & Austria to his
Confederacy, he had no doubt when he issued his secret orders
which bound Berkley &c, that you would crouch under his Insult;
or the U.S. would fall an easy Prey into his Hands.[2]

The great American manufacturer of woollens, David
Humphreys, confirmed from a different angle the opinions
of Barnes and Page. On a trip which he made to England,
he found that a large section of the British public favored
an immediate war with America, but he perceived that this
was contrary to the interest of the manufacturers and the
merchants trading with the United States, and he counted
upon their ability to influence the policy of the government.[3]
In a report to Jefferson, written soon after his return to
America, Humphreys says:

How long a period will elapse before their voice can be heard,
it is difficult to determine. The Ministry seemed solicitous to collect

[2] Jefferson Papers.

[3] This was alluded to by William Pinkney, our minister at London,
who wrote to Madison that "An attempt will, I think, be made by some
of the merchants trading to the United States to prevail upon their
whole body in the different parts of the kingdom to urge the Government, if not to an abandonment, at least to a considerable modification
of the orders, so as, perhaps to leave the trade of our country in its
native productions free. I do not believe that the attempt will succeed.
The orders in their present shape, are more popular than could have
been expected. *American State Papers,* Foreign Relations, III. 206.
See also *ibid.,* III. 203.

the sense of the Country, which is certainly no easy task.—In the meantime, Mr Monroe & Mr Pinckney entertained better hopes of success, at the eve of my departure, than they had done some time before.—I perceive little chance of enjoying permanent safety, but by our becoming in a great degree an armed & united People, in effect, as well as in name.[4]

Nevertheless, Jefferson hesitated to impose an embargo until a fair proportion of our shipping should have had time to be recalled.   On July 30, 1807, he intimated to General Smith, a politician of Baltimore, that "—Congress could not declare war without a demand of satisfaction, nor should they lay an embargo while we have so much under the grasp of our adversary."[5]   In October he gauged the temper of Congress to be "extremely disposed for peace,"[6] so much so, in fact, that there was danger that it would combat impressment by nothing more menacing than non-importation, a measure which would, however, be highly irritating to England, who would choose her own time for a declaration of war.[7]   But, by the close of November, Jefferson was confirmed in the opinion that the next dispatches from Monroe would offer to Congress no other choice than "War; Embargo or Nothing," with prospects favorable to the second of the three.[8]

Two persons who might expect to feel the weight of such a measure perceived the storm in advance and sought to stave off its consequences.   Both were friendly to the administration.   The one was James Sullivan, the Democratic governor of Massachusetts, whose political ascendancy would be immediately jeopardized by any party measure inimical to his constituents.   The other was Albert Gallatin, the secretary of the treasury, who, more than any other person, would be charged with enforcing the embargo.

[4] Jefferson Papers, September 25, 1807.
[5] *Ibid.*, Jefferson to General Smith.
[6] *Ibid.*, Jefferson to T. M. Randolph, October 26, 1807.
[7] *Ibid.*
[8] *Ibid.*, Jefferson to T. M. Randolph, November 30, 1807.

Early in December, 1807, Sullivan warned Jefferson that, owing to the composition of both state and federal courts in Massachusetts, the difficulties of carrying out any resolute course of action would be almost insuperable. At this time Sullivan thought that war would be the course determined upon, and he declared:

There is no way to carry on a war with that vigour which is necessary to success without the decisive aid of a Judiciary: our Judiciary here, would, under any circumstances that can take place, be decidedly against the Government of the United States and on the part of England.—The Judiciary of the United States in this district is still more unpropitious to the Safety of the country.—We shall, if a war takes place, be instantly plunged in a civil war in this State if the Judiciary continues as it is at present, and yet I do not conceive of a remedy.[9]

Nor was Sullivan's anxiety relieved by the news that embargo and not war was the decision of the government. He lost no time in painting for the benefit of Jefferson a most depressing picture of conditions in Massachusetts politics:

I would not make the residue of your administration more anxious and troublesome than is necessary: but you are now in a critical situation. . . . The machinations of the English party, for some years past have filled our State Judiciary with men who are determined to unite us again with great britain: ostensibly as an ally, but in reallity as a dependent on her . . . our militia does well to be talked about, but cannot be depended on. . . . Your Judiciary of the United States are worse than ours in this district. Your attorneys, in some instances for the United States, would be compleatly on the side of great Britain. . . . The federalists here openly avow that if a war takes place England will send an army to the Southern States to cause the blacks to cut their masters throats. They talk of a division between the southern and northern States as a matter of course, and are openly forming a party to be united under the protection of a british standard. You will not believe this until it shall be too late. Nothing but an alteration in the judiciary can save us from destruction in this way.[10]

[9] Jefferson Papers. James Sullivan to Jefferson. Boston, December 7, 1807.

[10] Ibid., James Sullivan to Jefferson. January 7, 1808.

Gallatin was less hysterical than Sullivan, but by no means friendly to a measure in the execution of which he could anticipate but little thanks. Three weeks before the enactment of the embargo, Gallatin hinted to the President that a repeal of the existing non-importation act and the substitution for it of another non-importation act more general in its scope was the most reasonable legislation for the time being.[11] When the embargo was finally determined upon, he expressed himself first upon a detail of treasury administration, as favoring a lenient treatment of foreign vessels already on the point of clearing from our ports.[12] Then, warming to his theme, he declared:

In every point of view, privation, suffering, revenue, effect on the enemy, politics at home &c., I prefer war to a permanent embargo. Governmental prohibitions do always more mischief than had been calculated, and it is not without much hesitation that a statesman should hazard to regulate the concerns of individuals. The measure being of doubtful policy & hastily adopted on the first view of our foreign intelligence, I think that we had better recommend it with modifications, & at first for such a limited time as will afford us all, time for re-consideration &, if we think proper, for an alteration in our course without appearing to retract. As to the hope that it may have an effect on the negotiation with Mr. Rose, or induce England to treat us better I think it entirely groundless.[13]

Having reached his decision, Jefferson ignored these counter arguments, whatever weight they may originally have had, and, on December 18, 1807, he submitted to Congress the brief message which follows:

To the Senate and House of Representatives of the United States:
The communications now made, showing the great and increasing dangers with which our vessels, our seamen, and merchandise are threatened on the high seas and elsewhere, from the belligerent powers of Europe, and it being of great importance to keep in safety these essential resources, I deem it my duty to recommend the subject to the consideration of Congress, who will doubtless per-

[11] Jefferson Papers. Albert Gallatin to the President. December 2, 1807.
[12] *Ibid.*, Gallatin to Jefferson. December 18, 1807.
[13] *Ibid.*

ceive all the advantages which may be expected from an inhibition of the departure of our vessels from the ports of the United States.

Their wisdom will also see the necessity of making every preparation for whatever events may grow out of the present crisis.[14]

Here was Jefferson's reply to the orders and decrees of both belligerents. It sought to reconcile neutrality and pacifism with dignity and national honor. It embodied the ideals of a statesman who kept his countrymen from war, even in the face of a direct insult like the affair of the *Chesapeake*. It ignored the more hostile aspect of British and French regulations, which might, after all, by a euphemism, he called "municipal."[15] Even where it made positive recommendation of an embargo, it stressed only the defensive advantages inhering therein. The message veiled such coercive utility as the embargo possessed under the ambiguous phrase "all the advantages which may be expected." War as the *ultima ratio* it hinted at only in the final clause.

So great was the necessity for action, swift and secret, and so smooth was the operation of the Democratic-Republican machine, that, within four days of the receipt of the message, its suggestions had become law. In obedience to the presidential mandate, Congress committed itself to a course of action the wisdom of which has never been fully resolved and which became for the President a source of greater unhappiness and more chagrin than any other event in his career, with the possible exception of his flight from the British in the Arnold invasion of 1781.

The act was no sooner passed than amendments were needed. On the very day of its enactment, Gallatin pointed out to his chief the absence of penalties for its violation, the

---

[14] *The Works of Thomas Jefferson,* X. 530-531.

[15] *American State Papers,* Foreign Relations, III. 205. Pinkney to Madison, November, 23, 1807. "The French decree . . . was no more than a legitimate, though possibly an ungracious exercise of the rights of local sovereignty."

neglect to mention coasting vessels, and the failure to prevent the export of specie in payment for foreign cargoes landed in the United States.[16] On December 24, he urged the necessary amendments, meanwhile undertaking to enforce the original act with revenue cutters and gunboats.[17] Gallatin's troubles began at once, for on December 31, before the embargo was ten days old, he mentions the receipt of "numerous letters stating gross evasions."[18] Nor were complaints at all slow in reaching Jefferson himself. The first was anonymous from New York, informing him as follows:

> We are the shipping interest and we will take care that, shall not be destroyed by your attachment to France, your implacable enmity to G.B, and in short, by your madness & folly—I have ever been a warm Republican but when I see my country on the verge of destruction, I am compelled to oppose those, whose measures I once approved.[19]

From the adoption to the repeal of the embargo, Jefferson was under attack. He became of necessity the chief apologist of his own pet measure. Defence of the embargo sometimes brought him into unaccustomed rôles, such, for example, as that of a protagonist of manufactures. Already in August, 1807, he had written benignly to say:

> No one wishes success, more than I do, to domestic manufacture, & especially under present appearances; & no one will more certainly give them the most important of all encouragements, the preference of all others, so far as my own wants go, but the establishing such works, the conducting them, & the having concern in them, are so entirely within the competence of private and patriotic citizens, & they are so much more competent & at leisure for them, that it would be a double abuse for me to become anything more than their customer.[20]

In January, after the embargo had become law, his interest was more keen:

---

[16] Jefferson Papers. Gallatin to Jefferson, December 22, 1807.
[17] *Ibid.,* December 24, 1807.
[18] *Ibid.,* December 31, 1807.
[19] *Ibid.,* December 26, 1807.
[20] *Ibid.,* Jefferson to John Gardiner, August 19, 1807.

I am much pleased to find our progress in manufactures to be so great. That of cotton is peculiarly interesting, because we raise the raw material in such abundance, and because it may to a great degree supply our deficiencies both in wool & linen.[21]

If New England had been as willing as Jefferson to recognize the possibilities for wealth in manufacturing, a trying chapter in her history might have been avoided. The Middle States, which had less capital tied up in shipping and were therefore more free to grasp the opportunity presented by immunity from the competition of Europeans, found the embargo a stimulus rather than a hindrance. But with Jefferson himself, the argument for manufactures was, at best, only an embellishment of the sounder doctrine that the embargo saved our shipping and averted war. This doctrine he preached again and again as the true milk of the word. To select but one from among many examples, a letter from Jefferson to Gideon Granger, his Postmaster General, is in point:

If we had suffered our vessels, cargoes and seamen to have gone out, all would have been taken by England or it's enemies, and we must have gone to war to avenge the wrong. it was certainly a better alternative to discontinue all intercourse with these nations till they shall return again to some sense of moral right. I only lament the situation of our seamen, and wish it could be relieved. as to the sacrifices of the farmers & citizens-merchants, I am sure they will be cheerfully met.[22]

These sacrifices were met with a far from uniform cheerfulness.[23] But, notwithstanding the numerous protests of

[21] *Jefferson Papers,* Jefferson to J. Dorsey, January 21, 1808.

[22] *Ibid.,* Jefferson to Granger, January 22, 1808. Cf. also *The Works of Thomas Jefferson,* XI. 7. Jefferson to Charles Thomson, January 11, 1808. "Time prepares us for defence; time may produce peace in Europe that removes the ground of difference with England until another European war, and that may find our revenues liberated by the discharge of our national debt, our wealth and numbers increased, our friendship and our enmity more important to every nation."

[23] Jefferson Papers. Anonymous, Boston, February 2, 1808. ". . . if you will go to war with Britain, you will be denounced, as the greatest traitor that history has exhibited. *We,* who live in the *Seaports* shall be ruined. Two or 3 ships will destroy our whole coast, left defenseless by Mr. Jefferson. Awake—arouse. French Philosophy will not do for *us Republicans.* We are for liberty: but we will not be destroyed," etc.

interests adversely affected by the embargo, Jefferson long held to a belief that the measure was not unpopular. He told his son-in-law, Thomas Mann Randolph, that definite news of the British Orders of November 11 had "entirely hushed all opposition to the embargo."[24] The news was indeed belated. Congress had acted upon rumor only. It was not until February 2 that Jefferson transmitted an official copy of the Orders, at the same time observing that they were "further proof of the increasing dangers to our Navigation and Commerce which led to the provident measure of the act of the present session laying an embargo on our own vessels."[25]

Jefferson had already come to the conclusion that war with England was not imminent, but he was satisfied that it was no time to discontinue the embargo.[26] Laudatory resolutions of the Massachusetts legislature,[27] carried through by Sullivan and the Republican machine, gave him encouragement. And assurances from a North Carolina correspondent, Colonel William Tatham,[28] that the planters around Newbern were in a mood to tax themselves voluntarily for the benefit of injured commercial men, if only the amounts could be justly ascertained, with a view of strengthening the President's hand so as "to overturn all the feeble theories of European policy," served to fill his cup of happiness. If anything was still lacking, it was made

[24] Jefferson Papers. Jefferson to T. M. Randolph, January 26, 1808. Cf. also *American State Papers*, Foreign Relations, III. 208. Madison to Pinckney, February 19, 1808. ". . . the appearance of these decrees has had much effect in reconciling all descriptions among us to the embargo."

[25] Jefferson Papers. Jefferson to Congress, February 2, 1808. Cf. also *The Works of Thomas Jefferson*, XI. 9.

[26] Jefferson Papers. Jefferson to T. M. Randolph, February 6 and February 22, 1808. The British Consul at New York reported to his government that war was unlikely, also that America was wearying of the embargo. See his letter of April 4, 1808, in George Lockhart Rives (ed.), *Selections from the Correspondence of Thomas Barclay*, p. 275. See also Jefferson to Governor Pinckney, March 30, 1808.

[27] Jefferson Papers. Boston, February 8, 1808.

[28] *Ibid.*, Newbern, February 10, 1808.

up by the instructions of the Massachusetts legislature to
its representative in the United States Congress to work
for a constitutional amendment which would place the
removal of federal judges under the control of the President, subject to the approval of a majority of the House
and two thirds of the Senate. Here was a step toward weakening the bench, one of Jefferson's pet aversions, and at the
same time an evidence that Massachusetts was setting her
house in order against the judiciary, the menace from which
had been alluded to in Sullivan's earlier letters to Jefferson.[29]

These cheerful considerations were, to be sure, at least
partially offset by a contraband trade with Canada, which
Gallatin was urged to prevent;[30] by the need for gun-boats
to enforce the government's regulations,[31] and, if Jefferson chose to take them seriously, by personal appeals for
help from individual citizens in distress. One such, who
implored assistance for his wife and seven children, declared
that he was a veteran of the Revolution and "ready to Lift
my musquit again should there be any invation."[32]

But, if all was not smooth in America, England, too,
had her difficulties.[33] Of these latter, Jefferson had confirmation through James Bowdoin, who was in London, on his

[29] Jefferson Papers. "Commonwealth of Massachusetts" in Senate,
February 11, 1808.

[30] Ibid., Jefferson to Gallatin, February 14, 1808.

[31] Ibid., Jefferson to Smith, February 14, 1808. See also The Works
of Thomas Jefferson, I. 421. A cabinet meeting on April 5, 1808,
agreed that twenty gunboats with twenty men apiece would be needed
at New Orleans, and "about half a dozen [to] be kept in different places
for enforcing the embargo with 8 or 10 men each." . . . "Let the
frigates & sloop remain where they are with about 20 or 30 men each
to keep them clean. Which will reduce the number of seamen to less
than 900." This in a time of crisis.

[32] Jefferson Papers. James Lewis, a citizen of New York, to Jefferson, February 16, 1808.

[33] William Pinkney, Life of William Pinkney, p. 192. "I am greatly
deceived if it will not in a few weeks be matter of surprise among all
descriptions of people here, that a manufacturing and commercial nation
like Great Britain, could have expected anything but disaster and ruin
from such a venture." Pinkney to Madison, January 7, 1808.

way home from Spain. Bowdoin wrote that so learned an
Englishman as Mr. Williams, the friend of Franklin, warned
America against any compromise. If America would but be
firm, she might place her commercial relations

upon the broad basis of Reciprocity to extend to every part of the
british dominions. The advocates of british restrictions, prohibitions, & navigation acts stand appalled at the perplexed & dangerous
situation in which this country, her colonies & commerce are involved: and with a governmt. so fixed in its habits as this is, & so
difficult of change on all questions of reform, it is necessary to seize
the occasion & to press home upon it, those points in favour of our
commerce which justice and reciprocity demand.[34]

Bowdoin's letter enclosed the pamphlet of Alexander Baring
denouncing the Orders in Council, certain to be cheerful
reading for the American President.

At about this time, in a communication to the Tammany
Society of New York, which, like the good Republican Club
that it was, had declared its approbation of the party platform, Jefferson set forth the underlying philosophy of the
embargo with a dignity which he never surpassed:

. . . but the ocean, which, like the air, is the common birthright of mankind, is arbitrarily wrested from us, and maxims conse-
crated by time, by usage, & by an universal sense of right, are
trampled on by superior force: to give time for this demoralizing
tempest to pass over, one measure only remained which might cover
our beloved country from it's overwhelming fury; an appeal to the
deliberate understanding of our fellow citizens in a cessation of all
intercourse with the belligerent nations, until it can be resumed
under the protection of a returning sense of the moral obligations
which constitute a law for nations as well as individuals: There can
be no question in a mind truly American, whether it is best to send
our citizens & property into certain captivity, and then wage war
for their recovery, or to keep them at home, and to turn seriously to
that policy which plant the manufacturer & the husbandman side by
side, and so establish at the door of every one that exchange of
mutual labors & comforts which we have hitherto sought in distant
regions, and under perpetual risk of broils with them.[35]

[34] Jefferson Papers. Bowdoin to Jefferson. London, February 17,
1808.
[35] *Ibid.*, February 29, 1808.

In one so sensitive to public opinion as Jefferson, March, 1808, must have been a season of conflicting emotions. From Philadelphia[36] and from North[37] and South Carolina[38] came the most enthusiastic encomiums; from Massachusetts came diatribes. For just as Jefferson was thanking Sullivan for the official approval of the state legislature, the Boston merchants put forth an independent protest, all their own, praying for light on the causes of the embargo and on its probable duration, asking help for their impoverished neighbors from a treasury so often boasted of as "overflowing," and closing with a gentle warning that unless this was *"speedily done* perhaps the United States will lose *New England* she not having the wish to bear insults & to let them go unrevenged, this notwithstanding the approbation of the Legislature is the sentiment of the Inhabitants of Boston."[39]

On March 7, Jefferson wrote to a private correspondent that the embargo was undoubtedly injurous to personal interests, but that for a limited time it was preferable to war. Just when that time would expire, he thought might well be determined at the next session of Congress.[40] Meanwhile, the embargo itself deserved a fair trial, and Jefferson felt alarmed for his pet measure because of a joker in the amending bill of March 14.[41] This provision would enable merchants who could prove their claim to property abroad to send a ship for it. Many merchants

---

[36] Jefferson Papers. "Delegates of the Democratic Republicans of the City of Philadelphia to Thomas Jefferson," March 1, 1808.

[37] *Ibid.,* Printed Resolutions.

[38] *Ibid.,* Resolutions of the South Carolina Legislature, forwarded by Governor Charles Pinckney, March 8, 1808.

[39] Jefferson Papers. "Petition of Boston Merchants and others, March 4, 1808."

[40] *Ibid.,* Jefferson to Major Joseph Eggleston, March 7, 1808. Also *Ibid.,* Jefferson to Levi Lincoln, March 23, 1808. Also *The Works of Thomas Jefferson,* XI. 13-17, March 11, 1808.

[41] Jefferson Papers. Jefferson to Governor Cabell, March 13, 1808.

applied for the privilege, and the whole purpose of the embargo legislation was in a fair way to be frustrated.

The merchants in question were merely seeking legal warrant for violations which others carried out in defiance of law. Thus protests of affection[42] for the embargo did not prevent North Carolinians from violating it.[43] An orgy of smuggling on Lake Champlain challenged the utmost efforts of the executive.[44] The coastwise trade in flour suddenly assumed unprecedented proportions,[45] mute testimony to illicit practices. Other problems confronting the executive were the proper regulation of the Indian trade, the continued fostering of manufactures, the maintenance of Republican majorities in disaffected states, and the interpretation of developments in Great Britain with a view to the wisest shaping of foreign policy. Concerning the first of these, Jefferson told Gallatin that simple justice required a free passage of supplies to the Indians, that the treaty with them guaranteed such a traffic, and that the treaty was more fundamental law than the embargo. If, however, doubt existed on this score, an amendment should be sought from Congress.[46] With reference to the second, North Carolina reports, which for that matter were usually encouraging, informed Jefferson that preparations were making for local manufactures sufficient to clothe the population "without being put to any non plus for supplies from any nation on earth."[47]

More perplexing than proper relations with Indians and manufacturers, was what to do for Republican majorities

[42] *Ibid.*, "Resolutions of the Grand Jury of the Superior Court of Law & Equity of the County of Brunswick held on the 12th day of April 1808."
[43] *Ibid.*, Gallatin to Jefferson, March 12, 1808.
[44] *Ibid.*, Proclamation by Jefferson, April 19, 1808.
[45] *Ibid.*, C. Rodney to Jefferson, April 22, 1808.
[46] *Ibid.*, Jefferson to Gallatin, March 26, 1808.
[47] *Ibid.*, James Lyne to Jefferson, March 30, 1808.

in districts where embargo losses were upsetting the party morale. Massachusetts presented an extreme example of restlessness. Yet local authorities, high in the councils of the party, themselves disagreed as to the condition of the patient. The protest of the "Inhabitants of Boston" has been already noted. But Levi Lincoln, the lieutenant governor of the state, maintained that such clamors were not to be taken seriously:

> It is the comparative few which make all the noise; the desperate in politics, the desperate in property, who wish by the risk of other people's capitals to take a possible chance of getting one of their own, & the unprincipled. The great body of the people, all the republicans, & many of the federalists beleive (*sic*) in the necessity & utility of the measure. The choice between it & National dishonor is unhesitatingly made by the citizens of the State. Their confidence is unabated in the wisdom, integrity, &· patriotism of their Govt. & they will support its measures, the vile attempts to prevent it notwithstanding.[48]

Over against this cheerful comment of Lincoln's, as if on the parallel columns of bull and bear advice in a broker's office, Jefferson might set the lugubrious views of James Sullivan, the governor of Massachusetts, and make his choice between them. Sullivan took the extremists at their word. On April 2, on the eve of the state elections, he wrote to Jefferson that an alliance with England was the avowed object of Federalist machinations:

> The attempt is to revolutionize this state in order to affect the election of a president of the united States, then to divide the nation and establish in this part of this hemisphere a different form of government, under the protection of Great britain. . . . They are now urging the Yazoo claim in favour of Clinton as the next president; but without any design to have him elected.[49]

Three days later, apparently from a fear that Jefferson would take the Republican victory at the polls as proof that he had been a mere alarmist, Sullivan repeated his warn-

[48] Jefferson Papers. Levi Lincoln to Jefferson, April 1, 1808.
[49] *Ibid.*, James Sullivan to Jefferson, April 2, 1808.

ings, only with greater detail. Dissolution of the Union by a separation of North from South and a new confederation under British patronage was the goal of the Tories:

and however you may treat the idea with neglect, it is on the request of this party in New England, that seven ships of the line, and ten thousand troops are on their way to Halifax. I know not what Lyman your consul is about in England; Williams, his predecessor the Nephew of Pickering is very vigilant there. His letters give assurance to the merchants in England, that the New England people will compel a repeal of the Embargo Act. His letters to his friends here give them assurance that great britian will cordially receive the returning northern States, and leave the Southern hemisphere to provide for its negroes, or to to (*sic*) submit to the french for protection. You will stand astonished to find that any considerable proportion of Massachusetts came forward in maintainance of such a project. But the old tories and old tory familys (*sic*) are resuscitated: the aristocracy of wealth; even though nominal in banks, and wrapt in the base corruption of speculation has crowded all principle from our community, and our people are essentially changed. There are open and public avowals every day, in the assurance offices, that great britian is our only protector, that we are unable to protect ourselves, that her fleet is our fleet, her navy our navy, and gunboats must be held in contempt. All the opposition they have made to gun boats, has arisen in this way: not that they wished or expected an American navy but wished to show that a connexion with England for the sake of her navy was necessary to us.[50]

Lest the pessimism of Sullivan should take too deep root in the mind of Jefferson, the more light-hearted Lincoln wrote him a victory paean, boasting that the Republican ticket had won by a majority better than last year's, that Pickering's seditious utterances, "sowed much thicker among us by the enemies to our Government than were the tares by the enemy of goodness, among the wheat" had not prevailed. In fine, Republicanism had been severely tested, "But is stronger for having been attacked."[51]

If conditions in New England were thus open to such opposite interpretations, those in old England were equally mystifying. A Liverpool correspondent wrote Jefferson

[50] Jefferson Papers. James Sullivan to Jefferson, April 5, 1808.
[51] *Ibid.*, Levi Lincoln to Jefferson, April 7, 1808.

that that town, "so long famed for its immense commerce with the U. S. A., in all probability, is shortly to experience a sad reverse." But, if the prosperity of Liverpool depended upon the American trade, and the American trade was in eclipse, why was there no greater price advance on American goods? "Although the United States furnish this country with $5/8^{th}$ of the Cotton she manufactures, yet the upland Georgia is only about 18^d. whereas in Holland 3/ & in France 4/2 the pound."[52]

Undoubtedly the embargo was imposing hardships in Great Britain, for the King, in April, instructed his warships and privateers to encourage the passage of all neutral vessels laden with lumber and provisions, and bound for either the West Indies or South America. The neutrals meant were Americans, and these fresh orders were an open bid to Americans to defy their own authorities, being assured of British licenses, even if they could get no clearance papers from their home ports.[53] From one point of view, this was a concession to the potency of an embargo which was depriving British colonies of sustenance. From another point of view, it was an insulting appeal to the people over the head of their government. Pinkney, our minister at London, adopted the latter interpretation, but concluded that its only effect would be "to add to the vigilance of the government in guarding the law, and to render more conspicuous the just pride and the public spirit of our citizens by an open disdain of all foreign allurements to break it."[54]

To Jefferson and his friends, the political life of England was as inexplicable as the economic. Notwithstanding all the protests from manufacturers and the American traders, Parliament was certain to confirm the Orders in

---

[52] Jefferson Papers. James Maury to Jefferson. Liverpool, March 15, 1808.

[53] *American State Papers*, Foreign Relations, III. 281.

[54] Pinkney, *The Life of William Pinkney*, Pinkney to Madison, p. 195.

Council;[55] the ministry was secure in its parliamentary majority, a circumstance boding ill for peace between Britain and America;[56] and the only real hope of any immediate adjustment seemed to lie in the possibility of a general peace in Europe, "in which case our embargo will cease, from that time."[57]

Amid cares so many and varied, Jefferson was not immune from petty annoyances, like the appeal already cited from the old soldier with seven children and a musket. A further importunity of this sort came from the guardian of a Boston orphan. He rendered to Jefferson the following bill for damages:

> Miss S.T. an orphan child: four months rent of a Store in Boston due this 29 March 1808—which Store the Tenant has left in consequence of the Embargo laid by Mr. Jefferson; and the said orphan is deprived of the past income without the least prospect of any future tenant occupying her store left by her departed parents, & has nothing but the prospect of poverty before her—The quarter
> Rent $100.[58]

Among so many tribulations, foreign and domestic, Jefferson was well nigh exhausted. When Congress finally rose at the end of April for its summer recess, he wrote to a member of his cabinet, Caesar Rodney, that "this six months session has worn me down to a state of almost total incapacity for business."[59]   Relief was not in sight, for with Congress adjourned to hear the voice of the country and to mend its political fences, Jefferson was left to execute

[55] The Jefferson Papers. Jefferson to C. Rodney, April 24, 1808. See *The Works of Thomas Jefferson*, XI. 29.

[56] Jefferson Papers. Jefferson to Col. Worthington, April 24, 1808. It was believed by Jefferson's enemies in New England that war was the very thing he desired. Cf. Bernard C. Steiner, *Life and Correspondence of James McHenry*, p. 544. Ben Stoddart to McHenry, March 31, 1808.

[57] Jefferson Papers. Jefferson to Mr. Strode, April 3, 1808.

[58] This bill is preserved in Jefferson Papers, March 29, 1808.

[59] Jefferson's handwriting confirms this.

the embargo and at the same time to negotiate for its suspension.[60] His experiences in this dual task are the subject of the next chapter.

[60] *American State Papers,* Foreign Relations, III. 222. Madison to Pinkney, April 30, 1808. ". . . the United States are ready to resume their export trade as soon as the aggressions on it shall cease; and that, in a hope that this might happen during the recess of Congress, the President is authorized, in such an event, to suspend, in whole or in part, the several embargo laws."

CHAPTER IV

SUCCESS AND FAILURE

The experiences which Jefferson was to encounter alone and face to face with the embargo were foreshadowed by the events of the previous months. Before the session came to an end, the chief difficulties of embargo enforcement, the ultimate division between supporters and opponents of the measure, and the probable effect of the embargo upon European developments were all fairly evident to the critical observer.

But the interval of personal government, in a test to the finish of liberalism as a substitute for war, affords a study, which can never be devoid of interest, of a humanitarian autocrat administering a panacea for the woes of mankind. Jefferson brought to the task of rendering the embargo an efficient engine of peace both the highest idealism and all the arts of the trained politician. No one knew better than he how to mould public opinion. No American of his time could rival him in the technique of party management and in the subtle machinations which build a strong machine. His endowments of heart and mind were both of the highest order. But they were pitted against forces which might baffle a superman, forces which, by their very success in overthrowing him, were to lift Jefferson into the noble army of martyrs who have fought the good fight for mankind.

Most fundamental of the obstacles to success were the facts of human nature. Jefferson was asking his countrymen to play a passive rôle. They were pitted against Europe, but the struggle was negative—a test not of aggression but of endurance. This in itself was a handicap, since the usual incitements to emotional patriotism were absent. It was to be a long pull and a hard pull, with the shoreline too distant to register daily progress. Worse still, it trenched upon the economic life of the entire American people. The rich merchant, who would willingly have given his son for his country, scorned a country which asked only for his moneybags.

If, in spite of these difficulties, Jefferson's extraordinary hold upon the imagination and affections of his countrymen were to insure the fairest possible trial of his new weapon of peace in time of war, how could he be certain that even a total cessation of American exports would bend the chancelleries of Europe to his will? The odds were certainly against him when, in May of 1808, he embarked upon an era of personal government which called for the arbitrary enforcement of a most inquisitorial act, for a tampering with what many men regarded as their dearest rights, and which put in jeopardy both his popularity and his fame, the cherished rewards of a long career. Yet it is during these six months of autocracy that Jefferson is most convincing as a democrat. A demagogue would have served his own fame. Jefferson preferred to serve his people by sparing them from what he regarded as man's greatest curse. He was in a position to test, as few reformers have been, the potency of those pacific theories by which he had chosen to guide his life. Among the sordid details of administration at home and negotiation abroad, pacifism, or a scheme of peace as a substitute for war, was on trial.

We are first concerned with the progress of embargo enforcement and with the state of American opinion, for upon these the negotiations abroad, whether successful or otherwise, would in a large measure depend.

One of Jefferson's first moves was a proclamation to the governors of Orleans, Georgia, South Carolina, Massachusetts, and New Hampshire, calling attention to the act

of April 25 authorizing him to detain all coasting vessels
and their cargoes upon suspicion of intent to evade the
embargo.[1] Flour in particular he designated as suspect.
At the same time, in order to insure a supply of flour to
communities which were not self-sufficing, he authorized the
governors to issue to trusted merchants warrants for the
importation of the amounts required by their respective
states, duplicates to be filed with the secretary of the
treasury.

The underlying idea in this plan coincided with Jefferson's whole political philosophy of distributing authority
whenever it was too centralized. At the same time, it relaxed the ironclad provisions of a law which represented the
very maximum of interference with the individual rights
of the citizen. To Gallatin, toward whom he may have felt
apologetic for a ruling which was bound to complicate the
workings of the treasury, Jefferson wrote on the same day,
urging the importance of a rigid execution of the new law,
for

the great leading object of the legislature was, and ours in execution
of it, ought to be, to give compleat effect to the embargo laws.
They have bidden Agriculture, Commerce, Navigation to bow before
that object, to be nothing when in competition with that. Finding
all their endeavors at general rules to be evaded, they finally gave us
the power of Detention as the Panacea, and I am clear we ought to
use it freely that we may by a fair experiment know the power of
this great weapon, the embargo.[2]

Jefferson went on to demonstrate to Gallatin that the
letters to the governors were a positive safeguard for such
enforcement, because the treasury would know that applications not properly vouched for were unwarranted. He
concluded with an obiter dictum that coast-wise trade "may

[1] Jefferson Papers. May 6, 1808.
[2] *Ibid.*, Jefferson to A. Gallatin, May 6, 1808. Cf. also *ibid.*, same to
same, May 15. "I place immense value in the experiment being fully
made, how far an embargo may be an effective weapon in future as well
as on this occasion."

be some trifling advantage to individuals . . . but it is not a farthing's benefit to the nation at large, and risks their great object in the embargo."[3]

The Governor of New Hampshire was the first to reply. He assured Jefferson that his constituents were almost wholly dependent for flour upon the southern states and that the trade therefore was vital. He was amazed that Jefferson construed New Hampshire as a *"revenue district* adjacent to The Territories of a foreign Nation," and reminded him that the Canadian border was a wilderness two hundred miles from the settled parts of the state, with no possibility of evasion. Besides, the people of the state were "nearly all in favor of the embargo, and the merchants of this place [Portsmouth] would not suffer a few enemies and speculators to make their fortunes, while they themselves were suffering every inconvenience and seeing (if permitted) it would defeat the intention of the government."[4]

Gallatin could not at once test the influence of the governors' warrants upon the general problem of enforcing the embargo. He did, however, feel that the law of April 25 giving the President complete authority to suppress the coastwise trade was too severe, and wrote Jefferson to that effect, at the same time reciting the extent of contraband trade along the St. Lawrence from Lake Ontario to Montreal.[5]

Jefferson recognized the validity of Gallatin's observation and agreed in the execution of the law to distinguish "between provisions, lumber, naval stores and such things as by the exaggerated prices they have got to in foreign markets would enable infractors to pay all forfietures [*sic*] & still make great profit, and cotton & such other articles as have not got to such prices. I am for going substantially

[3] Jefferson Papers. Jefferson to Gallatin. May 6, 1808.
[4] *Ibid.*, John Langdon to Jefferson, May 14, 1808.
[5] *Ibid.*, A. Gallatin to Jefferson, May 16, 1808.

to the object of the law, and no further; perhaps a little more earnestly because it is the first experiment, and it is of great *importance* to know it's full effect."[6]

If the letter just cited reveals Jefferson as a theorist, another, of the same period, demonstrates that in whatever new forms his theories found expression, he himself remained true to his faith in the common people. Though deprecating the evasions along the northern frontier, he rejoiced at the "spontaneous aid of our good citizens in the neighborhoods where there has been occasion," and concluded that "Through the body of our country generally our citizens appear heartily to approve & support the embargo."[7]

Jefferson's circular on the coastwise trade was directed to the governors of only five states.[8] Gallatin felt that other districts might require similar dispensations, and, on the twentieth, he accordingly directed a circular to all the collectors of the ports, ruling that, where shipments of flour and provisions did not exceed one eighth of the total cargo, they should be assumed to be bona fide, and, not being designed for evasion of the embargo, they need not obtain special warrants.

At this period Gallatin felt that the worst enemy of the embargo was not the coastwise trade, accountable to the officers of the treasury, but rather the secret loading and departure of vessels with no clearance papers whatever. He wrote to Jefferson on May 23:

I think that we have little to fear from any quarter. The great violations which have heretofore taken place have been, either on the frontier districts, or in the sailing of vessels before the penalties were in force. Of this I have clear proof in the returns of vessels arrived at Havannah (*sic*) from the United States till the 11th ult. & deposited by our Consul in the Department of State. I have analysed it; and taking two periods of 42 days each, the first from

[6] Jefferson Papers. Jefferson to A. Gallatin, May 20, 1808.
[7] *Ibid.*, Jefferson to General Benjamin Smith, May, 1808.
[8] A Printed Circular.

the 11th January to 29th Feby., & the other from 1st March to 11th April; I find that 43 vessels arrived from the United States during the first period, and only four during the last; one of which was in ballast, & only one had flour; an evident proof that the embargo operates & that since the penalties were enacted and the second supplemt. act was passed, the evasion (those on the British lines excepted) have been less than we had apprehended.[9]

Inasmuch as the control over sea-borne traffic had proved so successful, Gallatin felt that the provisioning of flour to needy districts might have been more wisely intrusted to the treasury than to local governors. The collectors were responsible to the executive; the state magistrates had their own popularity to consider. And the weaker of them might yield to a temptation to bolster this at the expense of an unpopular law. "Knowing Gov. Sullivan & Chas. Pickney [*sic*] as we do, we can have no confidence in the last, & must rest assured that the other will refuse no certificates. They begin already to arrive in large quantities."[10] Considering all the abuses which might creep into the system, Gallatin begged for its repeal, or at any rate that it be not extended to the other governors, and offered a plan by which the governors might submit advice rather than issue warrants.[11] A general rule rather than the caprice of politicians was the more essential, inasmuch as applications for coasting permits would necessarily exceed the anticipations of Jefferson, owing to the increasing dependence of the cotton states upon outside supplies of food, a condition especially true of "the greater part of the S. Carolina sea-coast and the whole of Georgia."[12] The treasury system of non-interference with cargoes in which food did not exceed one eighth of the total was, as Gallatin observed, "much less exceptionable, than the permission from the Governors under

[9] Jefferson Papers. Library of Congress. A. Gallatin to Jefferson, May 23, 1808.
[10] *Ibid.*
[11] *Ibid.*
[12] *Ibid.*

which whole cargoes of provisions will be perpetually transported and that perhaps done by persons who have violated the embargo without the knowledge of the Governors."[13]

To these suggestions Jefferson made a characteristic reply. He desired Gallatin to transmit his thanks to various subordinates who had aided in enforcing the law, assured him that his only desire with regard to the coastwise trade was a proper execution of the laws, for "I do not wish a single citizen in any of the states to be deprived of a meal of bread, but I set down the exercise of commerce merely for profit, as nothing when it carries with it danger of defeating the objects of the embargo,"[14] and made a profession of faith in the governors. "I cannot think that any of them would wink at abuses of that law."[15] Was Jefferson sincere in this rather unctuous sentiment, or was it a somewhat lame explanation for hasty action on his own part? He praised Gallatin's circular, however, and admitted that, "had the practicability of this mode of restraint occurred[sic] before the recurrence to the governors, I should have preferred it, because it is free from the objection of favoritism to which the governors will be exposed, and if you find it work well in practice, we may find means to have the other course discontinued. our course should be to sacrifice everything to secure the effect of the law. & nothing beyond that."[16] As for ships sailing without clearance papers, the naval department must prevent that.[17]

The response of the governor of New Hampshire had been immediate, doubtless because of the imputation concerning his state. Other governors were in less haste. But, on May 28, Charles Pinckney wrote that the normal con-

---

[13] Jefferson Papers. A. Gallatin to Jefferson, May 23, 1808.
[14] *Ibid.*, Jefferson to A. Gallatin, May 27, 1808.
[15] *Ibid.*
[16] *Ibid.*
[17] *Ibid.*

sumption of flour in Charleston and its vicinity was three thousand barrels a month, coming coastwise from Philadelphia, Baltimore, and Richmond. He promised to issue certificates for this only "to substantial houses which have always imported it," and denounced as nidering "those who for sake of gain are endeavoring to defeat the great purposes intended by the embargo."[18] Pinckney showed more circumspection than Gallatin had given him credit for. The weak reed was Sullivan, of whom, before he had been exercising his new authority a month, Gallatin complained that he had not the backbone to refuse certificates to any one. "One mail alone brought me permits for eleven thousand barrels, exclusively of corn and rye meal. As we must let those go at all events and without restriction there is really more danger from that quarter than from any other."[19] It looked as if Jefferson's philosophic confidence in the wisdom of Republican governors might cost him the efficient administering of the one measure nearest his heart.

Sullivan had only begun. Six weeks later, Gallatin filed with Jefferson a detailed report on Sullivan's licenses. They already amounted to 49,800 barrels of flour, 94,400 bushels of corn, 560 tierces of rice and 2000 bushels of rye; with permits issued but not yet acted upon to the extent of 7450 barrels of flour, or, if preferred by the importer, of 30,000 bushels of corn.[20] Some of these certificates, as Gallatin pointed out, were to merchants of Alexandria, or Georgetown, of whose commercial standing the governor must be entirely ignorant. But he admitted that Sullivan was the exception to a rule which otherwise was not working out so badly after all. "Govr. Langdon [of New Hampshire] has given four certificates for so many cargoes of flour—say 4000 barrels and two certificates each, for a

[18] Jefferson Papers. Governor Charles Pinckney to Jefferson, May 28, 1808.

[19] Ibid., A. Gallatin to Jefferson, May 28, 1808.

[20] Ibid., A. Gallatin to Jefferson, July 15, 1808.

cargo of rice. No certificates have been transmitted by the other Governors."[21]

Jefferson agreed with Gallatin that it was necessary to put some curb upon the headlong Sullivan. But how to accomplish this without offence was something of a problem. Jefferson attacked it by calling the governor's attention to the extent of his requisitions, intimating that "these supplies, altho called for within the space of two months, will undoubtedly furnish the consumption of your state for a much longer time," and urging him to discontinue the practice in question. He repeated his desire that no citizen be deprived of needed supplies, but reminded Sullivan that the coastwise trade offered special temptation to evaders of law. He requested a memorandum for the guidance of the administration as to the probable future requirements of Massachusetts.[22]

Though couched in the friendliest language, the rebuke was none the less real, and the recipient felt its force. He replied with ill-concealed vexation. In the first place, he had no desire to assume responsibilities so burdensome. He undertook the issuing of warrants simply to save the state from actual hunger, which would have multiplied the foes of the administration. So far as he personally was concerned, he would welcome relief. But he was sure that Jefferson would not grant it if he knew the circumstances.[23]

To begin with, Jefferson was probably ignorant that the importations had not affected prices. Here, of course, was an economic fallacy. Those prices were in the last resort determined by a world market, so long as any flour at all could reach it. And flour was certainly leaving the country by various channels. What Jefferson thought of the contention is not recorded. In the second place, it was certain

[21] Jefferson Papers. A. Gallatin to Jefferson, July 15, 1808.
[22] Ibid., Jefferson to Sullivan, July 16, 1808.
[23] Ibid., Sullivan to Jefferson, July 21, 1808.

that no flour was going to Canada, because Sullivan would not permit its unloading within two hundred miles of Passamaquoddy. In the third place, the amount so far certified seemed excessive only because nearly all contracts for the year were signed in the spring. And finally, the refusal of further certificates would "involve this State in mob riots and convulsions pretendedly on account of the embargo," which would mean "an additional triumph" for the enemies of Jefferson, and "new mortifications" for his friends. All things considered, Sullivan would take the liberty of ignoring Jefferson's request until further orders, which he trusted, if given, would be so explicit a withdrawal of the grant of May 6 that he might publish it to "satisfy the public claims."[24]

In the letter just cited, Sullivan was on the defensive. Two days later he carried the war into the enemy's country. He began in a vein of sarcasm. "I derive great relief from the consideration that the President is under no necessity to read it, and, that merely breaking the seal and glancing on the superscription, will take but a moment's time." In the body of the letter, he informed Jefferson of his growing conviction that the Federalists were plotting to renew their connection with Britain. Here the advance ended and retreat was sounded. Sullivan had evidently slept on the proposition of defying his party chief and pondered its unwisdom. He would hereafter evade the demands of the merchants, and would, moreover, furnish the estimate which Jefferson requested. Meanwhile, he assured the President that, "Upon the best calculation I can make of the persons who live on imported flour in the sea ports in this State, they are ninety thousand. This at one pound for each day will raise a demand for about 164,250 barrels per year or 13,687 barr. per month. This is to be sure an astonishing

[24] Jefferson Papers. Sullivan to Jefferson, July 21, 1808.

quantity but I do not believe the calculation extravagant."[25] Sullivan admitted that the coastwise trade afforded an opportunity to the wicked, but he maintained that too severe measures of repression would only serve notice to the northern states that the President had no confidence in them, but that he and the Virginia adherents upon whom he did rely were enemies by principle "to the commerce and navigation of the northern part of the nation."[26] In this seemingly impersonal way, Sullivan was touching upon a sore spot, as well he knew. His next statement is less cutting, really a very philosophical and detached estimate of Massachusetts for one who had lived through much of which he describes:

The habits of this State, contracted under the royal Government and yet continued lead to smuggling and the contravention of the embargo laws; and other laws restraining commerce. I believe the present embargo-laws have been as much respected as laws of this nature have heretofore been; nor do I believe, that until lately, there have been any evasions of them worthy of notice.[27]

Sullivan, who seems to have had the pen of a ready writer, was evidently in no hurry to bring his epistle to a conclusion. He proceeded to an historical sketch of Massachusetts opinion on the embargo. It had at first been popular with the Republicans. But failure to produce any apparent effect on Europe was costing it popular support, thanks to which and to the efforts of the Federalists, illegal acts were multiplying. In fact, many judicious men, former friends to the measure, now doubted the feasibility of its continuance, viewing it as an incubus to the party, "a decisive blow against the republican interest, now supported in this commonwealth."[28] With a rather fine irony, Sullivan concluded by an appeal to Jefferson, in the event that a continuance of

[25] Jefferson Papers. Sullivan to Jefferson, July 23, 1808.
[26] Ibid.
[27] Ibid.
[28] Ibid.

the coastwise trade was decided upon, to bestow the responsibility of issuing certificates upon someone else.[29]

On August 6, two months after the letter to the governors which had precipitated the correspondence under review, Gallatin once more admitted that his original fears were unfounded:

I would have preferred not to have written at all to the Governors & to have kept the coasting trade on the footing of my first circular of 29 of April which you thought not strict enough. It is, however, certain, that, with the exception of Govr. Sullivan's certificates, the mode which you directed has been perfectly efficacious on the sea-coast. No evasions can now take place worthy of notice, under colour of the coasting trade. The embargo is now defeated, as I have already mentioned, by open violations, by vessels sailing without any clearances whatever; an evil which under the existing law we cannot oppose in any way but by cruisers.[30]

Gallatin confirmed, however, the warning which Sullivan had uttered before ever the law was passed: namely, that the state courts would impede the operation of any act not popular with their constituents. Here was rising to taunt him a principle which Jefferson had invoked in his support of Roane against Marshall. The specific case was furnished by Rhode Island. With the connivance of the court, the state authorities at Newport strove to prevent detention under the act of April 25. Although these state courts had absolutely no maritime jurisdiction, their opposition was none the less embarrassing, and this, on top of all the wearying details of his office, drove Gallatin to his first admission of pessimism. He had opposed the embargo, but labored tremendously on its behalf. "I deeply regret," he sighed,

to see my incessant efferts [sic] in every direction, to carry the law into effect, defeated in so many quarters & that we will probably produce, at least on the British, but an inconsiderable effect by a measure which at the same time threatens to destroy the Republi-

[29] Jefferson Papers. Sullivan to Jefferson, July 23, 1808.
[30] Ibid., A. Gallatin to Jefferson, August 6, 1808.

can interest. For there is almost an equal chance that if propositions from Great Britain or other events do not put it in our power to raise the embargo before the 1st of October, we will lose the Presidential election. I think that at this moment the Western States, Virginia, S. Carolina, & perhaps Georgia are the only sound States & that we will have a doubtful contest in every other. The consciousness of having done what was right in itself is doubtless sufficient; but for the inefficacy of the measure on the Lakes & to the northward there is no consolation; and that circumstance is the strongest argument that can be brought against the measure itself.[31]

The times were indeed anxious for the statesman who had cast his all upon the die, and for his faithful associate. The warning of Sullivan as to the danger of flour riots in Boston greatly alarmed Jefferson. He wrote to General Dearborn, the secretary of war, then at home in Massachusetts, that "The Tories of Boston openly threaten insurrection if their importation of flour is stopped. The next post will stop it. I fear your governor is not up to the tone of these parricides, and I hope, on the first symptom of an open opposition to the laws by force, you will fly to the scene and aid in suppressing any commotion."[32] He also paid his respects to Sullivan in a note of the same date to Gallatin. "I have some apprehension the tories of Boston etc., with so poor a head of a governor may attempt to give us trouble."[33] Jefferson, it will be remembered, was on record as the advocate of a revolution every twenty years to purify the atmosphere. But that was the thought of a philosopher. To an executive, the idea was less attractive.

Between the instructions of Jefferson to the governors and of Gallatin to the collectors, the coastwise trade had a sufficiently brisk but decorous existence. That of North Carolina consisted of just the articles proscribed. Gallatin

[31] Jefferson Papers. A. Gallatin to Jefferson, August 6, 1808.
[32] Ibid., Jefferson to General Dearborn, August 9, 1808. See also The Works of Thomas Jefferson, XI. 40-41.
[33] Jefferson Papers. Jefferson to A. Gallatin, August 19, 1808.
[34] The Works of Thomas Jefferson, I. 422, June 30, 1808. "Agreed to continue the regulation of Mr. Gallatin's Circular of May 20, except

took note in a treasury circular to the collector at Edenton of the special conditions which differentiated it from the commerce of other states. To permit only one eighth of a North Carolina cargo to consist of food stuffs or of other articles in particular demand overseas was discrimination, owing to the fact that almost the entire trade of North Carolina consisted of just the articles proscribed. Gallatin, accordingly, left greater discretionary powers to the collectors in North Carolina, with a recognition that:

shipments even of provisions, naval stores, or lumber, which are made to the same places where it was usual to send. such articles, and which do not exceed in quantity or vary from the quantities thus usually shipped in former times, may in many instances be allowed without subjecting the vessel to detention, although their value should exceed 1/8th part of the bond.[35]

After its extreme frankness in July, the exchange between Sullivan and Jefferson assumed a milder tone. Perhaps it was because Sullivan had shot his last arrow; perhaps because he was hastening toward the tomb, where mundane matters cease to interest. But his words were more acceptable than his deeds. On August 24, he wrote as follows: "Sir—I have yours of the 12th and will continue to act as discreetly as I can in the business of certificates according to your request." He called the attention of Jefferson to a recent rise in the cost of flour, due to the prospect that its importation would be prohibited, and drew the proper moral that, "There is no engine but what is, and will be used here against your administration. Truth, Justice, and reason are expelled."[36]

that it may be relaxed as to vessels usually employed in the coasting trade. This has a special view to the relief of N. C. that her corn & lumber may be sent coastwise."

    [35] A. Gallatin to Samuel Tredwell, collector at Edenton, N. C., August 17, 1808. The Circular is in Jefferson Papers. See also *ibid.*, Gallatin to Jefferson, August 5, 1808.

    [36] *Ibid.*, August 24, 1808. Sullivan to Jefferson.

A few weeks afterward, Levi Lincoln, in the absence of the governor, wrote Jefferson that he had the admission from Sullivan's son that abuses undoubtedly existed but were most difficult to prevent. Like his superior, Lincoln believed ninety thousand persons in Massachusetts to be actually dependent upon flour imports, and felt that permits for these to the value of only one eighth of the bond value of a cargo were insufficient.[37]

It was evident that Sullivan and Lincoln, who in April had taken such divergent views of the Tory question and the general political situation, were in entire accord on the need of a liberal treatment of the coastwise trade. Both the standard bearers of Republicanism in Massachusetts were at cross purposes with the national leader of their party. Their position was natural. They represented, as it were, the sentinels of the party, and were most exposed to enemy fire. Their interests were endangered by legislation undermining the party domination of the state. They worked together to soften, if possible, the rigors of that unpopular legislation. A ready weapon for their genial purpose was liberal distribution of grain warrants.

But Gallatin, who favored the very minimum of commercial restrictions and belonged intellectually with the malcontents and party rebels, was not the man to wink at evasions of what it was his sworn duty to enforce. He again addressed to his chief a strong protest against the evasions which Sullivan condoned.

New York 16 Sept. 1808.

Dear Sir.

I am again compelled to address you on the subject of Governor Sullivan's certificates, which he continues, as I am informed from several quarters, pertinaciously to issue. Whether he still sends duplicates to the Treasury I do not know, but from the new form which he has adopted, rather think that he does not. I write how-

[37] Jefferson Papers. Lieutenant Governor Levi Lincoln to Jefferson, September 10, 1808.

ever to the principal clerk in my office to send to you along with this letter a memorandum of the gross amount of his permissions so far as they have been received there. But of the effect I can speak with certainty. Those permissions do not only create dissatisfaction & operate unequally in favor of those who obtain them: but they materially interfere with the execution of the embargo laws. As a proof they are granted without *discretion* & for districts where flour is not wanted, I enclose a letter from the deputy collector of Barnstable then at Boston. The provisions imported into Massachusetts in large quantities are intended for exportation and are the foundation of the violations of the embargo there. The facilities afforded by the immediate egress from the ports of that State to the sea, by the vicinity of Nova Scotia, & by the number of British vessels hovering on the coast for the purpose of receiving cargoes, give already sufficient temptations for violations of the law. The systematic opposition connected with the political views which prevails there, renders the execution of the embargo still more difficult: and the Governor's permissions supply the objects to be exported; as, otherwise, fish would be the only article that could be smuggled away. I think it really necessary that some efficient means should be adopted to put an end to his certificates, or to prevent their being respected by the collectors. With very few exceptions, the embargo is now rigidly enforced in every part of the sea border.

With great respect
and attachment
Your obedt. servt.
Albert Gallatin.[38]

In so far as these complaints concerned Sullivan personally, they were no longer necessary, as he had withdrawn from active affairs, convinced, as he wrote Lincoln, that in any event the treasury circular advising collectors at southern ports "not to detain any vessels whose cargo shd. be so apportioned as not to excite suspicion of a foreign destination," solved the problem of food supply for Massachusetts. If a further need for governor's warrants should arise, he intrusted their issuance to Lincoln, with a polite expression of willingness to be of any assistance possible. Lincoln promptly notified Jefferson of these developments, and assured him, meanwhile, of his own belief in the right-

---

[38] Jefferson Papers. A. Gallatin to Jefferson, September 16, 1808.

eousness of the embargo—and in the sinfulness of its evasion.[39]

The parting shots in this battle of the grain boats were fired by Jefferson in letters to Gallatin and Lincoln. To the former he said, "As we know that Sullivan's licences have overstocked the wants of the Eastern States, with flour; the proposal to carry more there is of itself suspicious, and therefore even regular traders ought not to be allowed."[40] And to Lincoln he refused supplies for Nantucket, on the ground that if that town lacked flour, it was only because she had exported her own stocks.[41] He reminded Lincoln that Sullivan's permits were bought on the open market in Alexandria and elsewhere. What Sullivan perhaps meant in kindness, but certainly continued in weakness, had thus assumed the proportions of a national scandal, contributing greatly to the ineffectiveness of the embargo and the embarrassment of the President. Here was the uncomfortable side of a theory which sought to link the governors with the President in a brotherhood of good works.

The controversy with Sullivan was far from being the only thorn in the flesh for Jefferson and Gallatin. The troubles on the Canadian border were even more mischievous. The extent of the illicit trade discouraged honest patriots and weakened European confidence in the sincerity and outcome of the American experiment. There was considerable smuggling even before Congress adjourned, and by the middle of May it had reached a pass where collectors at danger points were resigning their posts in order to escape the odium of enforcing the law.[42]

---

[39] Jefferson Papers. Lincoln to Jefferson, September 23, 1808, quoting a letter to himself from Governor Sullivan.

[40] *Ibid.*, Jefferson to A. Gallatin, October 14, 1808.

[41] *Ibid.*, Jefferson to Lincoln, November 13, 1808.

[42] *Ibid.*, A. Gallatin to Jefferson, May 16, 1808. ". . . Sackett has resigned, I believe from fear, or at least from a wish not to lose his

Jefferson treated the emergency more calmly than he
otherwise might have done because of his confidence that
the citizens of the danger zones would feel themselves personally responsible for enforcing the laws.[43]   To some extent
this faith was not misplaced, for, as he declared, "we have
experienced this spontaneous aid of our good citizens in
the neighborhoods where there has been occasion, as I
am persuaded we ever shall on such occasions."[44]

The strategic points for smuggling were the St. Lawrence, Lake Champlain, and Passamaquoddy Bay, on the
border between Maine and New Brunswick.   Gallatin was
inclined to eliminate Lake Champlain, as fairly well policed,
but he deplored the irresolution and final resignation of
Sackett on the St. Lawrence and felt positive alarm as to
conditions at Passamaquoddy.   Reports from there were
belated, but, at last accounts:

the opposition appeared still stronger, the revenue boats having been
fired at in the night & open violations continuing to take place.   It
must have been still more difficult in any degree to carry the law
into effect subsequently to that date as by return-vessels, it appears
that between 2d & 7th May there were entered 19,000 barrels flour,
4,000 of pork, 4,000 do. naval stores, &c.   The people are paid by
the British or disaffected; and no assistance to be expected till the
arrival of the Wasp which sailed from N. York on 7th inst.   Be
that as it may all the evil which can accrue both there & on Champlain is now at an end; and all we have to watch is our common
coasting trade.[45]

Both the sanguine Jefferson and the cautious Gallatin
were mistaken as to conditions on Lake Champlain.   Jefferson miscalculated the patriotism of its people.   Their sympathies proved to be not with the government, but with
their neighbors.   Gallatin put too much confidence in the

popularity with the people.   It is a fact that large quantities, particularly
of potash, have arrived at Montreal from his district which extends
along the St. Lawrence from the Canada line to Lake Ontario."

[43] Jefferson Papers. Jefferson to General Benjamin Smith, May 20,
1808.

[44] Ibid.

[45] Ibid., A. Gallatin to Jefferson, May 23, 1808.

insufficient forces levied for the emergency. The outcome was disappointing, showing "that we have not been properly supported by the people & that the love of gain & British agency had rendered the stoppage of intercourse so unpopular that even Sailly & other truly friendly characters were afraid to act."[46] Under the circumstances, Gallatin thought that a company of United States regulars and two gunboats would not be amiss.

Jefferson did not intend that the whole burden of enforcing the embargo should devolve upon the devoted secretary of the treasury. In July, in order to strengthen Gallatin's hand, he called upon the navy to maintain a more effective cooperation in the capture of offenders. Here again Jefferson found that one cherished ideal interfered with another. The pride of his administration had been his economies. A pet economy had been the navy, yet now the navy was summoned to a rejuvenation in order to battle some dozens or hundreds of individualists—no greater individualists certainly than Jefferson himself—into an enforced coöperation with their neighbors in submission to a hated law. Any philosophy carried to its limit encounters its own antithesis, but few philosophers have an opportunity like Jefferson's to press facts to this inevitable conclusion. Be that as it may, there was a sort of poetic justice—or was it dramatic irony—in a fate which compelled Jefferson to revive a navy in order to wage war on individualists. It is not at all likely that he realized the inconsistency. No longer the gentle philosopher, he was now the grim administrator, informing the secretary of the navy that:

Complaints multiply upon us of evasions of the embargo laws by fraud & force. They come from Newport, Portland, Machias, Nantucket, Martha's vineyard etc etc. as I do consider the severe enforcement of the embargo to be of an importance not to be measured by money for our future government as well as present ob-

[46] Jefferson Papers. A. Gallatin to Jefferson, May 28, 1808.

jects, I think it will be adviseable [sic] that during this summer all the gun-boats actually manned & in commission should be distributed through as many ports & bays as may be necessary to assist the embargo.[47]

Not infrequently Jefferson was in position to inform his secretaries of conditions within their special field. On July 19, for example, he forwarded to Gallatin the details concerning "habitual breaches of the embargo laws on the Canada line."[48] Jefferson had them from William Duane, a Philadelphia editor, who, for his part, learned them from a local correspondent. "I am sorry," the local observer laments,

to inform you that smugling [sic] is carried on from Lewiston to Canada to a considerable extent, and disgusting and humiliating as the practice is to every feeling that is American it is almost as publicly transacted as any common avocation. Merchandise Potash and Salt form, I am told the principle [sic] articles. Whether it happens through the neglect or connivance of the Collector or his deputies, it is hard to say; but from the nature of the place, certain it is that the least vigilance on their part, must effectually prevent it. But whatever the cause, the base and traitorous transactions ought to be exposed, and the government by some means Informed of them. It is some consolation, however, that I have not heard of one republican being implicated in the business: the Collector and his deputies; and all Concerned are of a very different Character.[49]

In transmitting to Gallatin the intelligence just quoted, Jefferson made the despairing comment that, "To prevent it is I suppose beyond our means, but we must try to harrass the unprincipled agents and punish as many as we can."[50] To which Gallatin assented, remarking that "the danger is much greater from New York northwardly, principally from Massachusetts,—than from either the Delaware, Chesapeak or North Carolina . . . until Congress meets, we must

[47] Jefferson Papers. Jefferson to the Secretary of Navy, July 16, 1808. On August 16, 1808, "The Navy reported the ff. captures—Brig Charles, Brig Montezuma, Sir Wm & Samuel, small boats, several Boats laden with goods and Cotton to amount of D^{rs} 80,000."
[48] Ibid., Jefferson to A. Gallatin, July 19, 1808.
[49] Ibid., Ez. Hill to William Duane. Buffalo Creek, July 29, 1808.
[50] Ibid., Jefferson to A. Gallatin, July 29, 1808.

depend entirely on force for checking this manner of violating the law."[51] For this critical situation he blamed defects in the original law, laxity on the part of the collectors on Lake Ontario, avarice among the border dwellers, and conspiracy among their Federalist leaders. He repeats that force alone will subdue all this stubbornness, but rather defends the wicked for not knowing where to turn amid the confusion of orders, decrees, and embargo. They are almost as sinned against as sinning, for, owing to the lack of "a single object which might rouse their patriotism & unite their passions & affections, selfishness has assumed the reigns in several quarters."[52] From all of which, Gallatin draws the inevitable conclusion that when Congress reassembles, it "must either invest the Executive with the most arbitrary powers & sufficient force to carry the Embargo into effect or give it up altogether. . . . I see no alternative but war."[53]

Jefferson evidently recognized the force of these considerations, for he dismissed the faithless collector at New Bedford, Massachusetts,[54] urged that his case be made an example, and invited Dearborn, as we have seen elsewhere, to be ready for instant action.[55] In New York, however, where opposition to the federal authorities fell little short of rebellion, he met a stumbling block in Governor Tompkins. The collector at Oswego, unable to enforce the federal regulations, had appealed for some detachments of militia, on the plea that the opposition amounted to armed insurrection. But Tompkins, who had no desire to risk the unpopularity of calling out state troops to enforce a federal law odious to so many citizens, wrote Jefferson that the

[51] Jefferson Papers. A. Gallatin to Jefferson, July 29, 1808.
[52] Ibid.
[53] Ibid.
[54] Ibid., Jefferson to S. H. Smith, August 2, 1808.
[55] Ibid., Jefferson to General Dearborn, August 9, 1808.

collector had overstated the case in order to secure the assistance which the militia law of the state did not warrant him in sending.[56]

To which Jefferson replied:

this may not be an insurrection in the popular sense of the word but being arrayed in war-like manner, actually committing acts of war; and persevering systematically in defiance of the public authority, brings it so fully within the legal definition of an insurrection, that I should not hesitate to issue a proclamation were I not restrained by motives of which Y.E. seems to be apprised.[57]

Gallatin also took the view that "The affair at Oswego has broken into insurrection."[58] But Tompkins refused to be convinced. He held to a pacific view of the question. In this, of course, he was in philosophical agreement with Jefferson himself, but his comfortable theorizing ignored the very palpable fact that Oswego and its neighbors were in open rebellion. Tompkins wanted to try court action before proceeding to force:

It is desirable that some competent legal character be sent to those places where violations of the Embargo laws are most frequent for the purpose of assisting the Collectors with advice and collecting and forwarding the requisite testimony to convict the offenders in the Courts of the United States. I am persuaded a few prosecutions and convictions would have a greater tendency to make the laws respected than the appearance of a Military force.[59]

Nevertheless, although he moved with reluctance along the thorny path of unpopularity, Tompkins did not, like his Massachusetts confrère, place actual obstacles in the way of the law. And Gallatin was able to inform the President by the middle of September that:

With the assistance of Govr. Tompkins & of Gen. Wilkinson, militia & regulars have arrived or are on their march to the Lakes, & I hope that by the 1st of Octer. everything will be there in toler-

[56] Jefferson Papers. Governor Tompkins to Jefferson, August 9, 1808.
[57] Ibid., Jefferson to Governor Tompkins, August —, 1808.
[58] Ibid., A. Gallatin to Jefferson, August 17, 1808.
[59] Ibid., Governor Tompkins to Jefferson, August 22, 1808.

able order, & the militia relieved every where but in Vermont by
the regulars. Nothing new or extraordinary from New England
or any other quarter. I did find it difficult to have the necessary
prosecutions instituted in the northern part of this State. [New
York] But the district Atty. of Maine has by going himself to
Passamaquoddy, collecting evidence, instituting suits &c restored
order in that quarter.[60]

Travelers testified to the effect produced by this vigorous conduct. Thus one friend of the administration, just
returned from a trip to northern New York, describes for
Jefferson's benefit his experiences en route: "The 22nd August retd. & embarked at Cumberland Heart in a sloop having
on board 66 bbls. ashes & 9 Firkins Butter seized the day
before by Gen. Woolsey for attempting to pass the line to
Canada."[61] He reports a conversation with a traveller
from Quebec who told him "That provisions were scarce;
that the pork of which I had seen so much, was principally
for Quebec, from whence it was shipped to Halifax, the W.
Indies, &c. That pot-ash had actually been worth $300
three hundred dollars per Ton, but was now lower; that bills
on London were at a discount of 7 per cent. & that he had
met at St. John's $50,000 going from New York to pur-
chase bills. He also mentioned the smuggling of English
goods into Massachusetts from the province with this observation, that it would destroy all political allegiance & morality, & that the present generation would learn a pernicious
trade, which they would not soon forget, but very probably
teach it to the next."[62] He concludes by expressing his own
opinion that "Avarice both in the Sea ports & in the remote
parts of this State appears to have effected (*sic*) 16-20ths
of the people."[63] Which was another way of saying that
only one New Yorker in five favored the embargo.

[60] Jefferson Papers. A. Gallatin to Jefferson, September 14, 1808.
[61] *Ibid.,* Charles Connell to Jefferson, New York, September 29, 1808.
[62] *Ibid.*
[63] *Ibid.*

Considering the embargo from the purely administrative side, one rather marvels at its efficiency. The permits to the governors had resulted in only one serious mishap, the weak and timid conduct of Sullivan. The coastwise trade, so threatening in its possibilities, with British ships in the offing ready to transfer cargoes if no other means afforded, had presented no serious difficulties, thanks to the moderate but well executed regulations of Gallatin. A state bordering on if not actually amounting to insurrection had developed, to be sure, on the northern frontier. But here Jefferson had acted with unwonted energy—a marked advance over his executive methods in Revolutionary Virginia. A combination of tact in his personal relations with local authorities and an unbending determination to enforce the law at all hazards, lifted Jefferson into the ranks of really great executives. The student of the period should not withhold from Jefferson his due meed of praise for excellence in an unexpected field.

There remains to consider, before we turn to the effect produced by this competent administration of the embargo upon the European nations against which it was aimed, a brief synopsis of how the country as a whole responded to the prolongation of the embargo and what progress, if any, it made along those lines which the embargo might be expected to stimulate.

Reports concerning domestic conditions varied greatly, not only by districts, but in accordance with the temperament of their senders. Colonel Tatham, for example, who had written so glowingly about the North Carolina planters, told quite a different tale about the commercial men of his neighborhood. He found them generally opposed to the government and much imbued with the doctrines of Pickering, whose pamphlet had been widely circulated about Newbern.[64] "So far as I can judge, the Majority of our Citizens in Town are as loyal subjects to John Bull, in their hearts, as any about St. James's; and would willingly mark similar lines of distinction in society."[65] He notes a disposition of sailors to turn to agricultural pursuits and prays that their example may be generally followed.[66]

Virginia sentiment was more reassuring, at least as reported by William Burwell, now returned from Congress to his district. He assured Jefferson that his constituents would continue to bear the embargo with patience so long as they believed it the only substitute for war. Merchants were dealing gently with their customers, and few lawsuits were pending—a circumstance contributing not a little to the tranquillity of the people under "a state of things however necessary, & unavoidable, extremely burthensome."[67] Burwell warned the President that it would be hopeless to continue the embargo beyond fall, when it would be "indispensibly necessary to remove the E. & give a new direction to the energies of the nation."[68]

Jefferson had an opportunity on his journey to Monticello to test for himself the loyalty of Virginia to the embargo. He found the people unanimous in preferring embargo to war and sanguine in anticipating a collapse of British tyranny and the repeal of the Orders in Council.[69] But this was in May; before Congress reconvened, sentiment seems rather to have veered. Such, at any rate, was the opinion of Wilson Cary Nicholas, a friend of Jefferson, who wrote him on the eve of the new session:

[64] Jefferson Papers. Wm. Tatham to Jefferson, Craven County, North Carolina, May 6, 1808.
[65] *Ibid.*
[66] *Ibid.*
[67] *Ibid.*, Wm. A. Burwell to Jefferson, May 21, 1808.
[68] *Ibid.*
[69] *Ibid.*, Jefferson to Mr. Lieper, May 25, 1808.

From the experiment we have made, I think there is not only excuse to distrust the firmness of our own people, but to doubt its being practicable to execute the law in a way to make it produce much effect abroad. . . . But if the complete execution of it and the support of the people cannot be counted upon, it will neither answer our purpose, nor will it be practicable to retain it.[70]

The context of Nicholas's letter suggests, however, that this view proceeded from a general survey of the Union rather than of strictly Virginia sentiment. Certainly that was not the attitude of one Virginia family, the Gunnells. Report had gone out that this entire clan had gone over to the Federalist opinion. Such slander demanded prompt denial, and one of the family rose to champion the honor of his kindred:

. . . feeling as I do the reproach of such a report, I have therefore taken the liberty to trouble you with this letter to contradict the report so far as it relates to myself in the most pointed manner and believe I may do the same with respect to most of the name, or perhaps all of them, for indeed I dont know of any of the Family that has changed their sentiments relating to the Government, tho there are some I have not seen since the passage of the Embargo Law . . . The Embargo certainly is a wise measure as a preventative against French aggression as well as against British taxation plunder and massacrees and should Congress think well to prolong the Embargo seven years and the belligerent powers should persist in their aggressions that long I should not withdraw my confidence but should think the prolongation wise provided War could not be waged to better advantage.[71]

If Virginia was wholly loyal, there was at least a shadow of doubt. In South Carolina, there was none. As the House of Representatives expressed it, "Thomas Jefferson, President of the United States in recommending, and the Congress of the United States in passing the Acts imposing and enforcing the Embargo, have *deserved well of their Country*."[72] Nor could it be said that this was mere lip

[70] Jefferson Papers. Wilson Cary Nicholas to T. Jefferson, October 20, 1808.

[71] *Ibid.*, Robert Gunnell to Jefferson. Minorca, Fairfax County, Virginia, October 29, 1808.

[72] *Ibid.*, House of Representatives of South Carolina, June 28, 1808.

service from a section which had not suffered,[73] for South
Carolina, only less than New England and the ports of
Philadelphia and Baltimore, was a commercial center. At
all events, it strengthened Jefferson's determination to press
the experiment to the utmost. It was as an investigator
in a huge laboratory of political science that he wrote to
Governor Pinckney: "I am determined to exert every
power the law has vested in me for its vigorous fulfillment.
That we may know the full value and effect of the measure
on any future occasion on which a resort to it might be
contemplated."[74]

South Carolina was, in truth, one of the surprises of
the year. Where opposition was expected, enthusiasm
reigned, and votes told the tale. The old stronghold of
Federalism was now a Republican fortress, and Jefferson
could count as one of his greatest assets the unwavering
loyalty of his Palmetto admirers. "Eight years are now
nearly ended," wrote Peter Freneau, in September,

since 69 members of our Legislature voted that you, Sir, ought not
to be the president of the United States, fortunately for America
87 said otherwise; One year ago when the Legislature resolved
that you had deserved well of the Country, there were but six
members to be found in the negative, and in June last, when a resolution was brought forward approving of the reasons you gave for
recommending the Embargo, not one arose in opposition. This
change in the minds of our Legislature, so honorable to your administration, is, in my opinion, a complete refutation of all the abuse the
federal presses have abounded with, and if the authors of it could
possibly have the feelings of honest men would drive them to
despair. . . . The Embargo bears heavy on us, but there are
no people, generally speaking, who bear it more cheerfully, they are
convinced that it was the only prudent measure that could be pursued at the time.[75]

[73] Jefferson Papers. Jos. Alston, Speaker of the House of Representatives of South Carolina, to Jefferson, July 6, 1808.
[74] Ibid., Jefferson to Pinckney, July 18, 1808.
[75] Ibid., Peter Freneau to Jefferson, Charleston, South Carolina, September 18, 1808.

Equally gratifying must have been assurances of fidelity from New Orleans, for no one knew better than Jefferson how tenuous had been the thread of loyalty binding the Southwest to the Union, and that but a few years earlier. With flowing heart he thanked the "Legislative Council and House of Representatives of the territory of Orleans" for their willingness to "submit to whatever sacrifices & privations may be necessary for vindicating the rights the honor, & independance [sic] of our nation."[76]

From Mississippi came protestations of devotion to the principle of the embargo, but a plea to escape its consequences. Mississippi was in the infancy of its agricultural and commercial life, and upon it the embargo fell like a blight. One cannot fail to sympathize with the pioneers as one reads their memorial to the President:

Cotton is the staple commodity of our Country. On it alone we depend for Cash. For this reason every Planter directs his efforts to that particular article. With this medium in our Barnes, we were prepared to meet the demands of Government & take one more step toward the fee simple title but these pleasing anticipations have been cut off from every hope of payment by an Act of that Government to which they are indebted. It has been deemed expedient to suspend by Embargo our Mercantile operations, and thereby our produce lies unsold and unsaleable in our Barns. The Policy of this measure is no where admired more than by the people of this Territory the promptitude with which it is maintained merits their fullest approbation & Support but at the same time we admire the Wisdom & Energy of the measure we deplore the severe and destructive effect which will inevitably accompany the operation of the Law if the payments due to the United States are rigidly executed. We therefore humbly solicit the parental interposition of the General Government and in the warmth of your highest confidence ask of the Government an extension of the time for the payment of the first instalment.[77]

One marvels at the detachment of people who could rise above the prospect of utter ruin to examine on its own

[76] Jefferson Papers. Jefferson to the Legislative Council and House of Representatives of the territory of Orleans, June 18, 1808.

[77] Memorial of the House of Representatives of the Mississippi Territory, September 19, 1808.

merits the cause of their sufferings, and then pronounce it
a measure of wisdom. Yet the memorial of the legislature
is confirmed from a private source. "Everybody wishes the
Embargo raised: but not until the object for which it was
layed is affected [*sic*]; or it is found insufficient to affect
it."[78]

Surveying the country south of the Potomac, the President might conclude that the people bore their yoke with
patience. Sentiment was submissive where it was not enthusiastic, and there was every disposition to give the embargo a fair test. The South was to Jefferson a rod of comfort as he faced the Federalists of New England, but even
there he did not lack friends.

New England, as we have seen, furnished a very special
problem. Here the embargo worked its heaviest injuries,
yet here were the best opportunities for its evasion and a
political organization to uphold the law breaker. That the
embargo had many enemies is not so surprising as that
it had many friends. These latter, while they could not
prevent breaches of the peace, did keep matters from
going to the last extremity of organized rebellion. The
troubles of the period constitute one of the most dramatic
chapters in the history of the section. But they will be
touched upon here only in so far as allusions to them in
the Jefferson Papers indicate that the President was influenced by them in the adherence to his policy.

The most detailed accounts which Jefferson received were
from the agricultural state of Vermont and the commercial
state of Massachusetts. From the former came an elaborate relation of the low prices of agricultural goods for
want of a market, the lawsuits by which creditors attempted
to collect from impoverished debtors, the distress of the
entire debtor class, the judgments against property to meet

[78] Jefferson Papers. John Sibley to General Dearborne. Natchi-
toches, October 12, 1808.

small claims, the increase of imprisonment for debt, and the temptation for the more reckless to recoup their fortunes by smuggling along Lake Champlain, where price inducements were high. Nor did the evil stop with this. Defiance of law brought inevitable punishment. Volunteers were called for; these failing, troops were drafted; and "military law with all its terrific attendants stalks before them and stares them in the Face and the Embargo is Cursed and Recursed again and again." Vermont would continue in this wretched state until some market was found for her produce. The way to right matters would be to use the money spent on coercing the state in finding employment and in providing an artificial market until normal trade might be resumed.[79]

While Vermont was thus groaning in travail, her neighbor of Massachusetts was bent on righting her own wrongs. In the senatorial elections, the anti-embargo men seated their candidate, James Lloyd, by a vote of two hundred and forty-six as against the two hundred and thirteen cast for John Quincy Adams, and, although it was six months before his term expired, the latter immediately resigned.[80]

A war of pamphleteers developed in Massachusetts, and the circulation of anti-embargo petitions went on at a merry pace. Even the untiring Jefferson found it impossible to reply to them all in long hand and caused an edition of one hundred and fifty copies of form letters to be struck off for this one branch of his correspondence. One type of reply was sent to the petitioners for an immediate suspension of the embargo by executive order. The other type strove to reach

[79] Jefferson Papers. Samuel Harrison to Jefferson, Chittenden, Rutland County, Vermont, May 28, 1808. For a parallel account with different accent, see William Pope to Jefferson. Montpelier, September 8, 1808. "It is said that the merchants at least sum of them, are very actively engaged in getting the new crop of wheat to smuggle that, like they did the last years crop, the only complaint in the Country, is that those traitors should be suffered to violate the laws with impunity, like Burr; get rich by continually practiseing treason, against their Country; while the virtuous patriot should suffer poverty distress and privation."

[80] Ibid., Governor James Sullivan to Jefferson, June 3, 1808.

advocates of "the calling of Congress if my power of suspension is doubted."[81]

These petitions, it may be noted, were not, even in
Massachusetts, uniformly hostile to the embargo. The ship
builders of Plymouth furnish a case in point. They described
at length the hush which had fallen over erstwhile hives of
industry, but assured the President that:

We venerate the laws of our country, we respect its constituted
authorities, we will submit to every privation necessary to preserve
our just rights and Independence as a nation—We bow in submission to your superior wisdom and patriotism, and with the most
sincere confidence in your integrity and good conduct, we pledge
ourselves to support the measures of the present administration of
our national government.[82]

But if the friends of Jefferson were numerous, his enemies were active, and the New England mail brought him
vilification in plenty. One epistle, commencing with the
friendly salutation, "You Infernal Villain," quite lives up to
one's anticipations. "How much longer are you going to
keep this damned Embargo on to starve us poor people
one of my children has already starved to death of which
I [am] ashamed and declared that it died of apoplexy."
There follows a fierce story of hardships and a wish that
Jefferson may have the same luck. "I am a Federalist."[83]

Of broader political bearing was confirmation from a
Connecticut source of the propaganda which Sullivan had
long declared to be rampant:

. . . a few weeks since a Reverend D.D. from the State of Massachusetts, and then standing in the Desk of the House, where I
usually attend divine worship, after describing the administration
of the general government in colours suited to his imagination;
declared that we ought no longer to *Confederate in such a Confeder-*

[81] Jefferson Papers. Jefferson to S. H. Smith, September 9, 1808.
[82] *Ibid.*, Elijah Haywood to Jefferson. Hanover, Plymouth County,
Mass., October 10, 1808.
[83] *Thomas Jefferson Correspondence. Printed from the Originals in
the Collections of Wm. K. Bixby,* p. 166. From John Lane Jones, Boston, August 8, 1808.

ation. this was the first time I had heard the sentiment avowed before a public assembly; tho I had for about four years perceived the leading Federalist[s] cautiously beating the pulse of the people to the tune of separation: the great body of the people, even Federalist, are still opposed to such a step, and did they but fully see its object, they would execrate its advocates, but they are impelled forward by the great phalanx of the *pulpit* the *bar* and the Monied Interest of New England. the headquarters of this spirit is to be found in the Town of Boston, and there is not a doubt to my mind what the object is getting Town Meetings, to express sentiments respecting the Embargo is not to effect its removal; but with a view of increasing discontents and wanton calumnies, and augmenting murmurs to a state of unworthy disafection to the government and to work up such a state of irritation as will furnish them with a favourable opportunity to boldly avow their objects. the *Centinel*, *Gazette* and *Paladium* of Boston since the 1st Sept carries strong evidence that the late success of Federalism in New England has thrown them off their guard and if the Vermont election (which is undoubtedly Republican) does not make them more cautious and less sanguine; they may rouse the spirit of an indignant people before they are aware of it.[84]

New England was, however, far from a unit in its hostility to the embargo. For in June, when the difficulties of enforcing the law were multiplying, the legislature of New Hampshire thought it the best of all possible times to tender its approbation, assuring Jefferson that "We will suffer any privations rather than submit to degradation, and will cooperate with the General Government in all its measures."[85] In spite of the growing burden, New Hampshire remained loyal throughout the summer, if one may accept the testimony of two social extremes, one an almost illiterate soldier, the other the governor of the state, sworn to defend her integrity against all her foemen, even the emissaries of the Essex Junto. The former, though willing for the embargo to continue, pleads for a moratorium on debts; the

[84] *Op. cit.*, p. 171. Elisha Tracy, of Norwich, Connecticut, to Jefferson, September 15, 1808.

[85] Jefferson Papers. Resolutions of the Legislature of New Hampshire June 14, 1808. Cf., also a letter of Wm. Plumer to Jefferson. Epping, New Hampshire, July 22, 1808: "I most cordially approve of the embargo, & the raising of the additional army," etc

latter decries the money with which the Federalists are trying to buy up the opinion of the state. The backwoodsman
secures the effect of pathos by a dialect redolent of local
color:

> Sir   I have respected your laws and your government for
> the younited Stats of merricia and I wish to have you continue
> your laws and goverment and keep the embargo on til you see fit
> to take it off, though it is very trying to the people in this country
> about thare debts and it is my wish that you would make some laws to
> pay our debts without paing the money and if the is a law to pay with
> produce & cattle and horses I think that the orter be a tender act so
> we can pay our debts without monay I sopose that you think strange
> of my writing to you but the reason of my writing is becase I have a
> father and a mother and thay cant take care of them selves and as
> times are I cant pay for thare place so that we could live & respect
> your laws and I hope that you will take som notis of me, and write
> to me as soon as you get my letter so I may know if your oner will
> do a little for me,
>
> Jonathan Hall Capt.[86]

The governor was the friendly Langdon, first of the
warrant purveyors to reply to Jefferson. He stood firmly
by the colors:

> Every candid and honest man must acknowledge the embargo to be
> a measure, that should and ought, to have been gone into, at the
> very time it took place, we must see that it has saved to our Country
> many millions of dollars and thousands of men and ships. . . .
> This Junto [Essex], are at this moment sending emissaries into
> every Town in this State, and I believe in other States, to effect the
> choice of federal Representatives to Congress no pains or money is
> spared to bring about a change of sentiment among the people;
> . . . [87]

Federalist influences, backed by the power of money,
finally carried the day in the state elections, and New Hampshire was lost to the Jeffersonians.[88] As Caesar Rodney
diagnosed it, "our friends in New Hampshire have been too
confident & have suffered themselves to be taken by sur-

[86] Jefferson Papers. Capt. Jonathan Hall to Jefferson. Charlestown,
New Hampshire, August 12, 1808.

[87] *Ibid.*, John Langdon to Jefferson, August 13, 1808.

[88] *Ibid.*, Caesar A. Rodney to Jefferson, Wilmington, September 16,
1808.

prise." The blow was all the more severe because the population of New Hampshire was of the backwoods type, on which Jefferson relied for support against the more sophisticated influences of an effete civilization as represented by the merchant princes of Newport or Salem.

If the entire strength of the country had been confined to the Southern States and New England, the great experiment could never have been carried to the lengths which it reached. But there was a vast region in between, whose opinion might easily prove decisive. The action of New York has already been sketched. The position of the state was essentially that of her New England neighbors. Unless Pennsylvania, the greatest state of the middle group, could be reckoned upon as friendly, the balance would certainly lie with the opposition.

In Pennsylvania, as elsewhere, opinion was of course divided. There were strong commercial and aristocratic elements in the state who found at best little to admire in Republicanism; who perhaps even welcomed ruin as the fulfillment of their prophecies. Many of these foes of Jefferson were to be found among the older Quaker stock, and the coldness of that sect puzzled Jefferson as much as it annoyed him. His insistence upon religious toleration had made him enemies in some quarters, but had raised up friends in others. That it had not won over the Quakers as a body was to Jefferson a source of amazement, for they, if any, had suffered at the hands of the intolerant. He seized upon the opportunity afforded by a testimonial of approval from one prominent Quaker to rebuke the generality of the brethren:

Th. Jefferson returns his thanks to Mr. Franklin for the address to the society of friends which he was so kind as to send him. The appeal both to facts and principles is strong, and their consistency will require an able advocate conscious that the present administration has been essentially pacific, and that in all questions of importance it has been governed by the identical principles professed by that society it has been quite at a loss to conjecture the unknown cause of the opposition of the greater part, & bare neutrality of the rest. The hope however that prejudices would at length give way to facts has never been entirely extinguished & still may be realized in favor of another administration.[89]

Philadelphia, as a great seaport, was naturally the center of such hostility as existed in the state. Men felt the blows of the embargo and did not hesitate so to inform the author. A vigorous petition was dispatched early in August by the seafaring men of the port, persons "engaged in the Mercantile service, since their Infancy with few exceptions, and accustomed only to conduct ships or vessels across the ocean", urging an amelioration of their lot.[90] The merchants who usually employed them also found cause for complaint in a permit which Jefferson granted to a Chinese, supposedly a Mandarin, to charter a ship for Canton and load a return cargo. The petitioners affirmed that many of them had themselves lived in Canton and knew the Chinese in question to be "a petty shopkeeper in Canton, utterly incapable of giving a credit."[91]

An individual Philadelphian contributed the verdict that any long continuance of the existing conditions would menace the peace of the Union. War would be less ruinous to the Eastern States than complete stagnation of trade. The planters were not earning even the rent on their lands. Fishermen were debarred from other ventures by the expectation that their trade might reopen. And the same was true of ship owners.[92]

[89] Jefferson Papers. Jefferson to Mr. W. Franklin, June 22, 1808. But cf. Jos. Binghurst to Jefferson, Wilmington, Delaware, July 20, 1808: "In this place, with a very few exceptions the Society of Friends is sincerely attached to our present administration. I hope the day is not far distant when the great body of the Society will rank among the warmest supporters of the pacific and dignified measures of our Government."

[90] Ibid., Petition. Philadelphia, August 8, 1808. A second petition from a similar source was signed August 10, 1808.

[91] Ibid., Philadelphia Merchants to A. Gallatin, August 10, 1808.

[92] Ibid., Wm. Montgomery to Jefferson, Philadelphia, August 16, 1808.

But seamen and shipowners were not the only spokesmen for Philadelphia. William Short, a trusted friend of Jefferson, wrote more encouragingly:

And this City has really acted as the government could wish on the subject of the embargo—I speak of those who are considered as of opposition politics & who are numerous.—They frequently & publicly speak their approbation of the measure, their determination to support it, & if on a jury to punish with rigor the violators of it. I have more than once heard it affirmed & not contradicted, that if the merchants of this City were assembled; confined to Federalists alone nine out of ten would approve the embargo, & of the Tenth disapproving, most of them would be men without capital.[93]

This message from Short was balm to Jefferson. He promptly replied:

I am much pleased with the account you give of the sentiments of the federalists of Philadelphia as to the embargo, and they are not in sentiment with the insurgents of the North. the papers have lately advanced in boldness and flagiciousness [sic] beyond even themselves. such daring and atrocious lies as fill the 3d & 4th columns of the 3d page of the U. S. Gazette of Aug. 31, were never before I believe published with impunity in any country.[94]

The truth was that, in the very capital of commerce, the embargo was creating a substitute therefor. And Pennsylvania, which had stood firmly by Jefferson for seven years, continued faithful even to the end. The secret of contentment in Philadelphia, even of positive enthusiasm, was the growth of manufactures. This growth absorbed a capital which elsewhere was stagnant. Jefferson appreciated the political as well as the economic importance of diverting men's minds from brooding over their losses to rejoicing over their gains, and he took a constructive interest in Philadelphia developments. In October, 1808, for example, he sent a fleece of Iceland wool to James Ronaldson, a correspondent in Philadelphia, "as this peculiar wool may possibly be useful for some manufacture here . . . I am

[93] Jefferson Papers. Wm. Short to Jefferson, Philadelphia, August 27, 1808.
[94] Ibid., Jefferson to Wm. Short, September 6, 1808.

encouraged to take this liberty by the zeal which your letter manifested for the promotion of manufactures."[95]

The fact was that, whatever New England and allied commercial interests might think, Philadelphia was in the midst of a positive boom. The variety and extent of her manufactures awakened civic pride and created the demand for a newspaper exclusively economic to keep good Philadelphians informed of the industrial progress in their city. It was called the *Philadelphia Price Current,* and its files reveal an economic progress truly notable. The editor recognized his indebtedness to Jefferson for a law which provided the initial impetus for most of this development. A letter to this effect deserves quotation in full:

The Editor of the Philadelphia Price Current, in the most respectful Manner, Solicits from the President of the United States, permission to lay before him, irrefragable testimony of the benefits, resulting from the Non Importation acts, and Embargo Laws, this he would beg leave to do by a reference, to an article in his paper of today, which he encloses, headed "American Manufactures", the sensation it has caused here is considerable, and has induced him thus to arrest the President's Attention, for which he will only make this Apology, that, his sole Motive is to prove that by the Presidents originating partial deprivations, he has ultimately bestowed on his country immense, and imperishable benefits.[96]

The political consequence of this promising state of affairs was, as Thomas Cooper congratulated Jefferson in October, that:

The embargo has not converted one republican in this State to tenets of federalism. Snyder had a majority of 1940 over M. Kean in 1805; this year he has a majority of 3061 over Ross. All the members of Congress from this State will be republican: & the success of Snyder ensures to Mr. Madison the electoral votes of Pennsylvania.[97]

No attempt has been made in these pages at an exhaustive study of the various sections of the Union in their

[95] Jefferson Papers. Jefferson to James Ronaldson, October 13, 1808.
[96] *Ibid.,* November 7, 1808.
[97] *Ibid.,* Thomas Cooper to Jefferson, October 16, 1808.

relation to the embargo. Such a study is of course essential to an understanding of the embargo in its fullest aspects. Only such references have been given in the present connection as are preserved in the Jefferson Papers and as can thus be positively identified as having influenced the thinking of Jefferson himself concerning the effect which the embargo was producing upon the country. Irrespective of what a more complete knowledge of the situation might have done for Jefferson, it would seem that, from the information at his command—and this came to him, as we have seen, from sources the most varied—the President was justified in thinking that if the country was not precisely with him, it certainly was not against him. He believed that the great body of Republicans throughout the country were loyal and felt that this was true of a majority of the Federalists as well, "but as they think it an engine which may be used advantageously against the Republican system, the[y] countenance the clamours against it."[98]   Certainly his confidence that the people stood behind him had much to warrant it.

This belief of Jefferson's that the great mass of the common people were capable of sharing in his grand experiment of pacifism lent confidence and strength to his conduct of foreign relations, on which hung the ultimate decision of failure or success. The rigor with which Jefferson enforced the embargo and the extent of his anxiety as to popular opinion concerning it were chiefly due to his interest in the great experiment of warfare without armaments, the final verdict as to which would be rendered by its effect upon the enemy. America would scarcely continue her sacrifices unless they could be demonstrated to bear fruit. So that every development, whether in England or on the Continent, looking toward the abandonment of the Orders and

[98] Jefferson Papers. Jefferson to Colonel D. C. Brent, June 24, 1808. See also Jefferson to La Fayette, July 15, 1808.

Decrees was watched with suspense. Jefferson knew the suffering which his policy entailed, but the poor felt it most, and he doubted, as well he might, the extent of their influence on the policies of government. He wrote:

Whether the pressure on the throne from the suffering people of England & of their islands, the conviction of the dishonorable as well as dishonest character of their orders of council, the strength of their parliamentary opposition, & remarkable weakness of defence of their ministry, will produce a repeal of these orders, and cessation of our embargo is yet to be seen.[99]

With so vast an experiment in progress, any testimonial to its success was more than gratifying. James Bowdoin made Jefferson his debtor with the good news that:

from what I observed when in England & from the best information I was able to procure, I think myself founded in supposing, that ye british cabinet will soon be constrained to modify or recall them in order to recover the advantages of our commerce: her critical situation with respect to the continental powers, the distresst state of her manufacturers at home, added to that of her west india colonies must throw so many embarrasmts in the way of her continuing the war without a better understanding with the U.S. that I expect not only a repeal of the orders of council, but ye most conciliatory overtures to place the commerce of the two countries upon a better footing than it has hitherto stood.[100]

However reassuring this confidence of Bowdoin's may have seemed, Jefferson did not develop any hasty spirit of exultation. In June, he expressed the conviction that the country could not know for two or three months yet the outcome of Anglo-American relations.[101] That this would be peace, not war, was the basic hope of the whole experiment, and intelligent correspondents of Jefferson shared the desire of their chief. A Baltimore observer called the attention of Jefferson to the foreign prints. "The English newspapers appear very anxious that this country & France, shd. be in actual war.—no doubt the French breath[e] the

[99] Jefferson Papers. Jefferson to Mr. Lieper, May 25, 1808.
[100] Ibid., James Bowdoin to Jefferson, Boston, June 9, 1808.
[101] Ibid., Jefferson to Dr. Leib, June 23, 1808.

same language between America & England but it is to be hoped, neither will be gratified."[102]

News from England was belated in those days of slow communication, and the trouble naturally worked both ways. Jefferson was content to allow a considerable time for American news to reach England, and more still for it to exert its natural effect upon British opinion. "I have never supposed," he said in July, "that we could form a final opinion of the British course until the public should be possessed of our communications to Congress and the Act of Congress hanging the discontinuance of the embargo on that of their orders in Council."[103] Since the act in question had been law for over two months, Jefferson could not be accused of undue haste, or of half-baked anticipations of the impossible.

If Jefferson was not prematurely elated by Bowdoin's sanguine conclusions as to the British outlook, it does not appear that he was cast down by Bowdoin's pessimism as to American resolution. In July, when evasions were at their worst and repression was most strict, Jefferson was too preoccupied with the management of affairs to pay more attention than circumstances called for to Bowdoin's conclusion that:

Considering the present posture of affairs, no measure could be better devised than the Embargo; but it is yet doubtful, whether the country has disposition, fortitude or virtue to submit to its privations, for a sufficient length of time, to procure those advantages which are contemplated from it.[104]

American resolution was indeed sorely tried, but if the American people could but realize it, so too was British. This was true more especially during the spring of 1808. By summer, Britain was buoyed by false hopes. Events in

[102] Jefferson Papers. John Hollins to Jefferson, Baltimore, June 27, 1808.
[103] Ibid., Jefferson to Mr. Vaughan, July 10, 1808.
[104] Ibid., James Bowdoin to Jefferson, July 18, 1808.

Spain, leading to the opening to British traders of the rich markets of South America, created a revival of commerce, which, superficially, at any rate, promised to counterbalance the loss of the American trade.

Americans, however, thanks to the slowness of sea voyages and an isolation which the embargo itself increased, were slow to learn of these changes in British opinion. As late as August 4, one correspondent, basing his statement on recent letters from England, wrote Jefferson what would have been in April a more faithful representation of British sentiment :[105]

By my letters from England, together with a tolerable knowledge of things in that Country, I have every reason to believe that the John Bulls are not only uneasy but alarmed at the state of things, & that the thinking or sensible ones among them are now anxious to withdraw those unjustifiable council orders, Edicts etc etc. under which our trade has been so injured & their own exports so diminished.[106]

The shift in British sentiment was known to Jefferson by August 10 at the latest, for in a letter of that date he alludes to the probable influence of these new Spanish hopes. His tone betokens an unusual bitterness. It is the voice of a profound disappointment. Significantly enough, in referring to the effect of the embargo upon England, he uses the past tense :

I believe that the English ministers as well as people were coming over to the opinion that peace with us was their interest. but it is a nation more puffed up by small events than any one on earth. it is not improbable that the turn in Spanish affairs may mount them on their stilts again. it is a government with which no stable connection can be depended on. their ministry is often changed, & with them their *system*. a new ministry so far from thinking themselves bound to observe what their predecessors had done make a point of reversing it. it is a government of no faith, and the same may be said of France & Spain.[107]

[105] It must be remembered that the letters alluded to were weeks en route.

[106] Jefferson Papers. Thomas Digges to Jefferson, August 4, 1809.

[107] *Ibid.,* Jefferson to Thomas Digges, August 10, 1808.

Canning, the minister with whom Jefferson had to deal, was a *Realpolitiker* without the least intention of yielding to either the overtures or the threats of America. He tried to manoeuver the American minister into admitting that the embargo was laid before the Orders were known.[108] And, when Pinkney set forth the desire of the President to remove the embargo if only Britain would take the lead,[109] he met him at first with tantalizing delays[110] and finally with open ridicule. Not that the embargo was impotent.[111] There was much suffering, particularly at first, until an industrial revival came, supplemented by opportunities for smuggling.[112]   But the cabinet was in a strong position, secure of support from the commercial interests and armed with dictatorial war powers. When, therefore, after months of delay, Canning spoke, it was, as Jefferson afterwards described it, "in the high ropes." Nothing would give him such pleasure as to restore American commerce. But to do so would be to admit that the embargo had produced some effect. Pinkney remonstrated in vain,[113] and he and Monroe were obliged to make a discouraging report.[114]

No better progress was made in the negotiations at Washington, though Erskine, the British minister, yielding to a natural temptation to make himself agreeable, held out false hopes. Of one of these diplomatic interchanges, Jefferson has left a memorandum:

Conversn. with Mr. Erskine. He was much alarmed at the conversn out of doors looking like a decln of war with Gr. Br. . . .

[108] *American State Papers*, Foreign Relations, III. 226, August 4, 1808; also III. 231, September 23, 1808.
[109] *Ibid.*, III. 228, August 23, 1808.
[110] Pinkney, *The Life of William Pinkney*, pp. 217-219, quoting Pinkney to Madison, September 10, 1808.
[111] *American State Papers*, Foreign Relations, III. 229-230. Pinkney to Madison, September 21, 1808.
[112] *Ibid.*
[113] *Ibid.*, III. 235, October 10, 1808.
[114] *Ibid.*, III. 197, October 22, 1808.

SUCCESS AND FAILURE

115

I told him that there were but 3 alternatives, 1. war, 2. embargo, 3. submission and that no American would look a moment at the last, he agreed it.

I told him I thot it possible France mt. repeal her decrees as to us, yet I did not understand from Mr. Pinckney's communicns that Engld. would even then revoke her decree; he declared in the most explicit terms she would. I then explain'd that the French repeal mt. only go to the high sea. He observed that he did not know that that cd. produce a repeal from Engld. because the exclusion of her merchandise wd. remain . . . I told him . . . I wished to correct an error . . . this was the supposed partiality of the admn & particularly myself in favr. of France & agt. England I observed that when I came into the admn there was nothing I so much desired as to be on a footing of intimate frdshp with England that I knew as long as she was our friend no enemy could hurt: . . . I observed that if we wished war with England as the Federalists charged us, & I feared his Govmt. might believe, nothing would have been so easy when the Chesapeake was attacked, & when even the feds themselves would have concurred, but on the contrary that our endeavors had been to cool down our countrymen & carry it before their Govrmt. . . . I told him in the course of the conversn that this country would never return to an intercourse with Engld while those orders of council were in force, in some part of it also I told him that Mr. Madison (who it was now pretty well seen wd. be my successor, to which he assented) had entertained the same cordial wishes as myself to be on a friendly footing with England.[115]

Thus, when Congress reassembled, negotiations, although by no means at an end, were at a standstill, and the hope of immediate results was gone.[116] England must discover the unreality of her castles in Spain; America's resolution must be tested with refiner's fire, before Jefferson and his policy could be vindicated. So far, the foreign outlook warranted no report of progress. Failing such a report, could Congress, freshly returned from an electorate groaning under the yoke, be persuaded longer to continue the experiment? This was a vital question, and it suggests that the final outcome of the embargo was determined not at Washington or in London but on the battle fields of Spain.

[115] *The Works of Thomas Jefferson,* I. 424, November 9, 1808.
[116] Jefferson Papers. Charles Pinkney to Jefferson, September 10, 1808.

Somewhat wearily, Jefferson wrote to Madison in September, when prospects were already growing dim, restating the alternative: ". . . if they repeal their orders we must repeal our embargo. if they make satisfaction for the Chesapeake, we must revoke our proclamation, and generalize it's operation by law. if they keep up impressments, we must adhere to nonintercourse, manufactures & a navigation act."[117] Nor did a letter from Pinkney, indicating a continued confidence in the repeal of the Orders, afford Jefferson much encouragement. He was an old man, disillusioned. As he wrote his son-in-law, John W. Eppes, "[Pinkney] infers this from a conversation with Canning, but I have little faith in diplomatic *inferences* & less in Canning's good faith."[118]

The cheerless aspect of foreign relations was known to Republican leaders. Wilson Cary Nicholas, one of Jefferson's Virginia friends, in an elaborate survey of the situation at home and abroad, written October 20, practically on the eve of the new session, tried to make it clear to the President that there were limits beyond which the party would not sustain him. Nicholas concludes that the American people have been none too firm in supporting the experiment; while as for Europe, "the sensation in England I suspect is more to be ascribed to the nonimportation act, than to the embargo, and the revolution in Spain will repair the effect of both."[119]

If the embargo seemed not to be winning its way over seas, it nevertheless opened the field for a diplomatic pronouncement closely akin to the Monroe Doctrine. The President anticipated as one of the consequences of the embargo a larger opportunity for expansion on our own continent. Thus, in August, 1808, he suggested to the secretary of war

[117] Jefferson Papers. Jefferson to James Madison, September, 1808.
[118] *Ibid.*, Jefferson to J. W. Eppes, September 20, 1808.
[119] *Ibid.*, W. C. Nicholas to Jefferson, October 20, 1808.

that, "The enforcing the embargo would furnish a pretext for taking the nearest healthy position to Saint Mary's, and on the waters of Tombigbee."[120]   And he unfolded the dazzling possibility that, "Should England make up with us, while Bonaparte continues at war with Spain, a moment may occur when we may without danger of commitment with either France or England seize to our own limits of Louisiana as of right, & the residue of the Floridas as reprisal for spoliation."[121]

The Spanish American situation, which, as we have seen, contributed to the defeat of Jefferson's object in Europe, was not wholly without its compensations.   The situation was not dissimilar to that of 1823, when the same Mr. Canning interested himself in a South American policy designed to checkmate the Holy Alliance.   Just as, at that time, President Monroe intervened to claim the fruits of South American championship for his own, to the ill-disguised chagrin of the British Cabinet, so, in 1808, when British *rapprochement* with Spanish nationalists threatened undue preponderance in South America, it was Jefferson who nipped the project.   His declaration is often quoted as a step in the evolution of the Monroe Doctrine.   But the parallels in the circumstances which called it forth have been ignored.   Writing to Claiborne, the Governor of Louisiana, he says, "The truth is that the patriots of Spain have no warmer friends than the administration of the U. S., but it is our duty to say nothing & to do nothing for or against either."   Natural sympathy was contending with diplomatic prudence, for the victory of the revolutionists would imply the profit of their British allies.   Yet no liberal could actually wish the republican defeat.   With this in mind, Jefferson continues:

[120] *The Works of Thomas Jefferson*, XI. 43, August 12, 1808.
[121] *Ibid.*

If they succeed, we shall be well satisfied to see Cuba & Mexico remain in their present dependence; but very unwilling to see them in that of either France or England, politically or commercially.

We consider their interests and ours as the same, and that the object of both must be to exclude all the European influence from this hemisphere. We wish to avoid the necessity of going to war, till our revenue shall be entirely liberated from debt. Then it will suffice for war, without creating new debt or taxes.[122]

In 1808, Jefferson stood alone against Great Britain and the Continent alike. In 1823, Monroe acted with a knowledge that the hands of Great Britain at least were tied by her own desire to thwart the Holy Allies. For this anticipation by Jefferson of the Monroe Doctrine,[123] the embargo supplied the motive. Jefferson was compelled to a decided attitude by his recognition that a commercial union between Great Britain and Spain would deprive the embargo of its sting. America would thenceforth suffer, with little power to injure.

If slight progress was apparent toward an understanding with England, our relations with France were no more promising. The enemies of Jefferson once and again raised the old cry of 1793, that he was hopelessly Gallophile. They declared that he and Napoleon were allies and that the embargo was a surrender of American sovereignty to the dictates of the Emperor. Party feeling had run so high and raged so long between the friends of France on the one hand and of England on the other, that neither side would accept foreign relations merely as facts and hope to make use of world conditions for the advantage of its own country. If Federalists were inclined to vent their spleen on Republicans,

[122] *The Works of Thomas Jefferson,* XI. 55, October 29, 1808.

[123] Jefferson's connection with the decision of Monroe to put forth the famous doctrine in his message of December, 1823, is well known. He is credited, too, with a long-time sponsoring of the policy of which it was the culmination. This is well expressed by Albert Shaw in "Jefferson's Doctrines under New Tests," in *Representative Phi Beta Kappa Orations,* p. 304. So far as the writer is aware, however, the influence of the embargo on Jefferson's development of a pre-Monroe Doctrine has not been noted hitherto.

once as "Jacobins" and now as "Imperialists," it was but a natural retaliation on men who had beheld in the entire period of Federalist control no other motive in foreign affairs than the basest truckling to Great Britain, the abandonment of sacred pledges to France, and the outrageous conspiracy of American and British Tories to overthrow the newly won liberties of the French.

Posterity knows that both parties, Federalists and Republicans, kept America first, whichever friendship abroad it seemed wiser for the moment to cultivate. If his enemies misjudged Jefferson, they did him no greater wrong than he had done them. But wrong him they did. Less was hoped, it is true, from the embargo on France than from that on Great Britain, but if its effect would be less damaging, that was due to the nature of things and not to the will of the President, who, although he conceived the conduct of the British to be more insulting than that of the French— the *Chesapeake* affair still rankled—was sufficiently alive to the injuries of the French to retaliate if possible. With war out of the question, as driving us into alliance with one or the other of our hated foes, the embargo was a logical means for coercing both, its unequal incidence being no fault of its sponsor. One looks in vain for evidences of cordiality in the attitude of Jefferson toward Napoleon.

As Armstrong, our minister at Paris, wrote Jefferson in June, "There is now a Champ de bataille between you and france. hitherto there has been none."[124] But it was difficult to persuade Jefferson that France would cling permanently to her obnoxious decrees. To his staunch supporter and good friend, John Taylor, he wrote: "I am not without hope that France will exempt us from the operation of her decrees of Berlin & Milan. if she does, England is bound by her

---

[124] Jefferson Papers. General Armstrong to Jefferson, Paris, June 15, 1808. See also *The Writings of Thomas Jefferson*, XI. 36.

declaration to do the same."[125]   This hopeful view was not shared by Armstrong, who was, in any event, too great a pessimist to please his superior:

> . . . Nor is France more disposed to change her system. She is as much attached to it as if it were both wise and honest. . . . The Emp. has taken it into his head to identify our trade with that of England. "You pay," said he "from ten to fifteen millions of a yearly balance of trade to G.B. and you receive from the rest of Europe, what enables you to pay this ballance. You are in fact, then, only agents between England and the Continent."[126]

To our other agent in Paris, Robert R. Livingston, the Emperor was equally uncompromising.   He made it a *sine qua non* that England act first.   "Tell the President from me," he commanded Livingston, in an audience at Bayonne, July 6, 1808, "that if he can make a treaty with England preserving his maritime rights, it will be agreeable to me—but that I will make war upon the universe should it support her unjust pretensions.   I will not abate any part of my system."[127]

Such arrogance as this of Napoleon deprived the British and patriot victories in Spain of part of their sting.   If they did threaten to prolong the deadlock between America and Great Britain, they at least gave pause to the archtyrant. In Jefferson's words, "I am glad to see that Spain is likely to give Bonaparte emploiment—tant mieux pour nous."[128]

Now and then some correspondent, ignorant no doubt of the importance which Napoleon attached to his commercial war upon England, assured Jefferson that all would yet be well.   "I have every reason," wrote one of these on September 8, "to hope sir, that all will soon be amicable [*sic*]

[125] Jefferson Papers. Jefferson to John Taylor, June 23, 1808.
[126] *Ibid.*, General Armstrong to Jefferson, July 28, 1808.
[127] *Ibid.* Quoted in Armstrong's Dispatch of July 28, 1808.
[128] *Ibid.*, Jefferson to A. Gallatin, August 9, 1808.   See also Jefferson to J. W. Eppes, September 20, 1808.   See also Jefferson to Governor Claiborne, October 29, 1808.

settled between this country & the United States."[129]   But, if a reconciliation should take place, it would be on the level of an *entente* with Tripoli, for, to Jefferson's way of thinking, Napoleon was no better than a pirate: ". . . his condemnation of vessels taken on the high seas by his privateers & carried involuntarily into his ports is justifiable by no law, is piracy, and this is the wrong, we complain of in him."[130]

In spite of the severity with which Jefferson judged the acts and motives of Napoleon, it was impossible for Federalists to regard an embargo which affected him so slightly— the British blockade of his ports being quite capable of sealing them up without our assistance—as really aimed at him at all.   Wilson Cary Nicholas, therefore, in the letter already cited, proffered the advice of wisdom, when he urged Jefferson to confide to Congress every detail of his negotiations with both France and England:

Take away all pretence that anything is concealed that ought to be made public.   Everything that has been said to the government of France in opposition to, or by way of remonstrance against their arts will have a good effect.   No motives of delicacy to that government ought to outweigh the great object of securing to the administration the entire confidence of the people.   Prepare the public for the course that ought to be pursued, and give to the well disposed in Congress and in the nation the full weight of your name and authority.[131]

In other words, it would be as well to make a clean breast of it that the embargo had not yet justified the expectations of those who beheld in it the equivalent of aggressive action.   England was in the "high ropes" over Spanish victories and Spanish-American speculations, and "The Emperor is too well satisfied with the slow & silent but sure progress of his experiment to wish a change on his own ac-

[129] Jefferson Papers.   N. Haley to Jefferson, Paris, September 8, 1808.
[130] *Ibid.*, Jefferson to R. L. Livingston, October 15, 1808.
[131] *Ibid.*, W. C. Nicholas to Jefferson, October 20, 1808.

count, and to expect it because it would be convenient to us, is expecting more than a knowledge of his general policy will justify."[132]

Such was the posture of affairs when Jefferson's personal administration of the government drew to its close. Congress would soon summon him to account for his stewardship, and the report would make dull reading. His achievements on the positive side were considerable. He could point to an enforcement of the embargo remarkable for its consistency and firmness. His admirers might even recognize in it hitherto unsuspected qualities of greatness. He could point with truth to rising manufactures, already transforming the country and destined ultimately to be the most significant factor in its life. He could present the documentary evidence of a sincere attempt to adjust our complaints with foreign countries and restore commerce to its own. But here the credit ended.

On the debit side was a growing restlessness among the people, in some localities amounting to and in others bordering upon revolution. Even districts which held fast to the faith based their trust on the evidence of things unseen and suffered in silence. Negotiations abroad had resulted in nothing tangible. The prospect of submission by either France or England was more remote than it had been in April. It was evident that the embargo, if persisted in at all, would need a term of years for permanent results to be secured.

By the irony of circumstances, Jefferson's positive achievements during these months of personal government would better be ignored in his reports to Congress, whereas the only hope of favorable action from that body would lie in the frankest possible setting forth of just wherein his hopes had been frustrated—not a happy situation for a

[132] Jefferson Papers. General Armstrong to Jefferson, Paris, October 27, 1808.

great idealist, who had staked his all on one of the mightiest experiments ever initiated in the laboratory of world peace.

It is with the manner in which Jefferson met this situation and with his handling of Congress and the country in a great battle for his principles that we are next concerned.

CHAPTER V

FAILURE AND SUCCESS

A repeal of the embargo on honorable terms was the hope of the country when Congress adjourned for the summer. Accordingly, when the new session convened after months of fruitless negotiation, the President's position was not easy. His message naturally took the form of an elaborate defence of the administration. He dwelt upon the promptness of his effort for suspension, the reasonable prospect for its success, and the unexpectedness of its rejection. Acknowledging his disappointment in the immediate objective, Jefferson fell back upon the actual achievements of the embargo, reminding Congress that it "has thus long frustrated those usurpations and spoliations which, if resisted, involve war; if submitted to, sacrifice a vital principle of our national independence."[1] To maintain these salutary effects, he urged the importance of the militia. The growth of manufactures he deemed to be another factor in the nation's independence. Without denying that "The suspension of our foreign commerce produced by the injustice of the belligerent powers, and the consequent losses and sacrifices of our citizens, are subjects of just concern,"[2] he nevertheless found a ray of encouragement in the new impetus to manufactures made possible by the release of so much commercial capital. "The extent of this conversion is daily increasing, and little doubt remains that the establishments formed and forming will—under the auspices of cheaper materials and subsistence, the freedom of labor from taxation with us, and of protecting duties and prohibitions—

[1] *The Works of Thomas Jefferson,* XI. 64, November 8, 1808.
[2] *Ibid.,* XI. 69-70.

become permanent."[3] In this renewed prosperity even commerce with the Indians was to share.[4]

The message admitted a failure in the chief objective. As a measure of conservation, the embargo served its purpose for a few months at most, during which ships and sailors could be gathered home. Its subsequent utility depended mainly upon forcing England and France to a repeal of their edicts. Failing this, the country would regard the incidental development of manufactures as insufficient compensation for commerce destroyed. Yet this, together with the assertion that the alternative was war, was all that the government could adduce in favor of the embargo. Its pressure upon Europe was undoubted, but no one could affirm when, if at all, Europe would yield. The message, therefore, was in a sense a forecast that the embargo was doomed. Nevertheless, so intimately was the prestige of both President and party bound up with the embargo that the chief legislation of the session revolved about its strengthening rather than its repeal.

The President held strong cards. He knew what he wanted. He possessed a Congress of his own party, the leaders of which were accustomed to his guidance. And, discouraging though the economic outlook was to many men in all parts of the country, there were in each section elements who found in the embargo no obstacle to self-interest. New England, for example, which had grown so rich as a neutral carrier, was already turning to manufactures, and these would suffer by a sudden reversal of policy. The Middle States had witnessed an even greater development in this same direction, and, if commerce and agriculture both suffered, the pronounced development of manufactures offered an equivalent. In the South, agricultural losses found

[3] *The Works of Thomas Jefferson*, XI. 70.
[4] *Ibid.*

no manufacturing offsets, and it is fair to say that the embargo contributed the final blow to the old tide-water prosperity, no substitute for which was ever found in the region affected. Yet here, by a psychological paradox, the embargo found its staunchest support.[5]

The economic interpretation of history wholly fails to explain southern loyalty to the embargo. To southerners possibly least among Americans was it possible to apply the hedonistic calculus. The economic man of Adam Smith still dominated the "dismal science," but that creature of the mind of economists never wore the homespun of a Georgia cracker or rode in the coach of a Virginia planter. The southerner, having once accepted Jefferson, accepted him fully. His mind made up, he walked with simple trust.

With so loyal a following, Jefferson was prepared to contend for his ideals, though he himself did not realize until the end how close the battle would prove to be. Congress was the chief arena, but the issue was joined wherever the embargo was felt. Thus, as so often happens in American history, it was a war of sections, commercial, manufacturing, agricultural.

In Congress the Federalists redoubled their clamor, hoping thereby to influence legislation directly. As Levi Lincoln wrote the President in December, "From the leading federalists we hear expressions of disapprobation of the embargo & of violence beyond anything which is seen in the papers"[6]—no small accusation, if one remembers the rare frankness of the early press.

[5] Cf. Henry Adams, *The Life of Albert Gallatin*, p. 380. "Her struggle saved her (*i.e.*, New England) ; necessity taught new modes of existence and made her at length almost independent of the sea. Virginia, however, friendly to the Government, and herself responsible for the choice, submitted with hardly a murmur, and never recovered from the shock; her ruin was accelerated with frightful rapidity because she made no struggle for life."

[6] Jefferson Papers. Levi Lincoln to Jefferson, Boston, December 5, 1808.

While Lincoln was making this alarming observation, the "Merchants Mechanics Traders and Mariners of the town of Boston in the State of Massachusetts" were denouncing the embargo in fifteen pages of solemn rhetoric, the sum of which was that "It would require the tongue or pen of inspiration to delineate the distresses which the Embargo has heaped on this people, a common mind cannot conceive must [sic] less a common hand pourtray them." Yet, in spite of it all, the Jeffersonian tradition was so strong, or the milk of human kindness so rich, or, perhaps, the temptation to irony so great, that the petitioners concluded their memorial with the pious hope that Jefferson might be happy in his approaching retirement. "They hope & pray that after a long life of pleasure & happiness, you may be received into Heaven & there enjoy eternal happiness & inherit everlasting Glory."[7]

Doubtless for the sake of removing him from his present sphere, some of the more tolerant Federalists would have consented to let Jefferson call Heaven his home. But on earth they could declare no truce, and he was obliged to scrutinize even rather minor appointments for fear the incumbent might prostitute his office to the enemy.[8]   No precaution could be too great with matters at such a pass as Jefferson outlined to his son-in-law at the beginning of January, 1809.   The "Monarchists of the North" had federalized five eastern states.   They threatened New York. Massachusetts was about to decide the question of separation from the Union "& to propose it to the whole country East of the North river."   Even good Republicans in that state were urging that a date be named for the repeal of the embargo, preferably in June.   Jefferson thought this might be necessary, even though it meant the defeat of the em-

[7] Jefferson Papers. Petition from Boston, December 2, 1808.
[8] Ibid., Jefferson to A. Gallatin, December 7, 1808.

bargo. "We must save the union: but we wish to sacrifice
as little as possible of the honor of the nation." Even a
surrender of the embargo, Jefferson feared, might not suffice to save the Union, because in the event of war with
England, the enemy might seduce New England by an offer
of neutrality and commerce. Nevertheless, Jefferson indulged a hope that things might not after all come to the
worst, for:

it is possible that England may be wrought upon, (1) by the documents published at the meeting of Congress which prove our fair
conduct toward both countries which she had affected not to believe;
(2) by the determination of the Presidential election; (3) by the
failure so far of expected insurrection in Massachusetts;[9] (4) by
the course of affairs in Spain, where there can be little doubt that
Joseph is re-enthroned before this day. Parts of the country will
hold out for a while, but the ultimate issue must very soon be visible.
If these things have the effect they ought to have on a rational government they will prevent a war with us. The nonintercourse law
will be past. This is a summary view of our present political
condition.[10]

The sinister influence of Old upon New England Jefferson attributed to community of language and customs and to
the friendly association of commercial men on both sides
of the water:

These circumstances aided by her intrigues and money have enabled
her to shake our Union to its center, to controul it's legislative and
executive authorities, to force them from the measures which their
judgment would have approved, & perhaps to constrain us to uncon-
ditional submission to her will, which can never again be opposed,
if such should be the present result.[11]

[9] Cf. *The Works of Thomas Jefferson*, XI. 84-85, January 14, 1809,
and more especially, *ibid.*, XI. 86-87.

[10] Jefferson Papers. Jefferson to Thomas Mann Randolph, January
2, 1809. Cf., also *ibid.*, Benj. Stoddert to Jefferson, January 25, 1809.
" . . . most sincerely believing, that even a few months further
perseverance in the embargo, will produce open defiance of the Laws—if
not disunion. . . . Believe me, sir—vast numbers of those who in
public meetings approve of the embargo, condemn it in private circles."

[11] *Ibid.*, Jefferson to Mr. McRae, February 8, 1809. Cf., also, for
Jefferson's suspicion of bribery, *ibid.*, "Republicans of Essex Co.,
Mass.," February 20, 1809: "But for the voice of Faction & the Bribery
of Britain, but for the efforts of a party headed by a man outrageous in

In a crisis so menacing with its constant undertone of secession, Jefferson should have taken some comfort from the action of the "Legionary Brigade" of Massachusetts. On January 31, its officers met to defend the honor of the organization against insinuations that it was no longer faithful to the government. Following a preamble, which recounted the honorable history of the body from 1775 to the present and set forth its contribution to the safety and glory of the commonwealth, resolutions were adopted vindicating the honor and patriotism of the troops. First, any attempt to alienate the men was "insulting to the Government, injurious to the rights and liberties of the people, dangerous to the quiet possession of honest property, and even hazardous *to life itself*. Second, the officers of the Brigade put themselves on record as viewing with indignation and abhorrence every attempt to disaffect the Militia from their known and uniform attachment and Fidelity, as *American citizen soldiers,* to their Country, its Constitutions, its Governments, and its Laws."

Other resolutions followed, testifying to the confidence of the officers in their men and their approval of the President's conduct, "and we will cordially unite with our Fellow citizens in affording effectual support to *such measures* as our Government *may further adopt,* in the present crisis of our affairs." The signers of this vote of confidence were a lieutenant colonel, three majors, twelve captains, ten lieutenants, and six ensigns.[12]

his passions and disgraced by his own friends, who to effect his purposes would ruin his Country & whose uneasy temper would disturb Elysium to gain the mastery;—But for him & his friends your exertions would have been crowned with the securement of the rights of our seamen and our Merchants."

[12] Jefferson Papers. "Legionary Brigade of Boston." Resolutions of January 31, 1809. Cf. also similar testimony to Massachusetts patriotism in *The Works of Thomas Jefferson*, XI. 84-85, January 14, 1809, and XI. 86-87.

Such expressions were as alarming as they were reassuring. Morale was attacked, or it would have needed no defense. And, if Essex County Republicans continued to praise Jefferson for his wisdom[13] and the men of Rhode Island to applaud his goodness,[14] it remained not a whit the less true that "our embargo has worked hard. It has in fact federalized three of the New England states. Connecticut you know was so before."[15]

Not even an embargo could "federalize" the South, though the warning of Wilson Cary Nicholas was well founded. He was not the only friend of the President turned pessimist by misfortune. John Taylor was another. He appealed to history:

Nonintercourse and embargo have been tried by us upon England for eight years, and failed. As measures preparatory to the revolutionary war, they inflicted privations both military and domestick, which would probably have caused that war to terminate differently except for French aid. Even provisions, as is usual in cases of embargo, became so scarce and dear, that it was nearly as difficult to feed as to clothe, a small army. And a deficiency of Indian corn itself for home consumption appeared as early as 1778 or 1779.

The incitement to a manufacturing spirit was at least equal during the same revolutionary war, to what it can be made now by law, or any other contrivance; it was kept up for eight years and also failed.[16]

[13] Cf. *The Essex Register*, Salem, Mass., January 16, 1808.

[14] Jefferson Papers. Bristol County, Convention, Bristol, Rhode Island: "You have all the glory as you had all the virtues of our beloved Washington. It is not enough for Americans to call you great; —we call you good."

[15] *Ibid.*, Jefferson to William Short, March 8, 1808.

[16] *Ibid.*, John Taylor to Jefferson, Port Royal, Virginia, December 23, 1808. Cf. also *The Branch Papers*, II. 298-299. John Taylor to James Monroe, January 15, 1809: "I entirely agree with you that the support of the administration has become absolutely necessary, not that I think it can now have much influence on our foreign relations, but for the sake of supporting republicanism at home. It is extreme folly to suppose that the bulk of the people are influenced by abstract political principles; such was never the case with any nation. Neither the principles of the former administration nor of the latter, caused their change of places or degrees of popularity. Both was done by taxes imposed and removed and the federalists and tories will work as effectually with whatever grates the popular feeling, as the republicans did."

Whatever may have been the case in Revolutionary times, no failure of the embargo, real or imaginary, could now dislocate the Virginia Republican machine. With well-oiled precision, it cast the entire electoral vote of the state for Madison and Clinton, for the latter, however, with great reluctance inasmuch as "his friends appear hostile to the administration, & have been so uncandid and illiberal as to oppose Mr. Madison on the score of the Embargo Laws while Mr. C. himself is said to observe profound silence on that subject."[17]

Thus, in Virginia, honest acting offset plain speaking. The case in Georgia was reversed. There speech was fair, and conduct dubious. The legislature was authority that "The citizens of this State . . . feel happy that a measure has been adopted which they conceive to be at once, pacific & manly."[18] This at the very time when Gallatin complained "that the system of illegal exportation is carried on the largest scale & embraces all the sea coast of Georgia."[19]

These lawless transactions constituted a romance of the sea. A friend in Savannah wrote as follows:

A merchant in this place has received advice that London merchants are fitting out ships of some say from 18 and 20 guns and 60 to 100 men to come on our coast with dollars the object said to be, the purchase of cotton at sea. in corroboration of this account I have been informed by a planter of South Carolina that a merchant from this place has been in his neighborhood offering 37½ cents pd. for cotton delivered at sea. I have also been informed by Mr. Williamson that a South Carolina planter has sold 100 bags at 30 cents altho the price at this market is but 22 cents.[20]

[17] Jefferson Papers. Archibald Stuart to Jefferson, Staunton, Virginia. But cf. Stuart's reflections on the embargo itself: "The nature of the Conflict in which we are now engaged with Europe does not appear adapted either to ye nature of our Government or the genius and character of Our people. . . . Many of our people are more capable of feeling than reflecting. . . . It would be almost worth the expense of a war to get rid of British influence."

[18] Ibid., The Legislature of Georgia, December 6, 1808.

[19] Ibid., A. Gallatin to Jefferson, December 28, 1808.

[20] Ibid., John Milledge to Jefferson, January 9, 1809.

Nor were Georgia and, by implication, South Carolina the only offenders. The Southern States, as we have previously noticed, found some outlet for their crops in a coasting trade with New England. And, in spite of the scrutiny of revenue officers and the system of bonded cargoes worked out by Gallatin, occasional shipments wholly eluded the Government. It is of these that Jefferson was speaking when he reminded Gallatin that "we see that N[ew] O[rleans] has exported flour the last 6 months, & that too to *the W. Indies.*"[21]

Unlike some of her neighbors, South Carolina continued to win golden laurels. "Every day furnishes fresh proof of the integrity, firmness, and unanimity of our Citizens in this State, to support you and our Government in whatever measures may be thought proper for our welfare."[22] Her electors, like those of Virginia, voted the party ticket naming Clinton for vice-president, but with equal lack of enthusiasm for one who had "discovered great hostility towards your administration, more particularly as related to the Embargo."[23] And her legislators, obedient to a resolution passed at the June session, "appeared clad in an entire Suit of Domestic Manufactures."[24]

More than most Americans, South Carolinians seem to have visualized the economic struggle as a veritable warfare, in which only true heroes could conquer. To men in such a mood, hardship was a stimulus. It was no time to mourn their losses. As their governor testified, "Our Citizens

[21] Jefferson Papers. Jefferson to A. Gallatin, December 8, 1808.

[22] *Ibid.*, House of Representatives, Columbia, South Carolina, Thomas Lehré to Jefferson, November 29, 1808.

[23] *Ibid.*, December 1, 1808.

[24] *Ibid.* Cf., also Samuel Alston to Jefferson, February 1, 1809: "Dear Sir: I received last evening from S.C. a few patterns of Homespun Cloth, manufactured under the direction of my industrious & truly republican wife, by her own servants, & calculated for the summer season—one of which I have the pleasure to send you as a present, the acceptance of which on your part, will be considered as a very high & most gratifying honor on mine & am with highest veneration," etc.

bear the losses of the Embargo with great great patriotism &
are ready to meet all events in defence of their independence
as a nation."[25] Their ardor was, in fact, quite ready for war
itself. As one member of the legislature expressed it:

> From my personal acquaintance with, and my knowledge of the
> sentiments of every member of both Branches of our Legislature, I
> am certain, that whatever measures our Government may think
> proper to adopt toward the Belligerent Powers will meet with their
> most cordial support. I never knew a greater rancor among us than
> upon the present occasion. Every man among us who has yet the
> least spark of the Fire of 76 remaining in him, is determined to
> stand, or fall by the Government of his choice.[26]

Yet virtue even such as this was not exempt from the
shafts of the wicked. The grand jury of Charleston found
it necessary to protest against violations of the law and to
recommend the offenders for trial. "From every information I have received there appears to be a very shameful
Traffic carried on about St. Marys River, it is said . . .
that English ships go there, & take in on the Spanish side
cargoes of Cotton, Rice &c. . . . I am fearful it will
have a very bad tendency,"—all the more to be deprecated
with Federalists showing symptoms of restlessness.[27]

From Maryland there came a most ingenious theory.
John Crawford, a citizen of Baltimore, contended that the
embargo should be kept in force for the very reason that it
encouraged smuggling. The temptation to this illicit trade
would lure people from "our crowdedly populous cities to
spread over the Country, where they would not so much
press upon each other, and thus obviate an evil—which their
collecting together so numerously occasions."[28] Less naive,

---

[25] Jefferson Papers. Governor Pinckney to Jefferson, December 8,
1808. Cf. also Governor Pinckney to Jefferson, January 2, 1809: "By
the average sales last year the Planters of this State lost one with another fifty percentum & yet you hear of no grumbling among us, but a
few, very few indeed violent federalists."

[26] Ibid., Thomas Lehré to Jefferson, Columbia, South Carolina, December 18, 1808.

[27] Ibid., Thomas Lehré to Jefferson, Charleston, January 21, 1809.

[28] Ibid., John Crawford to Jefferson, Baltimore, December 1, 1808.

but equally comforting, was a resolution adopted at Annapolis in February, 1809, to the effect that the embargo was "a wise, salutary and indispenşable measure; that the expediency of it was never questioned until the infamous production of *Timothy Pickering* taught the enemies of the government the use that might be made of it to their advantage."[29]

In Delaware near by, the friends of the embargo were said greatly to outnumber its enemies. They complained, however, that, in less patriotic districts, "the ingenuity of unprincipled speculators, whetted by avarice, has devised various means of evading it, and by their frequent violations of it have, in a great measure defeated its object."[30]   It was perhaps natural for a region so remote from the temptations which it denounced to assume the holier-than-thou attitude of self-proclaimed piety.

More constructive was the spirit of the manufacturing interest.   In this connection, the opinion of Thomas Cooper, the pioneer of American political economy, is suggestive. He wrote in December, after almost a year of embargo:

I hope Congress will take measures of *permanent* protection in favour of our infant manufactures. It will be horrible fraud to entice our citizens to embark in the troublesome and hazardous speculation of new manufactures, and then on a sudden peace leave them to all the malignancy of the British competition in our own market. I well know that Adam Smith's general doctrine is true, that bounties and protecting duties to encourage the raising at home at a dear rate, what can be purchased from abroad at a cheap one is neither more nor less than picking the pockets of one class of the Community to support the monopoly of another. But there may be cases, where necessity will call for this. With us, it will be, not a measure of economy, so much as a measure of protection and defence. Our markets ought to be more at home; more under our own command: and this will call for permanent not temporary regulations.   .   .   .

Of course, all the New England States are *ostensibly* and *apparently* adverse to the measures of Government. I do not believe

[29] Jefferson Papers. *Maryland Gazette,* (Printed) Annapolis, February 8, 1809.

[30] *Ibid.,* Wilmington, Delaware, February 2, 1809.

they are so really. Home manufactures are increasing to such a degree there, that e're long, in numbers as well as in opulence, that class of the Community will be a full match for the Sea-port merchants. The latter will separate from the Union and join England if they can. The Farmers and manufacturers certainly will not. They may be led, and misled, for a time, and their voice drowned by the mercantile outcry. But their wishes and their interest will be in favour of our own union. Would not some early and effective measure in support of domestic manufactures tend to strengthen the opposition in those States to the mercantile predilection for English goods, English politics and English government? It would certainly fix the manufacturing class decidedly in favour of the present measures, and probably frustrate the schemes of disunion now in contemplation.[31]

In this plea for protection, Cooper was ahead of the times. His recommendations were tabled till a day when manufacturers could outvote the commercial interests. Jefferson, meanwhile, lent to rising manufactures the encouragement of his personal patronage and ordered from Colonel Humphreys' woollen mills a suit of homespun for his New Year's reception.[32] To these overtures, the captain of an infant industry dryly replied:

Continuing to make some efforts to draw forth the Industry of a portion of the Community hitherto less usefully employed than it might have been; and waiting with patience the result of those efforts heretofore unaided and not particularly encouraged, I remain Very respectfully, dear Sir, Your Mt. obt. Servt, D. Humphreys.[33]

It was a season of great beginnings, and manufactures, though not of the same traditional influence as commerce, were increasingly diversified. In December, 1808, Charles Thomson, of Revolutionary fame, wrote Jefferson that within a mile of his home at Harriston, Pennsylvania, were three paper mills.[34] Of similar import was a Philadelphia boast that, "No one who does not take pains to keep him-

[31] Jefferson Papers. Thomas Cooper to Jefferson, December 4, 1808.
[32] Ibid., Jefferson to Mr. Bishop, December 8, 1808.
[33] Ibid., D. Humphreys to Jefferson, New Haven, Connecticut, December 12, 1808.
[34] Ibid., Charles Thomson to Jefferson, December 13, 1808.

self informed of the progress of things, can have any idea of the rapid strides we are making in mechanical knowledge and in manufactures." Wire for use in carding machines was an exception, and a scarcity of antimony was also deprecated. Lack of this essential was working great hardship among type-founders, many of whom were discharging their hands. Dyestuffs, too, were very scarce, a circumstance demanding attention, inasmuch as "The Consumption of those, is immense already; and will be increased, owing to the astonishing extent of Manufactures."[35] But occasional handicaps only emphasized the achievements actually accomplished. They were flies in an otherwise rich ointment. This being so, it is not surprising that "The Citizens of the City and County of Philadelphia in general Town Meeting assembled" testified to their enthusiasm for measures of "an enlightened and pacific policy, well calculated to advance the happiness and preserve the dignity and independence of these United States."[36]

Practical men were as keen as theorists like Cooper to recognize the importance of tariff legislation, if their industrial beginnings were to be assured of permanence. Jefferson himself was moved to recommend to Gallatin the placing of red lead "within the pale of protection."[37] He may well have listened with similar favor to a plea on behalf of white lead from one who forwarded

a sample of I believe the first White Lead ever manufactured in the U. States. This with many other manufactures of the first necessity that are now progressing speaks more forcibly the wisdom of the late measures of government than all that has or can be written on the subject, and should Congress deem it advisable to prohibit or to lay protecting duties on the importation of all articles that can be

[35] Jefferson Papers. James Mean to Jefferson, Philadelphia, December 6, 1808.

[36] Ibid., Philadelphia, January 23, 1809. For a similar plaudit, see Resolutions of Niagara County, New York, January 26, 1809.

[37] Ibid., Jefferson to A. Gallatin, December 24, 1808.

manufactured in the United States they will do more for the real independance [*sic*] of their country than has been done since the year 1783.[38]

Jefferson found in this constructive aspect of the embargo a solace for many an anxious hour over its destructive tendencies. And he wrote in good spirits to La Fayette that: "Our embargo, which has been a very trying measure, has produced one very happy & permanent effect. It has set us all on domestic manufacture, & will I verily believe reduce our future demands on England fully one half."[39]

Much of the credit for this hopeful prospect Jefferson chose to arrogate unto himself. He wrote in January, 1809:

I have lately inculcated the encouragement of manufactures to the extent of our own consumption at least, in all articles of which we raise the raw material. On this the federal papers and meetings have sounded the alarm of Chinese policy, destruction of commerce, &c.; that is to say, the iron which we make must not be wrought here into ploughs, axes, hoes, &c., in order that the ship-owner may have the profit of carrying it to Europe, and bringing it back in a manufactured form, as if after manufacturing our own raw materials for our own use, there would not be a surplus of produce sufficient to employ a due proportion of navigation in carrying it to market and exchanging it for those articles of which we have not the raw material. Yet this absurd hue and cry has contributed much to federalize New England, their doctrine goes to the sacrificing agriculture and manufactures to commerce; to the calling all our people from the interior country to the sea-shore to turn merchants and to convert this great agricultural country into a city of Amsterdam.[40]

---

[38] Jefferson Papers. Wm. Dalzell to Jefferson, Philadelphia, February 10, 1809. But for the obverse, see J. Branagan to Jefferson, Philadelphia, February 11, 1809. "Could you see the unspeakable distress of the poor in this city your very heart would almost weep blood." Cf. also W. Penn to Jefferson, New York, February 24, 1809: "All our citizens are become paupers, more than 10,000 now depend on Charity." But from Washington County, Pennsylvania, came praises for embargo as the sponsor of manufactures, February 21, 1809.

[39] *Ibid.*, Jefferson to La Fayette, February 24, 1809.

[40] *The Works of Thomas Jefferson*, XI. 90-91, January 21, 1809. Cf. also *Ibid.*, XI. 97-98. Jefferson to Benjamin Stoddert, February 18, 1809: "The converting this great agricultural country into a city of Amsterdam,—a mere headquarters for carrying on the commerce of all nations with one another, is too absurd . . .; it is essentially interesting to us to have shipping and seamen enough to carry our surplus produce to market; but beyond that I do not think we are bound to give it encouragement by drawbacks or other premiums."

He drew the conclusion that true prosperity depends upon a balance of activities, "and not in the protuberant navigation which has kept us in hot water from the commencement of our government and is now engaging us in war."[41]   Thus an effort to provide New England a substitute for her commerce awakened Jefferson to the possibilities of New England manufactures almost twenty years before the Yankees themselves were ready to accept the lesson.[42]

If the embargo made a positive contribution to Jefferson's thought upon manufactures and commerce, it did almost as much for his thought upon the means of enforcing the nation's will.   Notwithstanding a pride which led him to argue that "The pressure of the embargo, though sensibly felt by every description of our fellow-citizens, has yet been cheerfully borne by most of them, under the conviction that it was a temporary evil, and a necessary one to save us from the greater and more permanent evils—the loss of property and surrender of rights,"[43] Jefferson could not ignore the lawlessness of the "unprincipled along our seacoast and frontiers."[44]   As the executive, he was compelled to adopt a rigor wholly foreign to his character, though he cautioned officials "ever to bear in mind that the life of a citizen is never to be endangered, but as the last melancholy effort for the maintenance of order and obedience to the laws."[45]

This vigorous policy bore fruit, as already noticed, in a more or less general obedience to law.   And pride of opinion caused Jefferson to magnify passive submission under

[41] *The Works of Thomas Jefferson,* XI. 90-91.
[42] This statement does not seem unwarranted in view of New England opposition to the tariff of 1824.
[43] *The Works of Thomas Jefferson,* XI. 87, January 17, 1809.
[44] *Ibid.,* XI. 88-89.
[45] *Ibid.,* XI. 89.

threat of gunboats[46] and militia into active approval.[47] He
was loath to recognize the blow which the embargo dealt to
his own popularity and the party strength. With the turn
of the year, however, it became evident that the repeal was
only a question of time, though the majority still seemed
disposed to defer action until a special session of the eleventh
Congress, to be called in May, 1809. That this was Jefferson's expectation as late as January 28 appears from a letter
to Monroe:

The course the Legislature means to pursue may be inferred from
the act now passed for a meeting in May, and proposition before
them for repealing the embargo in June, and then resuming and
maintaining by force our right of navigation. There will be considerable opposition to this last proposition, not only from the
federalists old and new, who oppose everything, but from the sound
members of the majority, and that it is the only proposition which
can be devised that could obtain a majority of any kind.[48]

Confronting the repeal of his favorite measure, Jefferson was consoled by the reflecton that "There never has been
a situation of the world before, in which such endeavors as
we have made would not have secured our peace. It is
probable that there never will be such another."[49] He
pleaded for another eight years of peace at almost any price
until the happy hour when "our income liberated from debt

[46] *The Works of Thomas Jefferson*, I. 429, December 1, 1808. "These
11 small vessels to be sent immediately to the Eastern ports to enforce
the embargo."

[47] *Ibid.*, XI. 87-88. Circular from the secretary of war to governors.
"The pressure of the embargo though sensibly felt by every description of
our fellow-citizens, has yet been cheerfully borne by most of them, under
the conviction that it was a temporary evil, and a necessary one to save
us from greater and more permanent evils,—the loss of property and
surrender of rights." He goes on to threaten violators with the militia
power. January 17, 1809.

[48] *Ibid.*, XI. 95. January 28, 1809. He had already, January 14, 1809,
renewed his declaration that the embargo was never intended to be permanent. *Ibid.*, XI. 85.

[49] *Ibid.*, XI. 96. January 28, 1809. In this same letter, Jefferson finds
room for cheer over Napoleon's victories in Spain, for these would teach
Britain that her true interests lay in the North American trade, and they
might even lead Bonaparte to sue for our good will in order to obtain
our aid in subduing the Spanish Colonies.

will be adequate to any war, without new taxes or loans, and
our position and increasing strength put us *hors d' insulte*
from any nation." The measures to attain this desirable
end he relinquished to his successor.[50]

It was Jefferson's expectation that the new administration would usher in a new order, leaving to the old a retirement with flags flying and the honors of war. But as the
session wore to a close, sentiment against the embargo gained
new adherents, and the disaffection of the Massachusetts
Republicans, led by Ezekiel Bacon and Joseph Story, sealed
the fate of a law which was now sustained by sentimental
reasons only. It was, accordingly, in the bitterness of humiliation that on February 7, 1809, Jefferson sadly wrote his
son-in-law, Thomas Mann Randolph:

Dear Sir,—I thought Congress had taken their ground firmly for
continuing their embargo till June, and then war. But a sudden and
unaccountable revolution of opinion took place the last week, chiefly
among the New England and New York members, and in a kind of
panic they voted the 4th of March for removing the embargo, and
by such a majority as gave all reason to believe they would not agree
either to war or non-intercourse. This, too, after we had become
satisfied that the Essex Junto had found their expectation desperate,
of inducing the people there to either separation or forcible opposition. The majority of Congress, however, has now rallied to the
removing of the embargo on the 4th of March, non-intercourse with
France and *Great Britain*, trade everywhere else, and continuing
war preparations. The further details are not yet settled, but I
believe it is perfectly certain that the embargo will be taken off on
the 4th of March.[51]

[50] *The Works of Thomas Jefferson*, XI. 96. Cf. also XI. 74-75.
"I think it is fair to leave to those who are to act on them, the decisions
they prefer, Being to be myself but a spectator. I should not feel justified
in directing measures which those who are to execute them would disap-
prove. Our situation is truly difficult. We have been pressed to the wall
and all further retreat impracticable." November 13, 1808.

[51] *Ibid.*, XI. 96-97, February 7, 1809. For an illustration of the pacific
temper of this Congress, see J. Fairfax McLaughlin, *Matthew Lyon*, p.
114-115. "Lyon took just pride in the capture of Ticonderoga." "Now
is the time," he said in the debate of February 7, 1809, "to pause and
count the cost. I know a little of what war means." Jefferson thought
removal of the embargo presaged war. Cf. The Bixby Collection.
Jefferson to Daniel Lescallier, February 25, 1809: "Sir . . . We are

Jefferson's prophecy was correct, for the bill passed the House of Representatives on February 27 by a vote of eighty-one to forty.[52] Thus he retired from office with his great commercial remedy discredited, with the gloomy consciousness of having "refederalized" three of the New England States, and with the sincere belief that war was imminent.[53]

Jefferson and the embargo went out together, and the fame of the one is for ever associated with the fortunes of the other. Facing an unparalleled political and commercial crisis, he had chosen the embargo as a means to combine peace with honor in an assertion of the country's dignity. The injury which the enemy sustained demonstrated the wisdom of the choice,[54] though it was doubtless a miscalculation to count upon any temporary economic pressure for subduing the pride of the European belligerents, especially in view of the known strength of the opposition from the American commercial classes, which was as well understood in Parliament as in Congress. Still Jefferson continued to the end to believe that under any other circumstances the

a peaceable people and have sacrificed much to remain at peace with all the belligerents of Europe, but the hope of longer preserving that attitude seems desperate."

[52] *The Works of Thomas Jefferson,* XI. 101.

[53] *Ibid.,* XI. 104.   March 8, 1809.

[54] Cf. Pinkney, *The Life of William Pinkney,* p. 233.   Pinkney to Madison, January 23, 1809: "The documents laid before Congress and published have had a good effect here.   Your letter to Mr. Erskine I have caused to be printed in a pamphlet, with my letter to Mr. Canning of the 23d of August, and his reply.   The report of the committee of the House of Representatives is admitted to be a most able paper, and has been published in the Morning Chronicle.   The Times newspaper (notwithstanding its former violence against us), agrees that our overtures should have been accepted.   The opposition in Parliament is unanimous on this subject, although divided on others.   Many of the friends of government speak well of our overtures, and almost everybody disapproves of Mr. Canning's note.   The tone has changed, too, in the city.   In short, I have a strong hope that the eminent wisdom of the late American measures will soon be practically proved to the confusion of their opponents."

embargo would have achieved its peaceful aim.[55] Certainly
his persistence in championing a policy so odious to many of
his fellow citizens evinces a singlemindedness not easily
reconciled with that rôle of demagogue and popularity seeker
to which his enemies consigned him.

On the whole the embargo is a credit to both the heart
and the head of its originator. It marks him as a lover of
mankind, seeking a substitute for war, and at the same time
gives him credit for a sense of *Realpolitik*. He saw that
the war cloud over seas demanded the recall to safety of
American shipping. And he perceived that with equivalent
injuries from each belligerent, the utter impossibility of war
with both demanded an alternative. If the means he selected
were not completely efficacious, it is at any rate beyond
dispute that no better have since been found. To Jefferson
belongs the statesman's credit for a liberal project steadfastly
pursued. And as the years roll on, the shadow which the
embargo cast upon his popularity with contemporaries, melts
into the sunlight of his larger fame as a path-finder on the
road to peace.

[55] For support of this view, see *ibid.*, Pinkney to Madison, August
19, 1809. "I cannot subdue my first regret that it was found to be necessary, at the last regular session of Congress, to falter in the course we
were pursuing, and to give signs of inability to persevere in a system
which was on the point of accomplishing all its purposes. That it *was*
found to be necessary I have no doubt; but I have great doubts whether
if it had fortunately been otherwise, we should have had any disavowals."
(He refers to British disavowals of Mr. Erskine's agreement with the
United States.) Elsewhere, Pinkney wrote (see p. 148), "The embargo
was a noble and magnificent effort, suited to the extraordinary occasion
by which it was suggested, and adequate if persevered in to all its purposes. That great measure being abandoned, no half-way scheme of the
same family, can ever hope to stand in its place, and be effectual. . . .
It would have been successful, but that time and prosperity had alloyed
our virtues and unfitted us for such a trial. . . . Any other measure
than the embargo would have been madness or cowardice. For no others
were in our choice but war with both aggressors, or submission to both;
with the certainty too, that that submission would in its progress either
lead to war, or to a state of abject degradation."

CHAPTER VI

NEW ENGLAND AND THE EMBARGO

In one sense the object of the present study has already been accomplished, however imperfectly, by the preceding summary of the experience and philosophy which impelled Jefferson to attempt the great experiment and of the hardship and chagrin which it entailed upon him. But the approach has been up to this point almost entirely personal. And the inwardness of near success and final failure can be understood only through an examination of the political and economic reactions upon both America and Europe of a system which attempted to shake Europe to its foundations and did shake America. For that reason, it is proper to inquire into the effect of the embargo upon commerce, industry, and agriculture among the several states, section by section, and then to seek the explanation for the considerable but insufficient effects produced by it in Europe. Since, throughout the entire period of embargo enforcement, New England was by far the most vocal of American communities in her response to the measure, it is as well to consider her reactions first.

The attitude of New England toward the political and commercial crisis of 1807 was the result of her previous history. The meagre returns of a somewhat unprofitable agriculture and the discouragements to manufactures imposed by the British colonial office, had driven men early to seek for wealth in the commerce which New England harbors invited and in the fisheries which proximity to the Grand Banks encouraged. Long before the Revolution, New England was recognized as the commercial center of the North American colonies. The difficulties of the Revo-

lutionary period and the rivalries under the Articles of Confederation did not alter the primary dependence of New
England upon her commerce, and she entered the Federal
Union with that as her chief interest. Within the Union,
her welfare did not suffer under the watchful leadership of
three administrations of her own choice. She enjoyed the
additional and unhoped for advantage of membership in the
chief of neutral nations at a time when a great war in Europe
threw an unprecedented volume of commerce into the hands
of neutrals.

The first phase of the Great War, from 1792 to the Peace
of Amiens, gave an extraordinary impetus to American commerce, of which New England was the chief beneficiary.
But so abnormal a growth was artificial, and would be endangered either by a termination of the war and a resumption of trade by the belligerents, or, failing that, by any shift
in the policy of the hostile powers tending to convert what
had been a military and naval war into a commercial war.
Such a change was indicated upon the resumption of hostilities in 1803, when Napoleon finally discovered the impossibility of a direct attack upon Great Britain. As he turned
from Boulogne for the campaign of Ulm and Austerlitz,
Great Britain made the similar discovery that an indirect
method of attack offered the best chance against Napoleon.
The weapon for this was the blockade. As first employed
in 1805, it extended only from the Seine to Ostend. This
blockade in combination with Nelson's victory at Trafalgar,
pointed the way to a use of British sea power agreeable
neither to Napoleon nor to the neutrals who might wish
to trade with him. For the blockade, though somewhat ten-
tative at first, was capable of indefinite extension. And when,
in 1806 and 1807, Napoleon issued his Berlin and Milan decrees, imposing a paper blockade upon the entire British
Islands, the government of George III quietly retaliated by

Orders in Council of January and November, 1807, which rendered any neutral trade with the Napoleonic Empire a virtual impossibility.

The result for America was a staggering blow. With over one million tons of shipping destined to lie idle, except for a small fraction in the coasting trade, the nation faced a crisis of the first magnitude. For New England, where the single state of Massachusetts controlled about one third of the total tonnage of the country, with important shipping interests in Connecticut as well, conditions boded a catastrophe. Not only would shipowners and their dependent seamen face severe loss and privation, but farmers would be deprived of their customary market for lumber and potash, butter, grain, etc. Moreover, it was doubtful whether so huge a capital as that devoted to commerce could find a ready shift into the hitherto but little developed manufactures; which, in woollens, shoes, and the like, as yet gave only a dim forecast of the part they were eventually to play in New England economy. Accordingly, when the United States government, completing the work so well begun by the Orders and Decrees, declared a total embargo of American shipping, the temporary and artificial prosperity of New England shippers came to a sudden and disastrous halt.

The embargo shook to its foundations the entire economic structure of New England. Nowhere was its harvest of sectional self-consciousness and cleavage more marked, and the result was one of the most illuminating chapters in the history of American politics. But to estimate the interaction of economic interest and political opinion, it is essential to examine the state of political parties in the New England of 1808.

In the commercial centers the Federalists had found their original stronghold. Their appeal was conservative. Rich merchants, whether in Boston or New York, Philadelphia, or Charleston, supported a party which championed property. In turn, the party crowned the merchants with a shining halo as "the most honorable, the most benevolent, and in every respect the most important class of men in society."[1] Federalist America, in unison with aristocratic England, was horrified at the crimes against persons and property let loose by the French Revolution. In fact, during the last decade of the old century, the repressive and reactionary spirit which the French Revolution aroused in Federalist Tories, prepared the downfall of their party in the elections of 1800 and 1804. New England, like the rest of the country, went over to the Republicans, but her defection from first principles was political rather than economic. Her mercantile and seafaring interests had prospered under the Federalist régime. As we have noticed, she had reaped, more than any other portion of America, the profits which the Great War in Europe flung into the lap of neutrals.[2] These had continued, to be sure, under the cautious leadership of Jefferson. And New England, on the whole, submitted cheerfully to the Virginia dynasty so long as her commercial privileges remained uncurbed.

But European developments were now subjecting New England democracy to a hard test. Economic interest was coming into conflict with patriotism over an issue which aroused strong passions and brought to light determined leaders. In a section noted for sturdy mariners from the time when the men of New England first went down to the sea in ships, the commercial classes had exercised a preponderating influence in politics. It was to be expected that merchant princes and hardy ship captains accustomed to authority would defend their interests wherever threatened. The embargo was certain to counter the will and challenge

[1] *Annals of Congress*, XVIII. 1172, December 14, 1808.
[2] Moncure D. Conway, *Life of Thomas Paine*, II. 408, a letter "To the Federalist Faction."

the interest of the most articulate class in New England. No
economic class in American history—not even the planters
of the Old South—has more completely mastered its section.[3]
Once the embargo cut into its profits, this caste would
scarcely remain passive.

Nor were economic interests the sole objects of New
England concern. She was sensitive to the reputed Gallican-
ism of Jefferson. An embargo that twisted the tail of the
British Lion, however dear to the heart of a Jacobin like
Jefferson, would be anathema to all good men. If, with
Jefferson, an honest neutrality was hopeless and a breach
inevitable, New England would have favored her chief
customer, Great Britain, rather than a former ally, who
had used the twenty years of our connection to make demands
rather than to grant concessions. Old England held the ties
of blood and profit. France was an interloper. Whatever
respectability she once boasted had vanished with the old
régime. The new order, whether of sans-culottes or of
tyrants, was no fit object for American contemplation. To
play into French hands by an embargo speciously neutral
but covertly Gallophile was to insult the intelligence and the
virtue of New England.

Thus the embargo aroused aggressive opposition and
awakened dormant passions and prejudices. But there
were other and less hostile elements in the community.
Offsetting the merchants and their satellites were numbers
of men who looked to the Republicans to satisfy their
longings for democracy. There was a numerous frontier
element in New England of this period, with interests and
sentiments hostile to the merchant aristocracy. Giving
unity, moreover, to otherwise uncoördinated and sometimes

[3] Thomas Wentworth Higginson, *Life and Times of Stephen Higginson,* pp. 41, 42. "Salem was Federalist and the headquarters of Federalism was Salem. The strength of that strong party was in the
merchants of Essex County, most of whom had been ship-masters in
their youth." The name familiarly given to the party was "Essex Junto."

inarticulate masses was a strong party machine. Deriving
its power from party allegiance, the machine had everything
to lose by a sacrifice of party prestige. A small band of
the faithful was always assured.

Such was the background of interest and opinion behind
the New England delegates to the Congress that enacted
the embargo and its successive acts of amendment. While
the initial debate upon embargo was in progress, an anonymous delegate from New England sent to the *Connecticut
Courant* a communication which was published under the
caption, "Highly Interesting to Men of All Parties and Politics."[4] It sounded an alarm:

"Dear Sir,—Yesterday we received a message from the President of a confidential nature. We immediately closed our doors,
and they are still closed. Of course I am not permitted to inform
you either what the President has communicated to us, or what we
have done in consequence of it. But I may be permitted to tell you
that we are doing *no good*. I fear we are about to plunge the nation into the most dreadful calamities—unnecessarily and wantonly
—I am now more than ever persuaded that there is too much
FRENCH INFLUENCE. And it is well that those who succumb
to it, should act *in secret*. This is the reason, and I pledge myself to
you, almost the only reason why we sit with *closed doors*. Our deliberations no more require secrecy at this moment, than they did
when we were debating on the subject of fortifications. Nay, sir, we
are in my opinion, violating the great rights of the people, by sitting
at this moment with closed doors. I cannot express to you in terms
sufficiently strong my abhorrence of *what* we are doing, and the
manner in which we are doing it.[5]

The deliberations thus darkly hinted at resulted in an
embargo in which New England officially concurred.
Rapidity and secrecy were essential, lest ships in port put
out to sea and thus increase the very difficulties which the
embargo sought to avoid. New England Congressmen,

[4] See also Abraham Bishop, *Some Remarks and Extracts in Reply to
Mr. Pickering's letter on the subject of the Embargo*, p. 13. *"Even in
the short time, which the measure was under consideration, [four hours],
many letters were issued and published, stating the business of the secret
session and the probability of an embargo."*
[5] *The Connecticut Courant*, Wednesday, December 30, 1807.

therefore, offered slight initial opposition to the original embargo act of December 22, 1807.   By it, however, their
section was committed to a policy which would save her
ships but ruin their owners.   She stood to win and to lose.
Having garnered her gains, she would be the more certain
to bemoan her losses.

These latter she proceeded promptly to count.   The
Boston *Gazette* ran an extra, January 11, 1808, forecasting
in detail the losses to be sustained by New England.   The
author first showed how remarkably America had prospered by the Napoleonic War, our tonnage of shipping having mounted from six hundred thousand to one million
two hundred thousand, so as to carry a foreign trade worth
one hundred and fifty million yearly, all of which would be
sacrificed by the embargo, at a cost of twenty-five dollars per
capita including children and slaves.   Of this huge loss, the
Gazette demonstrated that Massachusetts would bear far
more than her share.   The editor claimed one third of the
nation's tonnage for his own state.   He anticipated a loss
of trade amounting to thirty-eight million, two hundred
thousand dollars, or somewhat more than one fourth of the
nation's total.   "Thus, then, Old Massachusetts will lose
by one year's Embargo, 38 millions being 38 times our whole
State Debt.   The Interest of this will be 1,980,000 dolls. a
year—Boston will pay of *this interest,* 310,000 dolls. a year
—and each town will lose 14 times the amount of its share
of the present State tax, only to pay the *Interest of one year's
loss by Embargo.*"   This, in the opinion of the *Gazette,* was
taxation without representation, since Massachusetts had
only nineteen representatives in Congress out of a total
of one hundred and sixty.   Yet she would bear one fourth
of the entire loss,—twice her rightful proportion on such
a basis.[6]

[6] The *Boston Gazette,* EXTRA, January 11, 1808.

Federalist editors affected in particular a deep concern for the misfortunes of farmers. But, according to the *Essex Register,* of Salem, most of this pity for the poor farmers was wasted. They were not complaining. "All the noise and clamor about their calamities and afflictions comes from—the merchants of Boston and their hireling editors!!"[7] The *Register* was sufficiently aware of the vast powers for mischief possessed by the press, and its comment upon the false impression of American politics to be derived from a reading of the Boston papers is an early recognition of the importance of propaganda:

If as the Boston tories pretend, the farmers are "distressed", "impoverished", "half ruined", and about to be utterly undone, it must be allowed that their patience and resignation was never exceeded by Job himself; for not one word of murmuring or complaint do we hear from *"our* poor farmers"!—All the noise and clamor about their calamities and afflictions comes from—the merchants of Boston and their hireling editors!! Yes—the monied speculators of our metropolis, with Park and Russell, and the Lord knows who, are raising their voice *in favour of the farmers,* while the farmers themselves are quietly pursuing their own business, regardless of the uproar of these new *defenders,* whom *they* never engaged or hired and who may be assured they will never be thanked for their pains.

If a foreigner were to arrive in Boston, read a few paragraphs in the newspapers, walk to Exchange, and saunter into a few compting rooms, he would think the country at the brink of utter ruin and destruction, in a blaze of commotion, and wonder why he did not see a mob parading the streets and plundering the houses—but let him take a ride into the country and there see the people tranquil, industrious and happy, united in support of government and ready to take upon their shoulders any burthen, necessary for its honor and its good, what must be his opinion of *Boston* politics? It is by the noise of a worthless faction in our sea-ports, that foreigners have conceived an idea of the confusion and distraction of the nation, they peruse federal prints, (for many of these are sent to England) and from thence form an opinion of the state of our politics; they see the most bitter and malignant abuse of the administration perseveringly continued, and are prepossessed with a belief that the measures of government are hateful and unpopular, they see our claims upon England discouraged, and her's justified; and are persuaded that the American people will surrender their rights

[7] *The Essex Register,* Salem, January 16, 1808.

before they will plunge into war; they see frequent misrepresen-
tations of the state of our affairs, continual murmuring at imaginary difficulties, and predictions of approaching ruin, and believe the
nation to be grievously oppressed and embarrassed. If the men who
create all this disturbance were constrained either to leave the country and take up their abode in what they seem to think the paradise
of the earth that *free* and *happy* Isle, *Great Britain,* or to keep their
peace and be silent with regard to our public concerns, it would be
much better for both the community and themselves.[8]

That the *Register* was correct as to contentment among
the farmers, at least in the early days of the embargo, was
virtually conceded by the *Connecticut Courant,* a leading
Federalist sheet, when it promised its readers that:

The first good snow that comes will bring down the pork, butter and
other country produce to market. Let our farmers come. They will
soon find their mistake if they have been dupes of Mr. Jefferson's
politicks. We trust that the price of country produce between this
and March next, will be compared with what it was last year.[9]

Let us postpone for the moment an estimate of agricultural opinion and examine the sentiments of a class more
immediately affected by the embargo; namely, the fishermen. It is possible to gauge for commercial and fishing
interests the degree of discontent, or at least the activity of
its fomentors, by analysis of the petitions with which Congress was bombarded between January, 1808, and the close
of the session in April. Among the petitioners, the selectmen of Hatfield, Massachusetts, for example, "with a humble
& confident boldness," asked for relief from the *"ruinous*
effects of the embargo," or at least for a straightforward
explanation as to why it was ever imposed. To a more
aggressive policy, they would cheerfully pledge their sup-

[8] *The Essex Register,* Salem, Mass., January 16, 1808. Quoting the
Worcester *Aegis.*
[9] *Connecticut Courant,* January 6, 1808. Some at least of the predicted
hardships were realized, if the following is at all typical. "A cow and a
calf, and two tons of hay were taken by execution a few days since in
Wolfboro, N.H. and sold at auction for seven dollars, not enough to pay
the cost of court." *Ibid.,* July 13, 1808.

port, assuring Congress that the spirit of 1776 was not dead in them.[10] This is typical of the wave of petitions coming out of New England. Some idea of the numbers who signed them may be gathered from the following list as now preserved among the Jefferson Papers. The record is doubtless incomplete:

Petition From	Date	Number of Signers
Barnstable Co. Mass., April 11, 1808		40
Barnstable Co. Mass., April 11, 1808		120
Barnstable (Provincetown and Truro), April 11, 1808		330
Barnstable, April 11, 1808		120
Ipswich, Mass., April 5, 1808		70
Essex County, Mass., Fishermen, April 16, 1808		285
Also "we the undersigned inhabitants of the town of Beverly, tho not actually engaged in the fishing business feel ourselves interested in its success; and do therefore join in the prayer of the foregoing memorialists."		324
Total		609
County of Plymouth, March 25, 1808		75
County of Plymouth, April 5, 1808		93
Hampshire County, Mass. (Hatfield), April 19, 1808		
Selectmen on behalf of the town		5
Hampshire County, Mass., Southampton, April 18, 1808		
Selectmen on behalf of the town		2
Hampshire County, Mass., Greenfield, April 19, 1808		
Selectmen on behalf of the town		5
Hampshire County, Mass., Goshen, April 19, 1808		
Selectmen on behalf of the town		3
Hampshire County, Mass., Easthampton, April 18, 1808		
Selectmen on behalf of the town		3
Hampshire County, Mass., Northampton, March 29, 1808		
Selectmen on behalf of the town		5
From Newburyport came a printed petition signed by		801
Bound with the same were from:		
Newbury		428
Ipswich		390
Gloucester		525
Manchester		114
Beverly		455
Wenham		61
Hamilton		122

[10] Petition of Hatfield, Massachusetts, April 6, 1808, in Jefferson Papers, Library of Congress.

Rowley 200
Boxford 126
Bradford 174
Topsfield 103
Middleton 62
Salisbury 137
Amesbury 153
Haverhill 250

This makes a total of 5571 actual signatures to Massachusetts petitions during this early period. The number of protestants was really far greater, since, in several cases, the selectmen signed on behalf of their constituents.

The petitions came before a Congress in which New England's varied opinions were brilliantly, if contradictorily, represented. Among Federalist politicians who would welcome every indication of hardship and discontent, the redoubtable and pugnacious Timothy Pickering was leader. His colleague and opponent, John Quincy Adams, already in the full tide of a great career, was fully competent to defend quite opposite convictions. In the House, the polished Josiah Quincy was a stalwart champion of particularism. These three men gave tone to the point of view and the utterances of the New England delegation.

Adams, in his support of the embargo, maintained an inherited point of view and carried on an inherited feud. His attitude was inevitably colored by the position which his father, John Adams, occupied in history. This position was, in fact, singularly detached. If, in a general way, it was evident that the prosperity of his native section was jeopardized by the embargo,[11] it ill became a former advocate of the embargo[12] to condemn his successor in office for putting it

[11] Manufactures had not as yet provided a sufficient outlet for energies otherwise commercial. See Francis Landon Humphreys, *The Life of Daniel Humphreys*, II. 376. Jefferson, though a nominal convert, was a weak reed for the manufacturers.

[12] *The Life and Works of John Adams*, IX. 606. See also the Frankfort, Kentucky, *Palladium*, June 2, 1808, quoting "Albany April 22:
"It is a fact highly creditable to the late President Adams, that he came out to the polls in *Braintree* and voted for Governor Sullivan and

into operation. And if t.ie difficulties of the embargo bade
fair to humiliate a victorious rival, who only a few years
before had been using his entire influence to undermine the
prestige of Adams himself, a high sense of honor forbade
Adams to seek a petty retaliation. Moreover, Timothy Pickering was fighting the embargo with all the vehemence of his
trenchant pen and bitter tongue. For John Adams to take
his stand with Timothy Pickering, was asking too much of
human nature. His successful rival and his bitterest enemy
being on opposite sides of the question, Adams was in a
position to judge independently. With due regard for consistency with his own record, he refused to condemn the
embargo outright. At the same time, he gravely doubted
its efficacy against the pride and resolution of world
powers,[13] though, when the consequences of the act appeared,
he deprecated the rising storm of protest.[14] Nevertheless,
as a constructive statesman he failed to come forward with
an alternative program, contenting himself with a pious
hope that neither embargo nor non-intercourse would long
continue.[15] The real alternative was war, and this Adams
was not prepared to recommend, although he intimated that
even war would be less disastrous than a too determined enforcement of the existing law.

For the elder Adams, the embargo meant, after all, only
a reconciling of current views with those long held. To
his son, John Quincy Adams, with a career still in the making, the decision was more vital. To cast in his lot with
Timothy Pickering, Harrison Gray Otis, John Cabot, Ste-

the Republican ticket—declaring that the man, who would not support the
administration in the present crisis, was an enemy to his country. *Al.
Reg.*"

    [13] *The Life and Works of John Adams*, IX. 605.

    [14] *Ibid.*, IX. 604, September 27, 1808. "The Union, I fear is in
some danger."

    [15] *Ibid.*, IV. 606-607.

phen Higginson,[16] the "old guard" of the Federalists, in a combat of one section against the rest, would be unbecoming the eldest son of a President of all the states united. Besides, the position of the professor in politics, then as now, harmonized with a social vision which could look beyond local needs and prejudices. It is conformable with his ultimate position in history that the statesman of the Monroe Doctrine and the defender of the right of petition already, in 1808, was upholding the liberalism of his day against Tory reactionaries, whose policy was obstruction.

In his memoirs and writings, John Quincy Adams sets at rest any possible doubt that the Orders in Council of November 11 were unknown at Washington when the embargo was urged on December 18.[17] He assures us that it was this knowledge of added injury from Great Britain that won his vote to the administration's measure. Even so, he was far from recommending its prolonged application.[18] Once committed to the policy, he was no lukewarm defender, though he wavered in January, 1808, to the extent of proposing a committee of inquiry into the possibility of removing the embargo and arming merchant ships.[19] This was in obedience to James Sullivan, governor of Massachusetts, who was alarmed at the state of home politics.[20] Again, when Congress was about to adjourn for the summer recess, he submitted a proposal for non-intercourse with France, Spain, Holland, and Great Britain, and the repeal of any embargo against all States not guilty of

[16] See Thomas Wentworth Higginson, *Life and Times of Stephen Higginson*, pp. 277, 292, 293, for a charming sketch of this New England merchant prince.

[17] *The Writings of John Quincy Adams*, III. 186, January 10, 1808; also III. 197; also III. 282-3.

[18] *Ibid.*, III. 168, December 27, 1808; also *Ibid.*, III. 187, January 10, 1808; and *ibid.*, III. 199.

[19] *Memoirs of John Quincy Adams*, I. 504, January 21, 1808.

[20] *Ibid.*, I. 502, January 4, 1808.

Orders and Decrees.[21]   This, too, was a concession to Massachusetts sentiment.   It failed to carry.

The desire of Adams to mitigate the extreme rigor of the embargo was apparently a concession to New England. More justly viewed, it was a bid for a united America capable of pursuing its own policy, without reference to the design of Great Britain and Mr. Pickering to force us into war with France.[22]   When his colleague, Pickering, appealed for state backing against the will of the nation, Adams was ready enough to denounce "the extraordinary interference of the commercial States, to control the general councils of the nation."   Union, not division, he deemed the crying need of the hour.[23]

Even in the early days of the embargo, conceiving the Union to be endangered, Adams pressed its cause with almost tearful urgency upon his kinsman, Josiah Quincy, a Massachusetts member of the Lower House.[24]   With a fervor which met no echo in Quincy's breast, he entreated him to lay aside the particularism of New England for a broader patriotism.   As for himself, he declared his readiness to die for the cause of nationalism in the civil war which he felt to be threatening.[25]

If Adams was the embodiment of nationalism, Pickering was the incarnation of sectionalism, a New England protagonist of a principle for which the South was eventually to lay down its life.   Notwithstanding Pickering's impetuous nature and headstrong opposition, he maintained courteous relations with Jefferson, but in the Senate and in his own Massachusetts, he was a fire-brand.   His strength lay in the intensity of his convictions.   One of these, most

[21] *Mémoirs of John Quincy Adams,* I. 530, April 30, 1808.
[22] *The Writings of John Quincy Adams,* III. 219-220.
[23] *Ibid.,* III, 223 to Harrison Gray Otis, March 31, 1808
[24] *Memoirs of John Quincy Adams,* I. 510, February 1, 1808.
[25] *Ibid.,* I. 510-511.   His sincerity commanded Quincy's respect.   See on this Edmund Quincy, *Life of Josiah Quincy,* p. 123.

tenaciously held, was a belief that England was our sole protection from the greed of France.[26]   He considered England's attitude toward us to be essentially benevolent[27] and
attributed the failure of the Monroe-Canning negotiations
for settling the *Chesapeake* Affair entirely to the nature of
Jefferson's instructions,[28] which coupled reparation for the
Chesapeake inseparably with satisfaction as to the entire
question of impressment at sea.   In the President's handling
of the existing crisis, Pickering found nothing to commend.   Face to face with the prospect of war, the government was making no other provision for defence save a
few gunboats.[29]   Yet the peaceful protestations of the President were belied by constant incitement to mob prejudice
against Great Britain.[30]   The embargo itself was aimed
solely against Great Britain and, but for the danger of war,
would have been avowed as such.[31]   The irony of it all
was that Great Britain stood to gain rather than to lose from
our hostility.[32]   For this reason, she was unlikely to make
aggressive protest,[33] but was likely rather to bide her time
till America should recover her own senses, for "Fifty or
sixty thousand seafaring people, and the many more thous-
ands absolutely dependent on commerce, will not be contented to starve to gratify the sheer folly of our administration in an experiment of which common sense would show
the futility. . . ."[34]

[26] Charles W. Upham, *The Life of Timothy Pickering*, IV. 121-122,
January 1, 1808, "but if Heaven permit this one to be subdued, the United
States will also fall, and one Tyrant govern the world."

[27] *Ibid.*, p. 122.

[28] *Ibid.*, p. 122.   See also *Ibid.*, p. 146-147.

[29] *Ibid.*, p. 122.

[30] *Ibid.*, p. 122.

[31] *Ibid.*, p. 122.

[32] *Ibid.*, p. 123.   "By shutting up all our own ports, and keeping all
our own vessels at home, we leave all the commerce of the world to
Britain.   She will enjoy this monopoly alone."

[33] *Ibid.*, p. 123.

[34] *Ibid.*, p. 123.

Convinced that opposition in Congress was futile against the intrenched majority of Jefferson, Pickering addressed himself to the legislature for state action against the embargo. His letter, nominally directed to Governor Sullivan, was returned unopened by the governor without presentation to the legislature. An acrimonious correspondence between governor and senator ensued, to the edification of their respective partisans. The immediate political consequence of it all was that Pickering's letter to Sullivan, following close upon Adams' letter to Harrison Gray Otis, brought to a head the issue between the ill-matched colleagues and resulted in the resignation of Adams from the Senate. The test of power brought to Pickering not only revenge upon the Adams family for his own dismissal from the state department, an old wound never healed, but it carried with it also a public approval immensely gratifying to the old agitator.[35] He was elated by the wide circulation accorded to his letter.[36] To his wife he confided that, while he had anticipated the raking up of many old scores, he had not looked for fame. "This has come unsought, and is, therefore, welcome."[37] Pickering's homecoming at the April recess of Congress gave occasion for "a large and respectable number of gentlemen of Salem, associated for the purpose" to bear testimony to their gratitude for his distinguished services.[38]

While at home these rivalries were moving toward their issue, in Congress the New England delegates faced

[35] Alden Bradford, *History of Massachusetts,* III. 99. ". . . it convinced a great portion of the citizens of Massachusetts, of the inexpediency of the embargo; and, some were even led to suppose that it was designed to favour the ambitious views of the Emperor of France."

[36] Charles W. Upham, *The Life of Timothy Pickering,* IV. 133. " . . . it has been read, by this time, probably by more than a hundred thousand persons. The public mind was in a state singularly fitted to hail the publication."

[37] *Ibid.,* IV. 134, April 4, 1808.

[38] *Ibid.,* IV. 134, May 17, 1808.

the thankless task of an opposition, apparently without hope. The embargo had been passed with strong majorities. The combination of West and South, which had twice swept Jefferson into power, gave no present indication of a breach. Moreover, support from New England itself was by no means negligible. What the opposition lacked in numbers, it possessed in spirit, however, and New England Federalists set to work to overcome their isolation.

The campaign opened with the series of petitions of which some notice has already been taken. These demanded either a total repeal of the embargo or special exemptions restricting its operation. Spokesmen for the fisheries were especially insistent, but their plea for leave "to export certain quantities of fish" met a cold response in the Senate.[39] The House was more sympathetic. Orchard Cook, of Maine, commiserated the poor fishermen on journeys of fifty to a hundred miles a week to take oath that none of their catch had been sold.[40] Josiah Quincy deplored the hardships imposed by the embargo upon dealers in perishable goods.[41] Tobacco, cotton, or even flaxseed, he pointed out, could be stored; not so, fish. The petitions bore no immediate fruit. The Republicans looked upon them simply as "the result of a deliberate electioneering plan."[42] A Republican victory at Marblehead, "notwithstanding the poor fish won't keep," was taken as a vote of confidence.[43]

More effective than the fisheries as a party lash and a goad to Republicans, was the perennial French question. New England leaders made adroit use of it to embarrass the President. The opportunity arose when, on February 26,

[39] *Annals of Congress*, XVIII. 375.
[40] *Ibid.*, XVIII. 1694-1695.
[41] *Ibid.*, XVIII. 1246-1247, 2072. For other lamentations on the fisheries, see *ibid.*, XVIII. 2070.
[42] *Ibid.*, XVIII. 2137.
[43] For rejoicings over Marblehead Republicanism, see Frankfort, Kentucky, *Palladium,* for January 26, 1809.

Jefferson submitted to Congress his embargo correspondence with both France and Great Britain. His enemies at
once raised an echo of the old battle between Congress and
the executive, the opening guns of which had thundered
about Jay's Treaty. Jefferson accompaned the correspondence
with a request for its return. Quincy forthwith urged Congress to take a copy before complying. His resolution to
that effect was voted down. Nothing daunted, he proposed
a second and more comprehensive resolution of similar
tenor,[44] which lacked only two votes of carrying. Even
friends of the embargo were not unwilling to tilt with the
President on a question of prerogative. Cheered by a defeat
which he construed as victory, Quincy returned in two weeks
to the charge. But this time the regulars had rallied. The
resolution failed by forty-four to sixty-six.[45]

On the subject of the relative importance of commerce
and agriculture, New England was hypersensitive. The
constant moan of her representatives was the injury to
the entire nation inflicted by any blow to commerce. The
efforts of Livermore[46] and other New Englanders to demonstrate their mutual interdependence were childishly simple.
It is difficult to believe that Congress needed serious enlight-
enment on the impossibility of a cotton planter's living unto
himself alone. Yet the dreary platitudes mustered in to
prove the point betray the debaters as the veriest tyros in economics.

The known and obvious was sometimes varied by excur-
sions into economic theory. The economics of the anti-
embargo men rested upon a substratum of philosophy equivalent to an early American formulation of the *laissez-faire*
idea, then winning many converts in England. America was
the natural home of individualism. The pioneer preferred

Annals of Congress, XVIII. 1693, February 26, 1808.
Ibid., XVIII. 1838.
Ibid., XVIII. 1700-1701.

to be his own lawmaker. Yet a race of pioneers suddenly found itself yoked under an extension of governmental authority which would have galled the most bureaucratic of societies. After electing Jefferson on a platform of democracy and strict construction, the country found itself straightway committed to the diametrically opposite, not only in the Louisiana Purchase instance, but, with actual individual hardship, in the less frequently cited but equally striking embargo as well. The embargo, quite as fully as the Louisiana Purchase, represented an extension of the power of Congress to cover matters not specifically granted in the Constitution. The commercial clause in the Constitution assigned to Congress the power to regulate foreign and interstate commerce. The carefully chosen wording of the fundamental law was far from an authorization to proscribe commerce altogether. Such a procedure rested upon war powers which had hitherto not been invoked. Yet Jefferson gave this most elastic interpretation to the commercial clause. Although some speakers in Congress called attention to the discrepancy between constitutional theory and Jeffersonian practice, posterity has remembered the dramatic example of loose construction afforded by the Purchase and has forgotten that which to contemporaries was equally real and far more irksome.

The embargo was, in effect, a challenge to *"Smithianismus,"* and Josiah Quincy took up the gauntlet in a vigorous speech. "This is the misfortune of the policy of the embargo," he maintained, "that you undertake by your laws to do what laws never did do—what they never can do. You undertake to protect better the property of the individual than his own personal interest would enable him to protect it. The interests which society has in the property of the merchant, are much better secured by his own prudence and understanding of his business, than by any general law."[47]   From this premise, Quincy hastened with entire confidence to a *reductio ad absurdum*. "The true course of policy in such a case," he urged:

would have been to say to the merchant, We will not defend you; here are facts; these are the orders of one nation, these the decrees of the other; you see your danger; we have given you all the information in our power; now do what you please. What would have been the consequence of this? The merchant has his eyes open; he buys up the produce of the country, and sends out ventures. The article is captured; it is lost. It gets to a foreign market; which being understocked, he receives a better price for it. If it be lost, who loses it? The insurer, sir, not the planter, farmer, grower, or fisherman; not industry in its first sources.[48]

The too active intervention of government was thus driving Quincy and those of like mind with him to anarchy and the virtual negation of all government. The highest function of government, in their judgment, was to give information. The function of protection and responsibility for its citizens was denied. Quincy is as unconsciously humorous in the wild fancy just cited as he is deliberately witty in his famous picture of the surgeon who seized a young man in the pride of health, and, after stretching him on a bed, stopping all his orifices, and sealing all his pores, left the patient at the very crisis of the treatment and went away into a far country. This sensible surgeon still further demonstrated his prowess and love of scientific truth by instructing his assistant to pay no attention to any internal symptoms. "Let the patient be convulsed as much as he will, you are to remove none of my bandages. But in case something external should happen; if the sky should fall, and larks should begin to appear, if three birds of Paradise should fly into the window, the great purpose of all these sufferings is answered. Then, and then only, have you my permission to administer relief."[49]

[47] *Annals of Congress*, XVIII. 2076.
[48] *Ibid.*, XVIII. 2076.
[49] *Ibid.*, XVIII. 2206-2207.

This little allegory was compiled by Quincy to fit the situation in April, 1808, when the House, on the point of adjournment for the summer recess, was debating what latitude to allow Jefferson in the conduct of negotiations with France and England growing out of the embargo. Lest the moral should not be sufficiently obvious, he appended his own interpretation. "The conduct of such a physician," he asseverated, "in such a case would not be more extraordinary than that of this House in the present, should it adjourn and limit the discretion of the Executive to certain specified events arbitrarily anticipated; leaving him destitute of the power to grant relief should internal symptoms indicate that nothing else would prevent convulsions. If the events you specify do not happen, then the embargo is absolutely fixed until our return."[50] Strange bedfellows, Josiah Quincy and Thomas Jefferson, but Massachusetts, however she might chafe at presidential authority in the hands of a Republican, did not propose to see Jefferson prevented, by any false notions of Congress, from removing the embargo if opportunity arose. Pro- and anti-embargo men for once found themselves in harmony, and, on April 25, 1808, the House, by a vote of seventy-three to twenty-six, vested in the President, until Congress should reconvene, a wide discretionary power over the embargo.[51] Congressmen, the New England delegation along with the rest, went home to mend their fences, leaving Jefferson to his ill-starred negotiations with Canning.

In the interval between the adjournment of Congress in April and the new session in December, New England experienced the natural resultant of forces friendly and hostile. In so far as men were the victims of commercial losses, inflicted by a government which they distrusted and in a

[50] Annals of Congress, XVIII. 2207.
[51] Ibid., XVIII. 2268-2269.

cause which they failed to comprehend, their attitude was bitter. Others there were who positively benefited through the stimulus to manufactures consequent upon the embargo. With them, though it was scarcely yet apparent, lay the future of New England.

The true salvation for New England depended, of necessity, on manufactures. And, in so far as she recognized this, she set her face toward the future. Commercial interests had, however, so long predominated, that the transition was made with reluctance, and New England manufactures experienced a much less striking expansion than those of Pennsylvania and the Middle States. That portion of New England capital which was fluid, nevertheless, found strong inducements to seek a manufacturing rather than a commercial vent, and actually, if not relatively, a considerable expansion occurred. Thus, at Providence, Rhode Island, there were thirty-four cotton factories, with a capacity of twenty thousand spindles. "That is at least four times as many as have hitherto been in operation." The oldest of these establishments had been set up at Pawtucket in 1792. Its original twenty-two spindles had grown into nine hundred.[52]

The most conspicuous among the entrepreneurs who directed the new industrialism was Colonel David Humphreys. He is best remembered as a breeder of fine Merino sheep, and a manufacturer of woollens. But his many sided energy found additional outlet in various other enterprises, so that he is to be reckoned quite literally as an early captain of found additional outlet in various other enterprises, so that by Daniel Mulford, a young graduate of Yale, who made a horseback journey through New England in search of health. His account is very detailed:

[52] The *Washington Expositor*, March 19, 1808. "Extract of a letter from Providence, Rhode Island."

These [Colonel Humphreys'] works are situated on the Nauga-tuck River, 5 miles above its junction with the Housatonic at Derby. They are a Grist mill, a Sawmill, a Paper mill, 2 fulling Mills & the Factory. They with their appendages, such as houses for the workmen, mechanic shops &c. have cost him $100,000. . He manu-factures cotton yarn, a course (*sic*) cloth for the southern market (cotton warp wool fitted) casimeres & broad cloths. I was shown a piece of casimere blue, a beautiful colour, softer than is common for imported, & equally fine. I saw no cloth finished, but a piece just wove, of an excellent thread, such a piece as ought to have fetched $7 a yard if properly finished. His best clothes and casi-meres are made of wool from the Spanish sheep he imported several years ago. He imported 100. He now owns between 1 & 2 hun-dred full blooded & many more half and quarter blooded. He sells the full blooded at 100 dollars apiece; and might ere this have sold his whole flock at that price. The legislature of New York have offered 50 doll's. bounty to the man who shall introduce that breed of sheep into the counties respectively, throughout the state. The Col. gave me specimens of his casimere and fine wool, to carry home. His best wool is worth a Dollar & half p. lb. for the com-mon half-blood wool, which the farmers in the neighborhood who have bred sheep from his rams bring in, he gives a Dollar a pound. Besides cloth, &c. Stockings are here manufactured in considerable abundance. I think here are a doz. stocking looms: these are cur-ious machines; as well as the water machines for spinning—both so complicated that from the slight views of the minute or so that I had of them, I got no complete idea of their construction.[53]

From another source it is evident that the Colonel, even with wool at a dollar a pound, made a handsome profit:

21 lb. of wool at a dollar	$21.
25 yards of cloth from loom at 60 cents	15.
21 do. from the clothier 21/-4	4.88
	$40.88
Sold 2134 at $2.50 the yard	54.37 1-2
Clear profit after paying every article of labor at common price	13.49 1-2[54]

[53] Daniel Mulford Diary. MS., Library of Yale University. Tran-script in the Library of Congress.

[54] *New York Evening Post,* September 27, 1808, quoting a letter from Mr. Rutledge of South Carolina, who had the figures from Colonel Humphreys himself.

Colonel Humphreys submitted specimens from his loom to the Philadelphia Premium Society, winning a nominal prize of fifty dollars, and, what was far more gratifying, an acknowledgment from the judges:

that the article of superfine cloth from the State of Connecticut, exhibited for the premium No.1, is not only superior to any other specimen, or to any idea they had entertained that cloth of such quality could be manufactured in the U. S. but that it is in goodness of workmanship, whether as it regards the spinning, weaving, dying or dressing, at least *equal,* and in fineness of wool *much superior,* to the best Broadcloth imported from any part of Europe.[55]

Massachusetts, for her part, was taking a position of equal note in the manufacture of shoes, a department in which she has since continued to lead. The indignation of a shoemaker of Lynn who, on a visit to Salem, heard a political speech in which manufactures were denounced and commerce extolled, is a symptom of the pride and class consciousness among the emerging class of mill operatives. Returning home, he hastened to remind the *Essex Register* that:

The town of Lynn owe all their wealth to the manufacture of shoes, and I shall not give my vote for a man who wishes to destroy the very sources from which alone we can acquire a livelihood. I can nowhere see the ghastly countenance painted by Mr. P. [ickman] and I believe our morals are as good and that our citizens attend upon the institutions of the Sabbath as well, at least, as they do in any *commercial* town in the Union. *A Lynn Shoemaker.*[56]

But manufacturing was the bright spot in a rather dreary scene. Commerce was depressed, and agriculture, which might have held the balance, was far from flourishing. The accumulation of crops and of farm products, such as dairy supplies, lumber, potash, etc., proved too great a temptation to smuggling for men who lived within hauling distance of the Canadian border. The entire line was a temptation. But the Bay of Passamaquoddy, on the border

[55] The *Independent Chronicle,* January 9, 1809.
[56] The *Essex Register,* Salem, October 29, 1808.

of New Brunswick, and the margins of Lake Champlain, as New England's natural outlets into Canada, were the chief danger zones. In these quarters, the efforts of the government to suppress illicit trade aroused a resentment amounting almost to civil war.

The spirit of insurrection on the frontier was no mean echo of the times of Shay's Rebellion. Boston papers, as early as January 29, reported an outrage against a reputed revenue inspector in the Kennebec district. His horse was killed, and he himself wounded. To meet the situation, four hundred militia were called out.[57] By February, the smuggling of goods into Canada was in full sway[58]—"*So much for starving the British.*"[59] Conditions did not improve with spring. In May, the Augusta papers announced that disturbances were still unsuppressed, "and but few places appear to be safe for civil officers to execute the laws. Several men were shot at last week and were deterred from doing their duty by men armed and masqued." Fears were expressed that society was on the verge of complete dissolution.[60]

Reports from Vermont were equally alarming. Rumor told of a pitched battle between revenue officers and smugglers on Lake Champlain, with a loss of one killed and thirty-nine wounded. "It is supposed that they [the law-breakers] were conveying large quantities of tea into Lower and Upper Canada."[61] In this emergency, the President acted with vigor. He summoned the state authorities "*by force of arms or otherwise,* to quell and subdue" the "insurgents." But he labored under the disadvantage of depending on local

[57] The *Connecticut Courant,* February 3, 1808, quoting Boston, January 29th.

[58] *Ibid.,* February 10, 1808.

[59] *Ibid.,* quoting Hanover, New Hampshire, February 3, 1808.

[60] The *Connecticut Courant,* May 18, 1808, quoting Augusta, Maine, May 6, 1808.

[61] *Ibid.,* May 25, 1808, quoting Bennington, Vermont, May 8.

authorities to enforce an unpopular measure. "We are sorry to say," is the comment from Keene, New Hampshire, "that the Proclamation *will not be regarded,* and that rafts valued at from 5 to 20 and 30,000 dollars, loaded with all kinds of produce, proceed as usual from the ports on the lake-to Montreal. The accounts also agree that these rafts have from 20 to 50, and even 100 armed men according to their size to protect them and bear down all opposition. From present appearances, we fear serious consequences."[62]

The government's efforts in Vermont to suppress trading with the enemy inspired the Federalist wags to mirth. A Massachusetts neighbor said of the enlistment of one hundred and fifty militia men for service on Lake Champlain, that it

Must convince the world, that the assertion that our *energetic* administration had ever shrunk from the menaces of a *pair of whiskers,* to be downright falsehoods. For can it be supposed, that an administration which could *nobly dare* to order a military force to attack with the bayonet, a race of hardy, though unarmed farmers, waggoners, and rafters, "seeking a market for their surplus products," would ever be intimidated at a bunch of hair on a Frenchman's chin, however black, huge, and curled?[63]

The "whiskers" were necessarily French, for French influence was the constant charge of New England protestants. If any proof were needed of Jefferson's submission to the French, his critics found it in the difficulty imposed by circumstances of expressing officially the sympathy actually felt by our government and people toward the Spanish struggle for liberty. For Washington to lend official countenance to Spain would have signified a sympathetic understanding with Spain's English protector, which was in the nature of things impossible. But, to Jefferson's numerous

---

[62] The *Connecticut Courant,* May 25, 1808, quoting Keene, New Hampshire, May 14, "From Vermont."

[63] *Massachusetts Spy* or *Worcester Gazette,* June 15, 1808. From Rutland, June 4, 1808.

enemies in New England, the sole explanation for hesitancy
was the deep-dyed hypocrisy of the man.   The present generation knows how easy it is to level such a charge, and how
impossible it often is for the person attacked to bring forth
the evidence which would acquit him.   It was so with Jefferson.   Such jibes as the following explain the charm which
retirement held for the weary statesman:

MR. JEFFERSON DISGRACED

Happily for the country, it will soon be well understood by the
world that THE PEOPLE of *America*, do not support Mr. Jefferson in his gallic attachments.—Next to the direful effects of the
Embargo Laws, (dictated by Mr. Jefferson to pacify Bonaparte,)
the indecent manner in which the government papers have treated
the cause of the Spanish patriots, has tended to wean the people of
this country from their attachment to this hypocritical mock-Phil-
osopher.

The people of these States have too much sincere love of liberty,
and with such feelings have had too much sympathy for the cause
of *Spain*, not to be disgusted with the contemptuous manner in
which Mr. Jefferson and his partisans have treated this interesting
subject.   The "Contest for Government" we trust will soon be ended.
—The vile instruments of the Tyrant are destroyed or driven before the Patriotic Armies of *Spain*, and eternal disgrace will justly
attach to all those, who not immediately under controul of the Des-
pot, had expressed an indifference to a cause SO JUST.—What
then can be said of the man who, though at the head of a FREE
REPUBLIC, has countenanced and supported the Despotic conduct
of BONAPARTE, and has endeavored to suppress the sympathy
of his fellow countrymen towards a patriotic people struggling for
their National Independence?   But he has his reward!   Even the
loss of his ill-earned popularity *at home*, and of his reputation
abroad.   .   .   .[64]

The object of this satire found abundant occupation in
his effort to reduce illicit traders to obedience.   That effort
divided itself into a naval patrol along the coast, and a close
system of inspection for Lake Champlain and other inland
routes. Collectors in the interior warned boat owners against
the movement of rafts,[65] warnings greatly needed, as mili-

[64] *New England Palladium*, Boston, October 14, 1808.
[65] The Van Buren Papers, Library of Congress, I. 1787-1813, quoting
New York *Republican Watch Tower*, June 14, 1808.

tary officers signed affidavits that "hostile demonstrations were manifested by many on both sides the line" and that "boats have been armed for the purpose of conveying property into the province of Canada, determined to effect their purpose by force, if they could not otherwise."[66] Blood was drawn in a pitched battle between a revenue cutter, manned by a lieutenant and crew of thirteen men, and the smugglers of the *Black Snake,* a large batteau. The cutter pursued the *Black Snake* up a small river. The law breakers abandoned their ship and then fired from shore upon the government forces, killing one man. The revenue men now came ashore. Here the outlaws opposed them with "a wall piece, about ten feet in length, carrying sixteen *ounce* balls." Two more fell. The villagers now lent a hand, one of their own number having been shot, and eight men were jailed to answer for "WILFUL MURDER." A price was set upon the heads of the Captain and several of his men.[67] The Captain was taken, found guilty, and paid the penalty. One of the crew, Dean, upon conviction of firing upon the soldiers, met his fate with levity. "He appeared perfectly composed and hardened; denied his crime, kicked his hat into his grave, spit upon his coffin."[68]

On the seacoast, similar conditions prevailed. Men vowed they would put to sea in defiance of law.[69] At Newburyport, revenue officers, seeking to prevent the departure of a sloop laden with contraband provisions, were "beaten with sticks and fired upon from the sloop." When a small revenue boat went alongside the sloop to inquire her destination, its crew were "insulted," whereupon their officer commanded them to retire. A schooner dispatched in their pursuit, after

[66] Van Buren Papers, *loc. cit.,* New York *Republican Watch Tower,* August 17, 1808. Affidavit signed June 24, 1808.

[67] *Ibid.,* September 13, 1808.

[68] Van Buren Papers, I. 1787-1813, New York *Republican Watch Tower,* December 2, 1808.

[69] Van Buren Papers, I. 1787-1813, *Salem Gazette,* August 5, 1808.

a ten hours' chase, apprehended such of the crew as remained upon the vessel.[70]

Years afterward transactions of this sort rose up to haunt their perpetrators. A campaign document of 1824 sought to discredit William King and Mark Langdon Hill, of Maine, for alleged participation in unlawful trade. King was a leading merchant of the time, subsequently governor of his state, and is now honored by Maine as one of her two representatives in the Hall of Fame at the National Capitol. The charges against him related more particularly to trade carried on by him under the non-intercourse act, which followed the embargo, and during the War of 1812. Hill's misdoings were under the embargo.

Affidavits were filed that Hill was part owner of the brig, *Mary Jane,* lying in the Kennebec River loaded, but prevented from sailing by a revenue cutter stationed a mile down stream. The deponent asserted that Hill sent for him and urged him in secrecy to make the finishing preparations for the brig's departure. He did so, "Mr. Hill being present, aiding, assisting and superintending the business." Guards were stationed nearby to prevent discovery of the operations under way. That night guns were carried on board for defence against revenue cutters, Hill still assisting. A company of fifteen men besides the crew gathered, their faces blackened to avoid identification, and the brig cast off. Being hailed by the cutter and giving no answer, the brig moved down the river past a United States fort, which was too surprised to use more than small arms, and sailed out to sea, whereupon the armed escort, leaving the crew to navigate the vessel, "returned and went to the house of Mr. Hill, who had in readiness, refreshments suited to the occasion," and who was well pleased with the night's work. The deponent concluded his testimony with a statement of the war-

[70] Van Buren Papers, I. 1787-1813, New York *Republican Watch Tower,* August 31, 1808.

like equipment of the piratical brig. It included "four cannon, small arms, and pitchforks." Other testimony follows from men employed in the same operation, all sworn to before justices of the peace, and all confirming Hill's share in the attack on the revenue cutter.[71]

This attack upon himself and Hill drew from King a declaration that he even anticipated the embargo by recalling most of his ships several months in advance, so that, when the act was proclaimed, he had in port at Bath ten ships:

In all 2475 tons; these vessels remained in port during the whole of the embargo, as it was a measure of our government to coerce the several nations of Europe, who were violating our neutral rights; no one ever heard any complaint from me, although the actual loss, at the most moderate calculation of charter, was 5558 dollars per month, being more than 185 dollars a day, exclusive of interest of money, on the amount of cargoes from 22nd December 1807, to May 1809.[72]

Testimony of fellow townsmen was adduced in King's defence to the effect that:

In relation to the embargo, it is well known, that every vessel owned by Gen. King was in port, entirely unemployed during its continuance; and that few individuals in the country suffered so severely in their commercial interests from this measure of the Government, as did Gen. King.[73]

Of the two cases, that against Hill is much the more convincing. If one accepts the favorable estimate of King —and that is the one made by the state that knew him best— he is to be reckoned as one great merchant, at least, who upheld the embargo in word and deed. Another merchant prince, about whose loyalty there is not even a question, was William Gray, of Salem. Perhaps the wealthiest of

[71] *The Disclosure—No. 1. Documents relating to Violations and Evasions of the Laws During the Commercial Restrictions and late war with Great Britain, &c.* Part First, pp. 34-45.

[72] *Mr. [William] King's reply to a Pamphlet published at Bath, Maine, 1825*, p. 7.

[73] *Ibid.*, pp. 11, 12.

American merchants, he endured his losses without a murmur, and loyally combatted the anti-embargo principles of the Federalists. It was hard for the rank and file among owners of anchored vessels to comprehend the calmness of the heaviest loser of them all. But a correspondence between Gray and the Federalist newspaper of Salem shows his ability to rise above personal losses to an impersonal view of the political situation:

Mr. Cushing

I observe in your paper of Friday last, over the signature "Cuesta," a piece imputing to me base and sordid motives for approving the embargo; in consequence of that, I am compelled to declare to the public FACTS, and leave them to judge how far selfishness has influenced my opinion and conduct.

It is suggested that I set the opinions of others at defiance.

I have presumed to think for myself, and made the Constitution my guide; however mistaken I may be, my intentions are at least correct, nor do I defy or condemn others for thinking differently; and so far from excusing the administration for submission to France, had I perceived symptoms of submission to that or any other foreign power, sooner than advocate such measures, I would devote my whole property for the support of the Independence of the United States.

When the embargo law passed, I thought it a constitutional measure, and I did not think proper to oppose it. The policy of the measure has been much questioned; yet I think the then existing circumstances rendered it prudent and necessary; as Great Britain had threatened, and had at that time passed (though not officially known to us) the orders of council of the 11th November, 1807, authorizing the capture and condemnation of all vessels bound from the United States, that should sail for France or the countries of her allies, after orders of council were known in America; which included all Europe, except Great Britain, Gibraltar, Malta and perhaps Sweden; at those places very few of those articles which we generally export, are admitted; and I think fewer still would have brought the cost and charges. Great Britain, it is said, would have permitted us, after touching there and paying duties, to go to France and the countries of her allies. Is there an independent American, who would submit to such impositions?

Bonaparte had threatened to put in operation his *Berlin Decree* which he had however forborne to do, so far as I know, except in one instance, of the Horizon, wrecked upon the French coast; but his severe and tyrannical decree of the 17th December last, called the *Milan Decree,* passed, declaring all vessels that should be spoken with by the British, liable to capture, which decree almost precluded the possibility of escape from capture or detention. After these restrictions on our commerce, had not the embargo been laid, I think a great part of our vessels, sent for the continent of Europe, would have, I think, been captured and condemned by the British, (as their orders authorized condemnation) and probably the remnants would have fallen into the hands of the French. Had these events taken place, the effect upon the public mind would, I think, have produced war; this, added to the immense loss which the Americans would have sustained by capture and condemnation, must, I think, have been a greater evil than the Embargo; though that, taken separately from these considerations is a serious evil; yet, as a proof that it was necessary, I find out of seven vessels, which sailed from this district for the continent of Europe, in the month preceding the commencement of the embargo, not one ever reached her destined port in safety.

It is insinuated that I am growing rich, while others are suffering by the embargo. I have not reaped any advantage from it, that I know of, in any form whatever; those who best know me can say, whether I have benefitted others, or taken advantage of their necessity. So far from reaping profit from the embargo, my estate has declined more than ten per cent. in value since its operation, which I am ready to demonstrate to any person desirous of investigating the subject. William Gray, Salem, Aug. 11, 1808.[74]

The kind of patriots who called forth Gray's defence were satirized by the Boston *Independent Chronicle* (Republican):

We often hear the disinterested patriotism of the mercantile interest of the United States spoken of in the highest terms, as though the very existence of the government depended on their exertions. There are not perhaps in the community (with a few exceptions) a class of citizens disposed to make so few sacrifices for the good of the country as the merchants. If they can promote their own interest, the indignities and outrages committed on our government by the British will not trouble them.[75]

The cynicism of New England commercial circles is self-proclaimed by their own organ, the *Boston Centinel*. A few years earlier a mere suggestion of peace on earth had called forth the following:

[74] The letter is quoted in The *Universal Gazette*, August 25, 1808. Gray's assertion concerning the seven lost ships led to further correspondence. He modified his statement to make it eight instead of seven. See the *National Intelligencer*, September 5, 1808, quoting Gray's letter of August 25 in the *Salem Gazette*.
[75] The *Independent Chronicle*, Boston, January 11, 1808.

The conclusion of a *gene[r]al peace* in Europe, will be the commencement of *the decline of our commerce*. Every friend to American navigation, *ought to pray as fervently* for a continuation of the war in Europe, *as a husbandman* for rain in a dry season! The one is as necessary to the filling our *warehouses*, as the other our *granaries*.[76]

From men capable of such sentiments, little could be expected that was patriotic or magnanimous.

The commercial interests found a crumb of comfort, and at the same time an additional ground for resentment, in the permission granted by Jefferson for a coastwise trade, under strict supervision as to the bonding and destination of cargoes. Massachusetts was permitted to import grain from states to the south of her, under licenses approved by Governor Sullivan.[77] Such licenses were notoriously easy to obtain. But men professed to see in the system merely a scheme for plaguing Federalists and rewarding Democrats. "Shew us," demanded the *Connecticut Courant,* "in any civilized government, we ask not for precedent from republicks alone—shew us in the modern monarchies of Europe, a stretch of tyranny equal to this."[78] The Salem *Gazette* was equally indignant. "If this is not despotic power, we know not what is—for Governor Sullivan to determine whether the people shall eat or not, and who shall feed them, if they are permitted to eat!!!"[79]

Grain licenses were compared to papal bulls and indulgences[80] and Jefferson was lauded as a mathematician who could not only foretell an eclipse, but produce one, "an eclipse of the *United States,* which he has contrived to render *visible* and almost total."[81]

[76] Quoted in the *Trenton True American* and from it in the *Republican and Savannah Evening Ledger,* Savannah, Georgia, April 30, 1808.
[77] The same privilege was extended to New Hampshire.
[78] *Connecticut Courant,* May 25, 1808.
[79] *Ibid.,* quoting Salem *Gazette.*
[80] *Ibid.,* June 8, 1808.
[81] *Ibid.,* June 22, 1808, from Hartford.

The somewhat scattered data just reviewed reveal a far from prosperous condition among New England farmers and shippers in the summer of 1808. In her fisheries, New England was even more vulnerable. The grain and lumber of the Middle States would be little the worse for a year of seasoning. The cotton, rice, and tobacco of the South might call for increased barns and longer credits. But, after all, they could bide their market. With fish it was otherwise. They must sell or spoil, and Europe was their normal market. The following table of fish exports, sufficiently unromantic in itself, is the record of genuine hardship for one of America's simplest and sturdiest groups, the brave and seldom overpaid fisherfolk:

Fish, Dried or Smoked. To All Parts of the World	To France	To England & Col.[82]
Quintals	Quintals	Quintals
1807 473,924	87,654	55,242
1808 155,808	16,144	26,998

That the trade survived at all was due to the independence of tough old salts who despised the laws of landsmen.

An economic situation so generally unfavorable produced a proportionate recoil in politics. Before Congress reassembled, state election returns showed the Federalists in control throughout New England. Yet there were several features of the election reassuring to the Republicans. In Massachusetts, for example, though the Federalists won the legislature, Governor Sullivan carried the state. And there seems to have been more than a grain of truth in the assertion that Republicans lost the legislature, not because of the unpopularity of the embargo, but because many towns which would have given a safe majority, in order to save the ex-

[82] *An address of Members of the House of Representatives of the Congress of the United States. To their Constituents on the subject of the war with Great Britain, Hanover.* Printed and Sold by Charles Spear, 1812.

pense of salaries, failed to send representatives to the legislature.[83]   Inequality of representation between Republican
and Federalist towns was, according to the Boston *Independent Chronicle,* a decided factor in the outcome.   Republican towns with a population of 67,383 are tabulated as sending forty-six representatives; while Federalist towns totall-
ing only 33,000 sent forty-seven.[84]

In New Hampshire also, the elections indicate a curious
reversal of the political norm.   As a backwoods state, the
upcountry should have been Republican, the short coast-
line, Federalist.   But the vote from the leading towns,
Portsmouth, Durham, Lee, New-Market, Stratham, Green-
land, Rye, and New-Castle stood 1620 Republican to 447
Federalist,[85] whereas the inland districts converted the total
into a Federalist majority.   From which, it was argued, and
plausibly, that the embargo was not responsible, since, on
the embargo hypothesis, the coast towns should have been
Federalist.   The explanation was found in propaganda:

To prove that the federal success in New Hampshire was not the
effect of any real pressure, of the Embargo, but was produced only
by *Embargo clamor,* we need only mention that in almost every town
near the sea-coast. and particularly concerned in trade, an increased
democratic majority was given.   In Portsmouth the majority was
vast and unexpected—and surely if the embargo were felt severely
in any part of the State, it must have been there.   The Portsmouth
Republicans have gained immortal glory, and deserve the applause
of every American.[86]

With New England Federalists returning to their own,
Connecticut felt entitled to a little boasting, for, of all her
sisters near by, she alone had kept the faith.   As the
Courant expressed it, "Connecticut, always faithful to the
true interests of her country, has, in the worst of times,

[83] Wilson Cary Nicholas Papers.   Library of Congress.   Ezekiel
Bacon to W. C. Nicholas, Pittsfield, Massachusetts, June 1, 1808.

[84] The *Independent Chronicle,* Boston, May 30, 1808.

[85] *Ibid.,* September 15, 1808.

[86] *Ibid.,* September 15, 1808.

successfully resisted democracy—She has stood firm while other States have fallen around her." But her welcome to the erring was not the less magnanimous. "With heartfelt joy we congratulate our sister States, Massachusetts, New Hampshire, Vermont and Rhode Island, on their returns to their first love. We hail them as worthy and beloved members of the American family."[87] Neighboring states might well regard Vermont, at any rate, as veritably a brand snatched from the burning, so loud and frequent had been her protestations of loyalty to Jeffersonian principles.[88] As one observer remarked, "New York and Rhode Island have set a glorious example—Massachusetts is treading close on their heels—let Vermont and the other New England States come out in their might, and the Virginia policy of destroying our commerce, will perish in embryo."[89]

Even while the issue still hung in the balance, the prospect of New England's return to the pale of respectability awoke the Muse. The following doggerel is a fair specimen of not the worst rhymes turned out. It is represented as the lament of Selleck Osborn, a poet of the administration, who, seeing the prospect of ruin, bursts into melody:

> O Jefferson! with deep amaze,
>   Thou'st overset our cargo;
> We've nought to do but stand and gaze
>   At thy own curst embargo.
> Old Massachusetts' o'er the dam,
>   Vermont is just a going,
> Connecticut—a stubborn ram,
>   Laughs at our sad undoing.
> Rhode Island too has run adrift

---

[87] The *Connecticut Courant*, September 28, 1808.

[88] *Ibid.*, May 25, 1808, quoting Keene, New Hampshire, May 14, "From Vermont."

[89] The *Connecticut Courant*, May 25, 1808, quoting Keene, New Hampshire, May 14, "From Vermont."

New Hampshire soon will follow,
New York's prepared to give a lift
And seize us by the collar.
Alas! the times are very hard,
They're filled with nought but evil,
Unless we better work our card,
'Twill all go to the devil.[90]

The prose equivalent of this rhapsody proclaimed that:

At length we have received the wished for good news from this State [Vermont]. The embargo party are Down-fallen, we trust like Lucifer, never to rise again. The influence of office would not answer. The prostitution of a batch of *paper money* banks to electioneering purposes would not answer. The infernal trick of imputing to the federalists a murder, committed by a notorious and active democrat failed of success. The opposers of Executive tyranny, foreign influence, and a tribute-paying Congress have completely triumphed.[91]

Such were the courtesies of victory!

Some account has now been taken of New England sentiment between April and November, 1808. To this sentiment Federalism owed a new lease of life. By gaining control of the state legislatures, it obtained a base for greater conquests, a fulcrum for operations at Washington. But before passing to New England's share in the Congressional debates of the new session, let us examine further the background of New England sentiment, upon which, after all, Congressional action would rest. Here also lies the clew to New England attitude toward the extremists of the Essex Junto, who favored a policy of independent action or secession. No verdict upon such a point can be final without reference to the clergy, who, in so God-fearing a community as New England, were potent moulders of opinion.

In the Reverend William Bentley, D.D., a sturdy theologian not unwilling to carry his religion into politics, Jeffer-

[90] The *Connecticut Courant*, June 1, 1808.
[91] *Ibid.*, September 28, 1808.

son possessed a useful champion against the fulminations of
rival divines,[92] who beheld in the President the new anti-
Christ and in his ideas the negation of all dignity and virtue.
Bentley's diary shows that in Church circles the tide against
Jefferson had set in long before the embargo was declared.
In September, 1805, he concludes that his friendship for Mr.
Jefferson is to cost him dear.[93] Four months later, Bentley
was for a third time the party candidate to preach the election sermon. But out of two hundred and seventeen votes,
he obtained only ninety-seven, "a less number than at any
former time."[94] He denounced the mob disorders accompanying the embargo;[95] and their indirect fomentor, Timothy Pickering, he anathematized as "the man that was a
scourge to Washington & Adams & is now the unfeeling political boot of political opposition to Jefferson."[96] It is in
the religious field, however, that Bentley is best informed,
and his alignment of the churches throws some light upon
New England opinion. Pillars of orthodoxy, whether Con-
gregational or Romanist,[97] were quicker to take offense than
Quakers, Baptists, and Methodists, who appreciated the
mildness and toleration of the administration.[98] The
Churches and the politics of the poor man felt themselves
akin.[99]

Political sermons invited their own rejoinders. Thus
when the rector of Trinity Episcopal Church in Salem ven-
tured to defend British conduct in the *Chesapeake* Affair and

---

[92] *The Diary of William Bentley, D.D.,* III. 151, April 14, 1805.
"Party have found that they profit much from the pulpit declamations."
    [93] *Ibid.,* III. 192.
    [94] *Ibid.,* III, 215, February 15, 1806.
    [95] *Ibid.,* III. 404-5, December 24, 1808.
    [96] *Ibid.,* III. 348, March 10, 1808; also p. 350.
    [97] *Ibid.,* III. 410, January 22, 1809.
    [98] *Ibid.*
    [99] For Baptist approval of Jefferson, see *The Diary of William
Bentley, D.D.,* II. 409, January 2, 1802.

to belittle American methods and manners in the months that followed, he was reminded that "Reason and experience forbid us to expect a strict and perfect adherence of uninspired clergy to the example of their heaven taught predecessors, the apostles; but we have a right to require that they should not be diametrically opposite."[100]

More immediately applicable to the final phase of the embargo, was a Thanksgiving sermon of Dr. John Lathrop, minister of the Second Church in Boston, representative of the best theological opinion in an excited time:

The present embarrassed state of our commerce, the threatening divisions which exist among the people, and the unhappy contention in which our government is engaged with the greatest powers of the earth, are circumstances of a very serious nature, and such as to take away a great part of the joy, which we might otherwise have felt on this festive occasion.—We rejoice indeed, but we rejoice with trembling.[101]

The reverend speaker concluded his discourse with an estimate of the state of the nation, admirably judicious and balanced:

In a review of the year, which has passed away since the last general thanksgiving, we find many reasons for gratitude and praise. Although the publick aspect of our country is now serious and alarming we yet enjoy peace. Our young men are not driven away to the field of battle; nor are our old men driven from their houses and theirs beds by an invading enemy.

We are favoured with unusual health, and the fields have yielded an abundance of meat. Our rulers are still of our own appointing and we still possess the highest privileges of religion.

We rejoice that God rules the world in righteousness, and all his ways are perfect. Let us hearken to his counsels. Let us resolve to be good subjects of his Son the Redeemer; we may then rest assured, that, whatever our circumstances may be in the present world, our happiness will be complete in heaven forever. Amen.[102]

[100] The *Essex Register*, Salem, Massachusetts, April 27, 1808.

[101] John Lathrop, D.D., *We Rejoice with Trembling, A Discourse Delivered on the Day of Publick Thanksgiving in the State of Massachusetts, Dec. 1, 1808,* Boston, 1808, p. 10.

[102] John Lathrop, *We Rejoice with Trembling,* p. 20.

Allowing, then, for partisanship among the clergy, there is at any rate no evidence that their ideas were revolutionary. Such extreme measures as the Junto may possibly have contemplated were not the work of the pulpit. More spectacular than pulpit declamation were anniversary processions and celebrations for denouncing the embargo. But even these were ebullitions rather than conspiracies. The anniversary of the embargo was, of course, a rare oportunity to press its lessons home. Parades and pageants were widely held. That at Newburyport is a fair specimen. Bells were tolled at sunrise; flags in the harbor were half-masted; and minute guns were fired. Bells tolled and cannon blazed at noon, and again at four. At nine A.M. a parade of sailors, "looking each of them a 'bloodless image of despair' " marched with muffled drums and crêpe on arms as escort to a dismantled ship, "Her yards a cock bill, a bell tolling in her bows, and her masts capped by inverted cans, denoting the want of grog." She carried a flag, denoting ship in dry dock, bore the name *"O grab me"*, and was commanded by an old sailor, who perpetually inquired, *"Which way shall I steer?"* When the procession reached the custom house, it found "a flag representing a terrapin; his head in *most dignified retirement."* The *pièce de resistance* was a speech suited to the times. *"It went from the heart, it reached the heart."* After such exertions in the cause of Federalism, it is refreshing to learn that "These honest tars afterwards dined together on Clams."[103]

As to whether, beneath these superficial evidences of discontent, a secession movement was actually under way, opinion varied. The Boston *Independent Chronicle* (Republican) noted the existence of a rabid class among the Federalists willing to go far in identifying American and British interests, even to the extent of war with France:

[103] The *Connecticut Courant*, December 28, 1808.

It is thought, if they could once connect this country with Britain upon their own terms, they would introduce monarchy among us, that being evidently their favorite scheme of government. A portion of the federalists do not act in unison with the Junto; and there actually exists at this moment in the New England States two classes of federalists, as distinct in their sentiments as are republicans and the followers of Mr. Pickering.[104]

J. B. Varnum, an influential congressman from Massachusetts, admitted that "the audatious paragraphs which appear daily in the public newspapers; the seditious Resolutions of County Convention—Essex, the Rebellious Handbills circulated in Newbury-Port; and above all the very Extraordinary Statements and principles, contained in the Instructions and Recommendations, to our Members in Congress, by the Senate and House of Representatives," all lent color to the fear of revolt. He contended, however, that "the Strong Arm of the Nation, would soon convince the deluded projectors of their mistake."[105]

John Quincy Adams was less sanguine. From his retirement, Adams watched the closing session of the embargo Congress with keenest interest. While grateful for disasters averted,[106] he found in multiplying difficulties a threat to the national morale. And, once the people should fail to sustain the embargo, the deadly alternative of war would present itself. If undertaken against England, war would precipitate the deep laid plan, for such it seemed to him, of New England to dissolve the Union.[107] War with France would be equally prejudicial. The Federalists would approve the idea, but thwart its prosecution.[108]

Impossible as he felt a retention of the embargo to be,[109] when alternatives came up in December for discussion, he

[104] The *Independent Chronicle*, Boston, July 18, 1808. Article on The Essex Junto.
[105] William Eustis Papers, Library of Congress, J. B. Varnum to William Eustis, December 5, 1808.
[106] *The Writings of John Quincy Adams*, III. 246, November 15, 1808.
[107] *Ibid.*, III. 248-249, to Ezekiel Bacon, November 17, 1808.
[108] *Ibid.*
[109] *Ibid.*, III, 250, November 17, 1808; also, III, 273, 283.

warned against the adoption of anything rash.[110]   Whatever change might be adopted should allow an outward vent for passions hitherto concentrated upon themselves.[111] This being so, the stubborn resistance of Republican leaders to even a hint of change seemed to Adams wretched opportunism,[112] a wilful playing into the hands of the enemy. New England, which was so well organized for trouble, would fall a prey to "projectors of *Disunion*, of *French war*, and of British alliance."[113]   Adams had in mind the Tories of his day, and no modern radical, cataloguing the crimes of capital, could draft a more ringing indictment than Adams of the "system" as it worked in 1808:

Consider [he tells Ezekiel Bacon] complications of the case: Two or three *file leaders* of disappointed ambition, hopeless of consequence under the present national union and building their castles of personal aggrandizement upon a separation and a British alliance. Under these *file leaders,* an organized concert of *banks* and other *monied corporations* holding great numbers of secondary characters in a state of dependence, by a return of discount days, and thus commanding their inaction, if not their assistance. A legislature perfectly under their guidance. A state judiciary, of which you must think what I cannot say. A militia so commanded as at least not likely to oppose much obstacle to their views, and a *plan* long since formed to seize the first favorable opportunity to divide the State, and set up a New England confederacy. What an engine in the hands of these people is a system of restriction which turns all political humors of your political body inward.[114]

Of Pickering and his followers, he goes on to say:

The sources of their influence are numerous and powerful, and there is but one possible motive which can deter them from proceeding to the last extremities, in case of war with England. That motive is fear. They are as selfish and timid as riches can make them,

110 *The Writings of John Quincy Adams,* III. 257, December 5, 1808.
111 *Ibid.,* III. 262, December 8, 1808.
112 Edmund Quincy, *Life of Josiah Quincy,* p. 146.
113 *The Writings of John Quincy Adams,* III. 273, December 19, 1808. See also, III. 279, "if a Measure is clearly for the interest of the Nation, the Government will reject it." December 27, 1808.
114 *The Writings of John Quincy Adams,* III. 278, December 21, 1808. See also, III. 263-264; III. 284-285; III. 287-288.

and in the hour of danger will shrink from their own doctrines, leaving bolder and more desperate characters to take their place.[115]

Some allowance must be made for Adams as a political storm centre, inclined perhaps to exaggerate the wickedness of his foes.   But his opinion is one of the weightiest arguments as to the Essex conspiracy.   It is probable that in her theoretical protest Massachusetts went farther than any other state.[116]   But Connecticut came equally close to decisive action.   It may be urged that the state of armed resistance in northern Vermont and on the Maine coast was rebellion in essence.   But the men involved were in no formal sense the spokesmen of their state.   Their defiance of revenue officers was nothing more than rioting.   And rioting, while it often features revolutions, never expresses their real significance.   Resistance to the extent implied in revolution or secession presupposes a legal or at least a quasi-legal formulation of principles.   This is what the General Assembly of Connecticut provided in February, 1809.   Its declaration may well be compared with the Virginia and Kentucky Resolutions, the chief previous land-marks of the secession movement in the United States:

Connecticut. General Assembly, 1809.
An address of the General Assembly, to the People of Connecticut.
The members of the General Assembly . . . have . . . decided, that in such a crisis of affairs, it is right, and has become the duty of the legislative and executive authorities in the State, to

[115] *The Writings of John Quincy Adams,* III. 285, December 26, 1808.

[116] The high tide of Massachusetts protest was the "Report of a Committee of the House of Representatives Respecting certain Military Orders issued by His Honor Levi Lincoln, Lieutenant Governor, and Commander in Chief of the Commonwealth of Massachusetts with the Documents referred to in the same." The Act of January 9, 1809, was declared "in many respects unjust, oppressive and unconstitutional, and not legally binding on the citizens of this State." Such being the case, Lincoln's summons to the militia, in violation of certain clauses of the State Constitution was an abuse of power, for "the militia cannot *legally* be employed by the President of the United States, or by any person empowered by him, till they have been called forth in the mode which Congress had previously prescribed." *Report,* p. 7.

withold their aid, and co-operation, from the execution of the act,[117] passed to enforce more effectually the embargo system. . . . While it is the duty of the Legislature to guard the sovereignty of the State, and your rights from encroachment, it continues to be your interest and duty, as peaceable citizens, to abstain from all resistance, against acts, which purport to be laws of the United States. Be advised to seek none but constitutional relief. Your character, for steady and firm, but peaceable and orderly conduct, is a sure pledge, that you will pursue this course. . . . .

We forbear to express the imminent danger, to which we fear, not only our constitutional rights, but those of all the people of the United States, are exposed from within and without. May heaven avert the danger, and preserve to us, our privileges, civil and religious, etc. John Cotton Smith, Speaker H. of R., Johnathan Trumbull, Governor.[118]

It was to obtain redress and guarantees in a constitutional manner that the General Assembly in special session drew up the following resolutions, February 23, 1809:

Resolved, That to preserve the Union, and support the Constitution of the United States, it becomes the duty of the legislatures of the States, in such a crisis of affairs, vigilantly to watch over and vigorously to maintain, the powers not delegated to the United States, but reserved to the states respectively, or to the people, and that a due regard to this duty, will not permit this Assembly to assist, or concur in giving effect to the aforesaid unconstitutional act, passed to enforce the embargo.

Resolved, that this Assembly highly approve of the Conduct of his Excellency the Governor, in declining to designate persons to carry into effect, by the aid of *military power,* the act of the United States, enforcing the Embargo, and that his letter addressed to the Secretary for the department of War, containing his refusal, to make such designation, be recorded in the public records of this State as an example to persons, who may hold places of distinguished trust, in this free and independent republic.

Resolved, That persons holding executive offices under this State, are restrained by the duties which they owe this State, from affording any official aid or cooperation in the execution of the act aforesaid; and that his Excellency the Governour be requested, as commander in chief of the military force of this state, to cause those resolutions to be published in general orders; And that the secretary of this state be and he is hereby directed to transmit copies of the same to the several sheriffs and town clerks.

Resolved, That his Excellency the Governour, be requested to communicate the foregoing resolution to the President of the United

[117] An Act Strengthening the enforcement of the Embargo.
[118] P. 5 of the printed "Address."

States, with an assurance that this Assembly regret that they are thus obliged under a sense of paramount public duty, to assert the unquestionable right of this State to abstain from any agency in the execution of measures which are unconstitutional and despotic.

Resolved, That this Assembly accord in sentiment with the Senate and House of Representatives of the Commonwealth of Massachusetts, that it is expedient to effect certain alterations in the Constitution of the United States; and will zealously cooperate with that Commonwealth and any other of the States, in all legal and constitutional measures for procuring such amendments to the Constitution of the United States as shall be judged necessary to obtain more effectual protection and defense for commerce; and to give to the commercial states their fair and just consideration in the union, and for affording permanent security, as well as present relief, from the oppressive measures under which they now suffer.

Resolved, That his Excellency the Governour be requested to transmit copies of the foregoing resolution to the President of the Senate, and Speaker of the House of Representatives in the Commonwealth of Massachusetts, and to the legislatures of such of our sister States, as manifest a disposition to concur, in restoring to commerce its former activity, and preventing the repetition of measures which have a tendency, not only to destroy it, but to dissolve the union, which ought to be inviolate.

General Assembly Special Session February 1809
John Cotton Smith
Speaker of the House of Representatives,
Johnathan Trumbull
Governor.[119]

While the anti-embargo sentiment, already well developed during the summer, was thus gaining momentum, Congress was once more in session. John Quincy Adams was absent, but most of the prominent figures of the previous session returned, besides several notable additions. Pickering, for one, came back full of zeal against the embargo. He reiterated the old point that the Orders in Council were unknown when the embargo was first passed[120] and scored the haste in its enactment.[121] He repelled the insinuation that he was under British influence,[122] though he pic-

---

[119] *Special Session of Connecticut General Assembly,* Hartford, February 23, 1809, pp. 7-8.

[120] Charles W. Upham, *The Life of Timothy Pickering,* IV. 144.

[121] *Ibid.,* IV. 145.

[122] *Ibid.,* IV. 146.

tured American commerce as not seriously damaged by the aggressions of either Great Britain or France.[123]

As he and his friends gained headway, Pickering ridiculed the government plea for yet a little longer trial of the embargo. He pictured Napoleon striding like a colossus through Spain. ". . . If heaven permits this sad catastrophe . . . what then? Are we to join his arms; and by conquering Canada and Nova Scotia—prepare those countries with our power for a new master? and hasten the glorious period when to the lofty titles of Emperor of France and King of Italy and Protector of the Confederation of the Rhine shall be added that of Emperor of the Two Americas? That, Sir, will be the natural course of things if, as some have wished, the British navy were destroyed."[124] Delay was, in fact, the last thing he meant to countenance. The "imposture"[125] must be laid bare, and "the great body of the people" freed from "the most miserable and mischievous delusion."[126] An ingenuous admission, this, that some Americans found the embargo not so insupportable after all. If Pickering can open their eyes, he avows it will be the most important service of his forty years in politics.[127] He defied the tongue of malice to turn him from his course. For the accomplishing of this purpose, he proposed to gather materials for a history of the embargo, which should set forth Jefferson as the chief of sinners,[128] whose only rivals were the insidious French.[129]

[123] Charles W. Upham, *The Life of Timothy Pickering*, IV. 146.

[124] *Ibid.*, IV. 153, December 21, 1808.

[125] B. C. Steiner, *Life and Correspondence of James McHenry*, I. 550. Pickering to McHenry.

[126] Charles W. Upham, *The Life of Timothy Pickering*, IV. 156, January 8, 1809.

[127] *Ibid.*

[128] B. C. Steiner, *Life and Correspondence of James McHenry*, Pickering to J. Wagner, I. 551, January 19, 1809.

[129] *Ibid.*

Ideas like these could be amplified ad libitum from Pickering's speeches before the Senate.   But details would only confirm the portrait of a belated Puritan, narrow but resolute, full of his high calling to lighten the darkness of others.   To this Puritan in politics, New England was the all-in-all.   Salvation was for the elect and chosen, among whom Jefferson and his wicked rout could claim no place.

In Joseph Story, Massachusetts sent a different and a saner type.   It was his first session, and he took his seat in December, 1808, just when the country was stinging from Canning's rebuff to the American appeal for mutual concessions.   At first he shared the official opinion that we owed this slap "to the false impression made upon the British cabinet by our own citizens, their exaggeration of discontent in America having strengthened the British will to resist."[130] Further reports from home soon convinced him, however, that popular discontent would not be trifled with, and he accepted non-intercourse as an objectionable but necessary substitute.   Republican though he was, Story felt that the interest not only of his section, but of the party demanded a right about face.   Personal conferences with Giles, Nicholas, and Campbell,[131] who sought to hold him steadfast in the faith, and examination of reports and statistics of the damage wrought in England, failed to convince him that the embargo deserved a longer trial.   He was doubtless clear-sighted in breaking the party leash.[132]   But his defection was the signal for the collapse of embargo support.   Although Story was absent from Washington when the final vote was taken,[133] to him more than to any other person, Jefferson attributed the abandonment of his pet measure.[134]   By one

[130] Wm. W. Story, *Life and Letters of Joseph Story*, I. 173, December 31, 1808; also I. 191, December 24, 1808.

[131] *Ibid.*, I. 185, 187.

[132] *Ibid.*, I. 184.

[133] *Ibid.*, I. 185, 187.

[134] *Ibid.*, I. 184-185.

of the ironies of politics, it was reserved for a staunch Republican and friend of the administration to achieve what the fiery diatribes of Pickering, Quincy, and other Federalists had failed to bring about. For this, Story was never forgiven by the retiring President.[135] The rift thus created rejoiced their foes. Not even the most dyed-in-the-wool Federalist could begrudge anti-embargo laurels to a Republican. Josiah Quincy, for one, viewed with a fine complacency the "dreadful distraction in the enemy's camp,"[136] but so strong was the spell cast by Jefferson that, even with victory in sight, his opponents could scarce trust their senses. So Quincy, writing to his wife as late as February third on the occasion of a skirmish won, warns her that "the wand of that magician is not broken.—But I hope his power is drawing to an end in this world."[137] A few days later, his hopes were rising.[138] But even when victory finally came, he failed to grasp its full significance. On what should have been a day of triumph, he complained of Jefferson, that "His intrigues have prevailed. Non-Intercourse will be substituted for Embargo. The Non-Intercourse bill passed, 81 ayes, 40 nays, all the Federalists voting against the bill except Taggart and Livermore."[139] Thus New England, in the very act of imposing upon Jefferson the deepest humiliation of his career, failed to comprehend the completeness of her conquest. The embargo having failed, non-intercourse would be little more than nominal.

The debates in Congress which led to this result were marked by no special eloquence or novelty of principle. The speakers were rather taking an inventory of where the country stood after a year of embargo. England, it was

[135] Wm. W. Story, *The Life and Letters of Joseph Story,* I. 187.
[136] Edmund Quincy, *The Life of Josiah Quincy,* p. 185.
[137] *Ibid.,* p. 185, February 3, 1809.
[138] *Ibid.,* 185, February 8, 1809.
[139] *Ibid.,* 185, February 29, 1809.

argued, had demonstrated her independence of our markets, thanks partly to smuggling from Vermont and elsewhere. She had, moreover, gained new fields, like those in Spain and her colonies, the more readily because of our failure to compete. As for ourselves, misery was sufficiently evident in the poor law statistics of Connecticut and in the political somersault throughout New England. Jefferson came in for a bit of fresh invective. "In this way our Chief Magistrate performs his duty. A storm is approaching; the captain calls his choice hands upon deck; leaves the rudder swinging; and sets the crew to scuffle about the alternatives."[140] Republican congressmen fared no better than their leader. Some merit was conceded to the embargo as a precautionary step. But its enforcement had violated the dearest rights of security from search and their guaranty in the Fourth Amendment. Speakers were at some pains to clear New England from the imputation of intended secession. But the impotence of a government which permitted Rhode Island militiamen to defy their own officers and Massachusetts citizens to substitute State for federal law was roundly scored.

The final decision came on February 27, as already noted, and by a vote of eighty-one to forty. This line of cleavage should have separated the friends from the enemies of the embargo, with New Englanders and their commercial allies for ayes and only the staunchest henchmen of the retiring President for nays. But the facts were less simple. Irreconcilables from New England, as well as fire-eaters from other states, had fought the embargo too bitterly to welcome a substitute like non-intercourse, which might prove equally disastrous.

Nevertheless, though some New Englanders refused to recognize their victory, their section had won its case. And

[140] *Annals of Congress,* XIX. 755-763.

this, notwithstanding the sectional cleavage already typical
of American politics, had been accomplished rather by the
general breakdown of embargo support elsewhere than by
any formal alliance with South or West. The centrifugal
influence of economic discontent broke up the political cohesion of Jefferson's machine. To New England the case
seemed simple. Ships idle and crews scattered sufficed for
those who refused to grapple with the merits of a bad peace
or a worse war. But, in addition to the positive damage
of customary profits forfeited, there was the negative distraction of new opportunities unseized. While New England merchantmen were straining at their hawsers, Old England's fleets were courting trade from Spanish colonies just
bursting their European yoke. And, in proportion as glow-
ing prospects in South America reconciled England to actual
losses in North America and strengthened her will to ignore
the embargo, by so much did the vision of an El Dorado
fading into mirage before a fleet which never sailed chafe
the very soul of New England, sick of present losses and
fearful of those to come.

Nor did the grieving merchants draw much consolation
from the field of national honor. Replying to the argument that the embargo spared us from the humiliation of ship
seizures and the consequent alternatives of war or dishonor,
the spokesmen of New England urged that the taint was
incurred by our very refusal to trade, our surrender of the
ocean paths being a cringing submission to the might of
lawless tyrants. Even the merit of saving us from war was
denied, because New England traders, safe in any case from
the casualties of war, were inclined to magnify their own
losses and to minimize the cost of war itself.

In the New England view, then, the administration had
ruined the old commerce, signed away our birthright on the
sea at the moment when the opening of South America

offered a new avenue for expansion, and betrayed the national honor by a surrender of fundamental and inalienable rights in preference to fighting for their support. From holders of these views, the country would seem entitled to a constructive program, fitted to the greatness of the emergency and free from the disadvantages of a condition which no one, either in or out of power, pretended to find comfortable. If New England had actually come forward with such a program, her record for patriotism would be spared a bar sinister. But the politicians preferred to gloat over the trap which the embargo was spreading for their foes. It was easier to criticize than to construct. Let the Republicans find their own way out.

In so far as New England Federalists did suggest alternatives, they were two; a novel form of *laissez faire* and non-intercourse. The former was a naive offer to commit the shipping interests to their own risks. Freedom of trade should be restored, with the definite understanding that losses and seizures should not involve the government as the sworn protector of American life and property. Shipowners were declared to be capable of estimating their own risks, and, on the basis of individual responsibility, it was urged that, if commerce continued to stagnate, its decline could no longer be attributed to the government. On the other hand, if the situation warranted a resumption of traffic, it was a shame to reject the profits. Moreover, if practical seamen lacked the wit to scan the probabilities of international politics, those very clever gentlemen, the agents of marine insurance, were trusted to regulate the outflow of shipping by means of their control of rates. The doctrine fitted well with current economic theory. It adapted the *laissez faire* of the classical school, already begininng to play its great rôle in England, to the extreme individualism of a new continent, where each shifted for himself, and of a section and class whose members attributed most of their misfortunes to the operations of a central government. It utterly ignored, however, the most elementary principle of politics; namely, that it is the first duty of a government to protect its citizens. It is difficult to credit the sincerity of experienced politicians who could advocate a scheme so ruinous to the interests of their section and the honor of the country.

Non-intercourse, though at first sight more plausible, was, when analysed, almost equally specious as a solution for the national embarrassments. It pretended to face facts squarely. These were, that Great Britain and France were the offenders and that it was folly for us to punish ourselves and the rest of the world by way of retaliation. Cut off trade with George III and Napoleon, and we should still have employment for our seamen, profits for our traders, and the credit of upholding our marine. Superficially this plan had merit. It apparently opened the door to profit and honor. But in reality it abandoned the advantages of the embargo and risked the menace of war without affording any real compensation. In the first place, any settlement which left our merchantmen free to trade meant non-intercourse only in name, because, even if the letter of the law were adhered to, France and Great Britain could secure their full American stock through neutral intermediaries. Thus the coercive element of the embargo would be wholly sacrificed. Its protective principle would be jeopardized by allowing our vessels to roam at will, subject to the whim of British and French courts of admiralty, whose decisions had frequently been tested and found biased. This carried with it the added danger of a naval war, for which even New England could not have deemed us prepared, since at no time did her discontent with the embargo urge her to the logic of war as its only real substitute.

Nevertheless, when New England found enough allies among the commercial and agricultural elements of the other states to overthrow the obnoxious embargo, non-intercourse was offered as the most dignified substitute. Jefferson and the embargo followed each other into retirement, each to be succeeded by a compromise; the one by a President who had signified in advance his assent to a settlement agreeable to the commercial interests; the other by a law feeble in its very essence but preserving the outward semblance of a defiance toward the lion of the sea and the tiger of the land.

Toward this emasculation of the embargo the purpose of New England had been steadfastly directed. In the process, the Federalists had recovered three Republican states. They had weakened the allegiance of New England Republicans to the Jeffersonian machine. They had played upon the discontent of commercial classes elsewhere and had capitalized the resentment of agricultural interests at the sight of successive crops piling up with no market in prospect. Even as the embargo hit New England hardest of all the sections, by so much was her reaction to it the most vigorous. To New England, most of all, belongs the credit or the discredit of the repeal of the embargo. The part she played has been justified again and again. But as long as the possibility remains that wise regulations of commerce may avert wars, so long will the action of New England in 1808 and 1809 lie open to the charge of selfish sectionalism and blind heedlessness of larger issues. The embargo was originally conceived as a preventive of war. Its trial, to be adequate, demanded perseverance through a number of years. This was not granted, and upon New England rests the onus of a diplomatic defeat which non-intercourse by no means concealed. The embargo was not allowed to avert war. Non-intercourse was incapable of doing it. Thus, in the irony of events, her sponsorship of non-intercourse was to urge New England, along with the rest of the Union, in the course of a few years, into the War of 1812, when New England was to learn that war suited her even less than embargo and was to forfeit even the political gains she had won by the embargo's defeat.

CHAPTER VII

THE MIDDLE STATES AND THE EMBARGO

Toward the embargo, as toward many other issues, the Middle States assumed a median attitude. The line between approval and opposition was not fast drawn. Lying at the heart of the older Union, the Middle States had sympathies common to both their northern and their southern neigh‑ bors, as well as interests peculiarly their own. Thus their mercantile marine was a link with New England, while their staple crops were a bond with the South. At the same time, manufacturers already possessed a foothold which made the Middle States the natural beneficiary of the stimulus which the embargo itself was to bring.

In respect to a marine and to staple crops, New York was typical of the section. To the extent of her great ship‑ ping interest, her sympathies lay naturally with New Eng‑ land. On her long Canadian boundary, moreover, the natural temptations to smuggling were multiplied by British in‑ ducements to evade the embargo. In addition, she was loath as any southern state to pile up successive crops against a market day which might never come. But these discourage‑ ments were compensated by the advantage, first, of rescuing her shipping, and then, of harvesting such gains as growing manufactures might offer. A strong party machine exercised a steadying influence, and DeWitt Clinton, Republican boss of the State of New York, though not a devotee of the Vir‑ ginia dynasty, was not the man to split his party by an open break with the national leaders.

Economic distress was, however, immediate. Early in January, Moss Kent wrote to his famous brother, Chancellor Kent, from Champion in the western part of the state, that:

this part of the country begin to feel the embarrassing effects of the embargo. It has destroyed the market for their produce, particularly pot and pearl ashes which is their principal dependence. In case of a war with Great Britain I calculate on emigrating towards the Hudson as my services will not, probably, be wanted in this part of the frontier.[1]

But the same general region of western New York sponsored the most contradictory declarations as to the effect of the embargo. A petition from Ontario County, dated October 10, 1808, and signed by 1,365 names, laments that "in no branch of agricultural pursuit do we find our customary profits," and grieves that the bustling industry of a pioneer community was giving place to "a constrained and sullen inactivity," rendered in no way more endurable by numerous evidences of a sudden prosperity across the Canadian line.[2] Yet, in face of this well considered statement of grievances in Ontario, a correspondent of Jefferson could write from the neighboring county of Niagara that:

. . . with respect to the embargo little difference of opinion exists in this quarter. With few exceptions, it is considered, both as to its origin and duration the wisest measure, which the administration under past and present circumstances could have resorted and adhered to.

The more optimistic view prevailed at Albany, for the state senate, on January 31, 1809, passed a resolution condemning the

. . . most unremitted and reprehensible attempts which are making with uncommon industry and malignity and by every art of misrepresentation to enfeeble and destroy the exertions of the general government in vindicating our national rights and honor by endeavoring to alienate the affections of the people by opposing the authority of the laws and by menacing a dismemberment of the Union.[3]

The legislature declared itself "fully satisfied that the conduct of the national government has been calculated to secure

[1] James Kent Papers, Library of Congress, Vol. III. Moss Kent to Chancellor Kent, Champion, New York, January 10, 1808.
[2] Petition of Ontario County, New York, to the United States Congress, October 10, 1808.
[3] Jefferson Papers, Library of Congress, January 26, 1809.

the resources to preserve the peace to maintain the honor and to promote the interests of this country."[4]

Wherever the balance lies between these conflicting opinions, and it must be admitted that the pessimists had probably the weight of argument, there was at least some compensation in an awakening of manufactures. In a season when opponents of Jefferson and his policies could see no ray of cheer, the pew holders of St. George's Chapel, in New York, were sufficiently prosperous to install a five thousand dollar organ built by the Messrs. Geibs, of their own city, who, it may be added, had "just completed a very elegant and splendid organ which is now erected at Salem in Dr. Barnard's house of worship."[5] The clothing industry was encouraged by premiums on the introduction of merino sheep.[6] And the raw products thus favored by legislative bounty needed not to go to Connecticut for manufacture in Colonel Humphreys' mills, as there was at Poughkeepsie a plant, less extensive to be sure than the Colonel's, which manufactured an article of similar quality running in value to eight dollars a yard.[7] Some activity was manifest in the iron mines of northern New York.[8] Similar progress was noted in tin manufactures, one entrepreneur in the latter urging his claim to patronage on the basis that:

as every citizen, who by his genius and industry, aids in perpetuating the independence of his country, has a claim on the community for their patronage, the subscriber presumes that the liberality of his fellow citizens will enable him to persevere in his present undertakings.[9]

While the embargo was modifying the economic life of the people, the politicians were not idle. Jefferson no sooner

[4] Jefferson Papers. State of New York, Senate, January 31, 1808.
[5] The *Repertory* (Boston), June 17, 1808.
[6] *Ontario Repository*, quoted by *Federal Gazette* and Baltimore *Daily Advertiser.*
[7] The *Diary of Daniel Mulford.* Poughkeepsie, September 3, 1808.
[8] The *Repertory* (Boston), September 27, 1808.
[9] The *Public Advertiser*, New York, April 25, 1808.

made known his intention to retire into private life than the question of succession stirred New Yorkers into potential opposition to the Virginia dynasty. Of this movement Governor Clinton was the natural leader,[10] and James Cheetham its chief spokesman. But even Federalists, who would have rejoiced at schism, doubted its likelihood,[11] for only the closest unity among New Yorkers would have withstood the Virginia machine, and unity was conspicuously lacking. As Chancellor Kent reminded his brother in July, 1808: "The news from New York is that the Democrats are all by the ears. Cheetham has been publicly denounced by two ward general meetings and DeWitt Clinton goes down with him."[12] The following philippic against Cheetham bears witness to Republican discord in a manner leaving little to the imagination:

James Cheetham. This is the wretch who has the unblushing impudence to speak of himself as a man of character, of gentlemanly deportment, &c. This same being, who on the files of his own paper, stands recorded as an *unprincipled calumniator,* a *registered liar, libeller* and *assassin* of private character.

From this rather mild beginning, the attack warms to some heat, reminding the reader of "how lost, even to the honors of the *halter* and the *gibbet,* must the man be, who does not stand, in the estimation of the public, in point of character, at least upon a level with James Cheetham."[13]

But if there were quarrels among the Republicans, and if the Clintons showed no reluctance to capitalize for their own benefit the unpopularity of Virginia measures, the party nevertheless retained sufficient cohesion to preserve its local

[10] Wilson Cary Nicholas Papers. Library of Congress. J. Nicholas to W. C. Nicholas. Albany, February, 1808. "I think there is little doubt that the ruling party here [New York] expect something to grow out of inconveniences of the embargo favorable to them". etc.

[11] *The Balance,* Hudson, New York, January 5, 1808.

[12] James Kent Papers, Vol. III. Chancellor Kent to his brother. Albany, July 7, 1808.

[13] The *Public Advertiser,* New York, August 6, 1808.

ascendancy. The governor of the state undertook personally to refute the charge that the embargo represented a submission to French influence.[14] And the Republicans of the county and city of New York adopted strong resolutions approving the embargo and promising aid in its enforcement.[15] The New York Republicans united in an appeal "to the Republicans of the United States" to hold together and declared their unbounded indignation over the tactics of the opposition, serving as they did only to increase the obstinacy of the belligerents and to hinder the success of our own diplomacy.[16]

Such solidarity as the Republicans were able to maintain was in face of much discontent among the people, especially the frontiersmen. There were numerous violations of the embargo and much sympathy for offenders along the Canadian boundary. But discontent was not confined to these informal outlets, however disconcerting. Anti-embargo New Yorkers possessed in Barent Gardenier an intrepid spokesman, a veritable fire-eater. There was in the man a certain nobility of character, well displayed in a duel which his rabid utterances provoked. But in an age when duelling was rampant, this final test of his convictions was less remarkable than his very curious defense of Josiah Quincy for refusing to do what he himself had done. He shamed the southern leaders for baiting Quincy into a duel which Quincy's own moral code and that of Massachusetts forbade. In the courage to defend another for not fighting, Gardenier showed a finer spirit than in his fearlessness on the field of honor. His own qualities, as well as the morbid political

[14] The *Palladium*. Frankfort, Kentucky, April 7, 1808.

[15] *Ibid.*, October 20, 1808. This or a similar demonstration was referred to in Congress as proof of the loyalty of New York. *Annals of Congress*, XVIII. 2078.

[16] *Ibid.*, October 27, 1808. Contrast this, however, with the petition of Third Ward, February 6, 1809, against interfering with transportation of provisions and necessary supplies. *Annals of Congress*, XIX. 1779.

atmosphere of the times, are displayed in a speech which ascribed our entire foreign policy to French influence, an extreme example of the kind of suspicion that poisoned the early political controversies of America. "It does appear to me, sir, that we are led on, step by step, but by an unseen hand. We are urged forward by a sort of spell, to the ruin of our country." When Gardenier named Napoleon's as the unseen hand, a tumult arose, but the speaker was allowed to proceed,[17] though not to escape the consequences of his zeal. He was challenged by George W. Campbell, of Tennessee, severely wounded, and for several weeks was an invalid. But he returned to his seat in Congress with ideas unchanged, their expression, however, a bit less wild. He talked thereafter less of foreign influence and more of domestic injuries, defending in particular the northern New Yorkers for their traffic with Canada.[18]

The chief effect of Gardenier's outburst was to eliminate him from the reckoning. His place was to some extent taken by Josiah Masters, a man of similar views but less impetuous expression, who wished the embargo wholly removed before the adjournment of Congress in April. His remedy for maritime troubles was to arm the merchant vessels and let them give a good account of themselves. A show of force on our part would bring France and Great Britain both to their senses.[19]

This policy was not adopted, and when the New York delegates returned from the summer recess, they renewed their attacks with a hostility which seems excessive, in view of other evidences of sentiment in their state. Gardenier, once more in harness, declared that the embargo and nonimportation acts were tantamount to war.[20] But when it came

[17] *Annals of Congress*, XVII. 1652-1656.
[18] *Ibid.*, XVIII. 1705-1706.
[19] *Ibid.*, XVIII. 2110.
[20] *Ibid.*, XIX. 826.

to a vote on, "*Resolved, That the United States can not, without a sacrifice of their rights, honor, and independence, submit to the late edicts of Great Britain and France,*"[21] he and William Hoge, of Pennsylvania, were the only negatives against one hundred and thirty-six affirmatives. Perhaps the two were more sincere than the one hundred and thirty-six, for many of these warriors of the council chamber were soon voting for a submission which no disguise concealed.

When the administration asked Congress to put teeth in the embargo which would render evasion more difficult and dangerous, Josiah Masters commandeered a vengeance, "which will hurl you down into that detestable and abominable place where the worm never dies and the fire is not quenched."[22] He credited the executive with good intentions at best, but not with wisdom, called the embargo and non-intercourse paper threats, and even insinuated, but with a caution inspired by Gardenier's recent experience, that America was a tool of France.[23] His caution was perhaps needless, for opposition to the embargo in December, 1808, and January, 1809, was less dangerous than once it had been. The heresy of one year had become the orthodoxy of the next, and Gardenier himself was less of an outlaw. His was at best, however, a negative and destructive genius. For constructive statesmanship he seems to have shared the general aversion among Federalists at this period, but he liked to ferret out weak points in the government's position. When sentiment finally veered toward a repeal of the embargo and the substitution for it of non-intercourse with Great Britain and France only, Gardenier ridiculed a policy which rendered shipping precarious and then released the

[21] *Annals of Congress*, XIX. 853.
[22] *Ibid.*, XIX. 938.
[23] *Ibid.*, XIX. 991-993.
[24] *Ibid.*, XIX. 1262-1263. January 31, 1809.

ships.[24]   On this point he carried with him but two delegates from New York.   The remaining thirteen voted with
the majority in Congress for a submission which should
preserve at least the semblance of dignity.

Less important than New York in every way, New Jersey
took a less conspicuous position on the embargo.   But the
two states had one very striking resemblance in the fact that,
while both remained true to their essential Republicanism,
and both upheld the state and national tickets of their party,
each found its most eloquent spokesman in the party of the
opposition.   New Jersey's decision in the presidential election was correctly forecast early in the summer, when a
good Republican of Trenton asserted that:

our political prospect is, in this State as favorable as at any past
period.   The Republicans to a man, and many federalists, approve
the embargo, and the correspondent measures.   On the subject of
the presidential election, there is no division of sentiment in the
Republican party; all are decidedly for Madison.[25]

But a letter in October announcing the victory admits that
the contest was not easy:

I have just time to inform you, for the gratification of the Whigs
of New York, and the dismay of the *Tories,* that REPUBLICAN-
ISM has completely triumphed in New Jersey, and that in both
branches of the legislature, there will be a democratic majority.
The *Tories* made a dreadful struggle, and we had to combat all the
federal lawyers, British pensioners and agents; but thank God, the
Whigs were as ready to oppose them now as in the American
revolution.

Of fifty-three members in the legislature, the Whigs secured
a majority of seven.[26]

Much of the local color in the campaign which led to
this result is imbedded in some rather spirited doggerel,
which originally graced the pages of the *Trenton True
American*:

[25] The *Universal Gazette,* Washington, D. C., July 14, 1808.   Extract
of a letter dated Trenton, New Jersey.
[26] The *Public Advertiser,* New York, October 18, 1808.   To the Editors, Newark, October 18, 1808.

THE EMBARGO

There's knaves and fools, and dupes and tools,
   Debas'd enough to argue,
That every ill the people feel,
   Is owing to The Embargo.

Does some loose tongue, like a clapper hung,
   Delight in constant dinging,
The Embargo well supplies the bell
   Against which to be ringing.

Do party men incline to pen
   A false and foolish farr'go,
No other themes so fruitful seem
   As *"Jefferson's d——d Embargo."*

To pelf and power would villains soar,
   Mid uproar and confusion;
With hearts well pleas'd, the Embargo seiz'd
   To work the dire delusion.

Should Hessian fly our wheat destroy,
   Or granaries crawl with weevil,
The Embargo's curst in language worst,
   As source of all the evil.

Does wind or wave or watery grave
   Consign ship crew and cargo,
'Tis chance but some in visage grum,
   Ascribe it to *the Embargo.*

Does cold or heat, or drought or wet,
   Work hay or harvest's ruin
'Tis made appear as noon-day clear,
   'Tis all *the Embargo's doing.*

Or should our crops exceed our hopes,
   Right round about they dare go,
And in a trice, the lessen'd price
   Is charged upon *the* Embargo.

Should boat or ship lose tide or trip
   By gale, or ice, or freshet,
The Embargo 'tis, puts all amiss,
   And merrily they curse it.

Do vermin bold on trees lay hold,
   And make their limbs quite bare go,
'Tis ten to one the mischief done
   Is saddled on *the* Embargo.

Has drunken swab or idle drab,
　　Become forlorn and needy,
Both he and she will find a plea,
　　"*Embargo*," always ready.

Is buck or blade bankrupt in trade,
　　By sloth or vice or folly.
He's not to blame—the fault and shame
　　Rests on *the Embargo* wholly.

Does some vile knave, his cash to save,
　　Pay all his debts with paper;
"*The Embargo laws*" are made the cause,
　　And loud he'd rant and vapor.

But though such knaves and fools and slaves
　　Paint it a frightful scare-crow,
The good and wise their arts despise,
　　And cling to *the Embargo*.

They know it keeps from pirate's grips,
　　Our vessels, crews and cargoes;
Which were they lost, would much more cost
　　Than half a score Embargoes.

They know that this most punishes
　　The nations that oppress us;
While it involves our injur'd selves
　　In least and few'st distresses.

They know that that would cost us more
　　Monthly than this does yearly;
While every blow some blood must flow
　　From kin or friends lov'd dearly.

Then let who will, to work our ill,
　　Against it lie and argue;
Columbia's sons, in loudest tones
　　Will laud *THE WISE EMBARGO*.

　　　　　　　　　　—"*Jersey Blue*."[27]

The jaded Muse may well have winced at verses such as these. But when sung, as recommended, to "Yankee Doodle," "Moggy Lawder," or the "Vicar of Bray," they

---

[27] The *Independent Chronicle*. Boston, October 27, 1808. Quoting from the *Trenton True American*.

no doubt aided the chorus to fight the good fight and keep the faith. The more solid opinion of New Jersey found its expression in the debates of Congress. In James Sloan, the state was represented by a man of wit; in Henry Southard, by a man of sense. Sloan's first sally upon the embargo question was in reply to Key, of Maryland. Key had been pouring forth at endless length a most lugubrious picture of the sad fate of his constituents. Sloan reduced it to an epigram: "I discovered only this solid argument in all he said: that the constituents of some gentlemen have power to evade the law, while his have not."[28]

Sloan took a higher flight when he attempted an allegory along the lines of Josiah Quincy's famous parable of the young man and the birds of paradise. Sloan's *dramatis personae* were an orchard and some pruners, Congress being the latter; the country, the former:

Suppose I employ a man a number of days to regulate my orchard, do I authorize him to cut it down? Certainly not. There is a power given to commissioners of this city to regulate the markets; have they, therefore, a right to prohibit them? I contend not; they are appointed to keep them in order and improve them.[29]

Similarly, Congress was created to regulate and cherish, not to destroy. Yet the embargo was proving the great destroyer. And, though Sloan voted for it twice, he could not stomach its third and revised version.[30]

Once converted to the opposition, Sloan advanced into the enemy lines and tackled the general himself. Jefferson, in his long career, had written much which he doubtless believed at the time, but which could hardly be expected to fit all occasions. When Sloan dragged forth the *Notes on Virginia,* written in the eighteenth century, to show that

[28] *Annals of Congress,* XVIII. 2126.
[29] *Ibid.,* XIX. 572-573.
[30] *Ibid.,* XIX. 573.

Jefferson ought to be acting on its principles in the nineteenth,[31] his method was clever, but hardly fair.

With much less pretense of rhetoric, but more of optimism and constructive thinking, Southard called attention to the good which the embargo had already accomplished, to the infant industries it had established, now "rapidly progressing to perfection," and to the probability that it would have accomplished its whole purpose in six months if the American people had given it loyal support. But this they had withheld, and, in Southard's judgment, it would not pay to prolong the experiment. He even preferred March to June as the date for its repeal.[32] It was men like Southard, friends of the embargo, not its enemies, who finally sealed its doom.

Among the Middle States, Delaware was the most hostile to the embargo. There was, of course, within the state a Republican faction, and "a very numerous and respectable Meeting of the Democratic-Republican Citizens of New Castle County" drew up, as late as September 3, 1808, resolutions highly laudatory of the embargo.[33] The faithful at Wilmington even went so far, in February, 1809, as to assure Thomas Jefferson that:

had such honorable generous principles [as theirs] universally predominated the shackles imposed upon our commerce would before this, we believe, have been removed, and peace and prosperity would again have resumed their sway over our country.[34]

Testimony such as this is offset, however, by an emphatic denunciation of the embargo, signed by four hundred and fifty-six citizens of Smyrna and its vicinity, prepared after the law had been in effect over a year, as well as by the more significant fact that the entire delegation from

[31] *Annals of Congress*, XIX. 928. December 27, 1808.
[32] *Ibid.*, XIX. 1307-1308.
[33] *Broadsides*. Library of Congress, Vol. 8.
[34] Jefferson Papers. Wilmington, Delaware, February 2, 1809.

Delaware consistently opposed the embargo in Congress.[35] Senator White opposed the passage of the law.[36] His colleague, Bayard, joined him in opposing the various amendments designed to render it effective.[37] And, in the House, Van Dyke, the sole delegate from Delaware, was too hostile to any sort of restriction even to vote for the act which repealed the embargo. Delaware was a commercial center and a stronghold of Federalism. She could not anticipate the boom in manufactures which was to compensate her neighbor, Pennsylvania, for present sufferings, but she did realize that the embargo was a god-send to Federalism, which had been perishing for a real issue with the Republicans. Delaware was the little man with the one idea. Pennsylvania was too rich and varied to be so confined.

Even as the Middle States were the pivot for the entire seaboard, so their own keystone was the State of Pennsylvania. As the Middle States decided, so went the Union. Theirs was the balance of power between North and South. The balance within the balance belonged to Pennsylvania, and at the heart of Pennsylvania lay the decisive influence of Philadelphia. The conflict of sentiment in that city offers, therefore, an important clew to the sources of national action throughout the period of the embargo.

In so far as Philadelphia was rich and commercial, a proper nursery for Federalists, her merchants were necessarily hostile to the embargo. Their petitions against its enforcement proving unavailing, they shared in the general stagnation of trade; and, save as they were individually able to recoup their fortunes by ventures outside their usual field, they and all the seamen whom they employed felt the pinch of the times.

---

[35] Jefferson Papers. Petition from Smyrna, Delaware.
[36] *Annals of Congress,* XVIII. 51. For hostile speeches by him, see also *ibid.,* XIX. 55, 59.
[37] *Ibid.,* XVIII. 63.

It is not surprising, therefore, that Philadelphians were among the first to seek a loophole for evading the new legislation. Undaunted by their former experience with Congress, they now came forward with a second petition, this time for a grant of clearance papers to those vessels already in cargo when the embargo act was published.[38] To grant this would have liberated from three to four hundred vessels in the various ports of the country, in contravention of the entire purpose of the act, and Congress, after but slight debate, tabled this petition also by the decisive vote of ninety-one to sixteen.[39]

These two experiences with Congress practically ended direct action on the part of the merchants. They did, however, make one further protest, this time not against the embargo itself, but against an exception to it, permitted by the President in his executive capacity. A certain Chinese, who claimed to be a great mandarin of Canton, by imposing upon the credulity or the internationalism of the President, had obtained permission to proceed in a vessel to Canton, and there to load a return cargo. This was too much for plain American citizens who had no flowing robes and peacock feathers wherewith to unlock the gates of commerce, and a group of Philadelphia merchants wrote to Albert Gallatin, the secretary of the treasury, their opinion of the transaction. They assured the secretary, in the first place, that men of mandarin rank never emigrated from the Celestial Empire and, in the second, that several of their own number had lived in Canton and personally knew this *soi-disant* mandarin to be a person of no consequence. "To some of us he is known only as a petty shopkeeper in Canton, utterly incapable of giving a credit; and to the remainder he

---

[38] *Annals of Congress*, XVIII. 1272.

[39] *Ibid.*, XVIII. 1275. Of the approximately eight hundred thousand tons of American shipping in 1808, Pennsylvania, *i.e.*, Philadelphia, possessed 86,723. Cf. *Richmond Enquirer*, December 17, 1808.

is altogether unknown; which would not be the case were his character and standing in any degree respectable." They considered him an impostor and a tool in the hands of others and allowed the government to realize that it had been duped.[40]

These formal communications from rich and conservative merchants were not the only anti-embargo protests which emanated from Philadelphia. Thomas Leiper, a friend of Jefferson, described for the latter's benefit the hardships of poor flatboatmen under regulations compelling a bond of $300 a ton for little sloops in the coastwise trade; $9,000, therefore, for a vessel of 30 tons, worth all told no more than $300. In the case in point, the owner had only a half interest, and Leiper exclaims:

Nine Thousand Dollars, is this *reasonable,* is this *just* to require a man his bond to follow his lawful business for Nine Thousand Dollars who is only worth One Hundred and Fifty—But he must give it too for his all is in the Flatt and he most [sic] keep soul of Body together abstracted from his being able to pay for his other half of his Flat.[41]

On no other class in the community did the embargo weigh more heavily than on the officers of merchant ships, men bred to the sea as a profession, who could not lightly turn to the first new work that offered. Their complaint is full of pathos. In terms the most respectful, they urge Jefferson to keep their situation near his heart, "that means may be had to prevent our Families beging there [sic] subsistance." As for themselves, they declare, "We become irksome to our friends; and no means by which we can subsist left us."[42]

The common sailors, too, were wretched enough, and one can not but commiserate them. In one sense, however, their

[40] Jefferson Papers. To Albert Gallatin, August 10, 1808.

[41] *Ibid.* Thomas Leiper to Jefferson. Philadelphia, January 27, 1808.

[42] *Ibid.* Philadelphia petition of August 10, 1808. See also a similar petition of August 8, 1808.

situation was less serious than that of their officers, because
they had less to surrender in leaving the sea and might have
been expected to adjust themselves with less difficulty to the
lot of a laborer on land. Be that as it may, their actual condition was wretched enough.[43]

Ship owners, ship captains, common seamen, and long-
shoremen, like the protégé of Leiper, of necessity bore the
full burden of the embargo. Yet their sufferings may be
admitted without seriously affecting the question of Philadelphia's prosperity in 1808, which would depend upon the
welfare of many classes, not of one. That the city was far
from presenting one unbroken front of misery is plain from
the *United States Gazette* of October 8, 1808, which, though
an opposition paper endeavoring to make out the worst possible case, reluctantly admitted even a certain degree of prosperity. Said the *Gazette*:

> The Embargo has as yet produced *comparatively* little inconven-
> ience in this city and its neighborhood. During the last winter, we
> began to suffer from the domiciliary visits of labourers, *in forma
> pauperis,* who could not find employment and were obliged to beg;
> but, generally, the stores, laid in by poor men before the embargo,
> were sufficient "to keep want from their doors" until the spring
> opened; since when, the unexampled improvements in our city have
> given constant employment to eight or ten thousand of them.[44]

To preserve the proper tone of opposition gloom, the *Gazette*
predicted a hard winter, as soon as frost suspended these
building operations. Meanwhile, the fact would not down
that Philadelphia was in the midst of a wholly unprecedented
boom.

A rather playful explanation of this era of construction, involving the building of possibly one thousand[46] new
houses at Philadelphia alone in the single year of the em-

---

[43] Jefferson Papers. Thomas Truman, of Philadelphia, to Jefferson,
November 14, 1808.
[44] *United States Gazette,* Philadelphia, October 8, 1808.
[46] *Annals of Congress,* XIX. 100-03.

bargo, attributes it to the prosperity of the Philadelphia lawyers. To these virtuous citizens the embargo brought a blessing in disguise. The very act which restrained commerce multiplied marine lawsuits, the effect of which upon the gentry of the bar is humorously described by Horace Binney, one of its own distinguished ornaments:

The stoppings, seizures, takings, sequestrations, condemnations, all of a novel kind unlike anything that had previously occurred in the history of maritime commerce—the consequence of new principles of national law, introduced offensively or defensively by the belligerent powers—gave an unparalleled harvest to the bar of Philadelphia. No persons are bound to speak better of Bonaparte than the bar of this city. He was, it is true, a great buccaneer and the British followed his example with great spirit and fidelity, but what distinguished him and his imitators from the pirates of former days was the felicitous manner in which he first, and they afterwards, resolved every piracy into some principle of the law of nations, newly discovered or made necessary by new events; thus covering or attempting to cover the stolen property by the veil of the law. Had he stolen and called it a theft, not a single lawsuit could have grown out of it. The under-writers must have paid and have been ruined at once and outright. But he stole from neutrals and called it lawful prize; and this led to such a crop of questions as nobody but Bonaparte was capable of sowing the seeds of. For while he did everything that was abominable, he always had a reason for it, and kept the world of the law inquiring how one of.his acts and his reasons for it bore upon the policy of insurance, until some new event occurred to make all that they had previously settled of little or no application. In many instances the insurance companies got off; in others, though they failed, it was after a protracted campaign in which, contrary to campaigns in general, they acquired strength to bear their defeat. In the mean time, both in victory and defeat, and very much the same in both events, the lawyers had their reward.[46]

It is hardly necessary to remark that, although Philadelphia lawyers were reaping a harvest that has made their name a byword for shrewdness and success, this could not represent a net gain to the community. The real expansion of Philadelphia lay in industrial enterprise, and progress in this direction appears to have more than compensated for commercial losses.

[46] Charles Chauncey Binney, *Life of Horace Binney*, pp. 60-61.

In the very nature of things, the embargo proved a stimulus to manufactures, and nowhere was this stimulus more promptly felt than in Philadelphia. Manufactures were of course not unknown before 1808, but in that year they assumed an altogether fresh variety and significance. The *Philadelphia Price Current* devoted to them an article which produced a local sensation, and which the editor at once forwarded to Jefferson "to prove that by the Presidents originating partial deprivations, he had ultimately bestowed on his country immense and imperishable benefits."[47]

The inclosure, which must have given keenest satisfaction to the harassed Jefferson, is here quoted in full notwithstanding its length, as proof conclusive of the manufacturing impetus of the period:

AMERICAN MANUFACTURES

The following new American Manufactures, we quote with pleasure, as an evidence of public spirit, and a sure pressage of future prosperity and independence.

Floor Cloth Carpets of any size with or without border per sq. yard	$2.25	
The same with three colours	2.00	Manufactured
The same with two colours	1.75	by
The same with one colour	1.50	John Dorsey

The patterns are in great variety and the colours bright, hard and durable.

Cotton Bagging, per yd. 50 cts   Apply to Maclure & Robertsons.

Printed Calicoes (war'd fast colours)

pr yd.			20c	Manufactured
	4--4———25 a		27	by
Shawls assorted	9--8 per shawl		21	John Thoburn
	4--4	do.	32	& Co.
	5--6	do. 50 a	58	
Bed spreads	10--4		$1.	

EARTHEN WARE

Yellow—Tea Pots, Coffee Pots and Sugar Boxes per doz.	$3.	Manufactured
Assorted Ware per doz.	$1.25	by
Red—Tea Pots, Coffee Pots and Sugar Boxes per doz.	$2.50	Binney & Ronaldson.

[47] Jefferson Papers. Editor of the *Philadelphia Price Current* to Jefferson, November 7, 1808.

GLASS WARE

Green hlf gall. Bottles per doz	$2.	
Do. quart Do do	1	
Green hf. gall. Jars. do	2	Manufactured
Do. quarts Do do	1.	by
White hlf. gall. Jars do	7.50	T. Harrison
Do. quart Do do	3.75	& Co.
Green Pocket Bottles do	80	
Glass per pound do	50	
Windsor Soap per lb.	35	Manufactured
Fancy do. per dozen	$2 a 3.	by W. Lehman,
Sealing Wax per lb.	50 cts. $3	W. Smith & Son.
White Lead per cwt.	$17 a 18	Manufactured
Red Lead do	15	by Dr. Joseph
Litharge do	15	Strong.
		This extensive
Shot B B B la 12 cwt	$11.	Manufactory
Do. S G G and Buck	13	(Paul Beck's)
Bar Lead	10.50	goes into opera-
		tion this day.
		Manufactured by
Shot B B B 10 per cwt	$12.	Bishop & Sparks.
Do. Goose and Buck	10.50	
Bar Lead		
Floor Cloths per square yard	$1.75	Apply at Domes-
Do. do do	2 a 2.25	tic Manufactory.
Cotton Flannel per yard	47	
Acet. Distillat.....................gall	$ 60	
Acid Muriatic............................lb		
Aq. Fortis dup.............................	45	
Alcohol ....gall	2.	
Aq. Amon c Cale...................lb	20	
————c Tart........................	22	
Calomel Crud.	1.90	
——Ppt	2.10	
Camphor Refin...............................		
Ether Vitriol.....................................	1.75	
Liq. Anod. Min. Hoff..	.75	
Lunar Caustic.....................................oz.	1.50	
Merc. Corros. Sublim...............................	1.50	
Ol. Vitriol	.15	
Sp. Nitri Dulc.....................	34	
—Vitrirol Dulc	75	
—Salis. Volat. Arom	75	
—Nitri Fortis		
—Vinos. Rect. G. P. Proof.....................gall.	1.50	
—Turpentine	40	
Patent Green ....lb	67	

Vermilion ....lb 1.50
Tartar Emetic .... lb 1
Vitriol Roman 25
Varnish Bright ....gall

Manufactories of various other articles are in operation, and several rapidly progressing; we could not, however, for the present number ascertain with precision the just denomination of articles or their quotation, but shall soon increase our paper so as to embody them in the general prices of Domestic Articles, and for that purpose *invite communications*.[48]

It will have been noticed that white lead receives mention in this *Price Current* of November, 1808. Yet, three months later, in February, 1809, William Dalzell of Philadelphia, apparently ignorant of the output of Doctor Strong, sent Jefferson "a sample of I believe the first White Lead ever manufactured in the U. States." He complimented the President on the wisdom of the embargo as the measure which was making possible the industrial growth on every hand, and concluded with a fervent hope that Congress would adopt the one means which could insure permanence to these infant industries, namely a protective tariff.[49]

Curiously enough, neither Dalzell nor the *Price Current* speaks of the heavier manufactures depending upon iron and steel. But an advertisement in Duane's paper, the *Aurora*, supplies the missing evidence:

AMERICAN MANUFACTURES

The acting committee of the society of Iron-mongers, of the city of Philadelphia, give notice, that agreeable to a resolution of the society, they will receive proposals for manufacturing any of the following articles, to wit:

Cast WAGGON BOXES, neatly ground inside.

Cast SAD IRONS, made agreeable to the Dale co. patterns, and neatly ground to the face and edges.

FRYING PANS with long handles.

PLAIN IRONS, Socket and Firmer CHIZELS and GOUGES, Carpenters ADZES, FILES, RASPS, STEELYARDS and HOES.

[48] Hope's *Philadelphia Price Current and Commercial Record* in Jefferson Papers.

[49] Jefferson Papers. Wm. Dalzell to Jefferson, Philadelphia, February 10, 1809.

The proposals must be in writing, stating the probable quantity that can be furnished within a stated period with their price, delivered in this city, and in all cases to be accompanied with samples. Application to be made to either of the subscribers.[50]

The wording of this advertisement is obscure, it must be granted, casting some doubts as to whether the articles were to be manufactured in Philadelphia or elsewhere. It is clear, however, that a society of ironmongers existed, and the presumption is strongly in favor of their being in active business.

From time to time, the *Aurora* contained other advertisements bearing witness to still greater diversity in Philadelphia manufactures. Thus machines for repairing weavers' reeds,[51] felting superior to the imported,[52] satinets, muslinets, cotton stripes, bed tickings,[53] Germantown stockings, socks, and gloves, fleecy hosiery, and cotton and woolen yarns,[54] all contributed to American self-sufficiency, and to the enrichment of their entrepreneurs.

It is thus apparent that Philadelphia prosperity in 1808 was not a mere shifting of wealth from merchants to their lawyers, but a genuine progress, resting on an active and diversified industrial basis. As Charles Jared Ingersoll summarized it:

Who that walks the streets of Philadelphia, and sees, notwithstanding a twelve months stagnation of trade, several hundred substantial and elegant houses building, and the labouring community employed at good wages, who reads at every corner advertisements for workmen for factories of glass, of shot, of arms, of hosiery and coarse cloths, of pottery and many other goods and wares; who finds that within the last year rents have risen one-third, and that houses are hardly to be had at these prices; that land is worth, as Mr. Brougham observes, much more than it is in Middlesex; in a word, who perceives, wherever he goes, the bustle of industry and

[50] *Aurora*, Philadelphia, March 21, 1808.
[51] *Ibid.*, April 14, 1808.
[52] *Ibid.*, June 3, 1808.
[53] *Ibid.*, October 18, 1808.
[54] *Ibid.*, November 2, 1808.

the smile of content; who, under such circumstances, that is not too stupid to perceive, and too prejudiced to believe when he does perceive, can doubt the solid capital of this country?[55]

Nicholas Biddle also, though he has less to say about the embargo and its effects than one would expect from so important a man of affairs, confirms Ingersoll's estimate of Philadelphia prosperity. Writing to a friend in Paris, he says:

> You would scarcely recognize Philadelphia, so much has it grown and improved. Among your former acquaintances, Cadwalader is always here and prospering. His wife has just presented him with a third child. Chauncey is making a fine fortune, and surely no one deserves it more than he. As for politics, our actual position is not the most agreeable. The embargo presses heavily on the people, but it has been put in execution without difficulty, and as the people is very sane, the session of Congress soon to meet will be peaceably awaited. In spite of this the embargo appears to have wrought some change in New England, where the elections have terminated in favor of the Federalists. There is even an appearance . . . that the Government of the United States will pass once more into the control of the Federalist Party, or at least that the embargo will be raised before very long. In all these matters I do not mingle. After my long absence, it is impossible to become a very zealous partisan, and I am occupying myself with my profession.[56]

Interesting testimony this, as to the possibility of living in 1808 without worrying over the embargo, its wisdom, or its consequences, although no Philadelphian could quite ignore the prosperity his own city was harvesting.

If confirmation of these estimates of Ingersoll and Biddle is needed, it is to be found in a communication of William Short, a friend of Jefferson, to the President. Short possessed a handsome fortune and, like Biddle, would have seen little to recommend in the embargo had it proved as ruinous as its enemies alleged. He wrote:

[55] Charles Jared Ingersoll, *A View of the Rights and Wrongs, Power and Policy of the United States of America* (1808), p. 49.
[56] Nicholas Biddle Papers. Library of Congress. I. 1775-1809. Nicholas Biddle to Mr. J. M. de la Grange, September 26, 1808.

And this City [Philadelphia] has really acted as the government could wish on the subject of the embargo—I speak of those who are considered as of opposition politics & who are numerous—They frequently & publicly speak their determination to support it, & if on a jury to punish with rigor the violators of it. I have more than once heard it affirmed & not contradicted, that if the merchants of this City were assembled; confined to Federalists alone, nine out of ten would approve the embargo, & of the Tenth disapproving, most of them would be men without capital.[57]

But the best test of the economic situation, better than the enthusiasm of Ingersoll and Short or the contentment of Biddle, was the state of political parties in 1808. Economics and politics are so interrelated that if commercial stagnation had proved ruinous to any considerable proportion of the citizens, popular discontent would have registered itself in the overthrow of the Republican machine. Nothing of the sort occurred. The state legislature passed a resolution most reassuring to Federal authorities.[58] And, although the campaign for the Governorship in 1808 was warmly fought, the Federalists thinking that they had even made inroads upon the Irish vote,[59] which already by tradition belonged to the Republicans, nevertheless the final victory for Snyder and the party of Jefferson was decisive, the Republican majority being "immense," to use the language of an enthusiastic contemporary.[60] As one of the President's correspondents in Philadelphia stated it:

A stranger from reading our antirepublican newspapers, might have anticipated a different issue, but we are sound to the core. We believe the General Government has, by its measures, consulted our true interests, and we wished in the day of election to express that sentiment in the strongest possible terms.[62]

In Congress, the Pennsylvania delegation was not wholly united. One of its members, William Hoge, was irrecon-

---

[57] Jefferson Papers. William Short to Jefferson, August 27, 1808.

[58] *American State Papers*, Foreign Relations, III. 294, 295.

[59] *United States Gazette*, October 8, 1808.

[60] The *Palladium*, Frankfort, Kentucky, November 3, 1808.

[61] Jefferson Papers. Elijah Griffith to Jefferson. Philadelphia, November 14, 1808.

cilable, being the only one in December, 1808, to vote with Barent Gardenier of New York for a frank submission to the edicts of Great Britain and France.[62]   But his colleague, Smilie, who led the pro-administration forces of the state, made in the early debates a strong speech on behalf of the embargo[63] and consistently maintained his position.[64]   The Pennsylvania record varied only slightly between the eleven to five with two not voting, for the original embargo act of December 18, 1807,[65] and the ten to six with two not voting, for the non-intercourse act, which succeeded it on February 27, 1809.

Whatever the temptation to oppose the embargo, congressmen, at least from Philadelphia, were not allowed to forget the favor it enjoyed among the people back home. As some staunch defenders of the administration expressed it :

We behold in a temporary suspension of our commerce an ephemeral & doubtful evil, producing a great, a growing & a lasting good. We see arising out of this cause the prolific sources of our internal wealth explored & with industry & ability directed thro' channels, which while they benefit the enterprising, enrich our country with solid wealth & make her more independent & happy.[66]

When, in January, 1809, the friends of embargo were called for a last rally in its defence for the passage of amendments which would make its operation iron-clad, Philadelphians, at least the numerous element among them whom a share in the industrial prosperity previously alluded to served to strengthen in their fidelity to party, lent their fullest measure of support.

In Philadelphia, it may be admitted, the ruin of powerful commercial interests brought a real and somewhat wide-

[62] *Annals of Congress*, XIX. 853.
[63] *Ibid.*, XVIII. 1710.
[64] *Ibid.*, XIX. 574.
[65] *Journal of the House of Representatives*, VI. 320-321.
[66] Jefferson Papers. "Delegates of the Democratic Republicans of the City of Philadelphia" to Jefferson, March 1, 1808.

spread distress. But there much more than in many other localities subject to similar commercial losses, men found compensation, and frequently much more than compensation, in the development of large-scale industrialism. On this basis was reared the superstructure of building operations which made Philadelphia the wonder of the times and at least one great commercial center to which Jefferson could point for the vindication of his system. A prosperity in which so many types of citizens participated encouraged political constancy and served to hold in the Republican household of faith a state whose defection would have been peculiarly embarrassing at a time when Federalism was regaining so much lost ground in New England.

Conditions in Maryland bore some striking resemblances to those in Pennsylvania, though in the aggregate they were probably less favorable. As in Pennsylvania, the impetus given to manufactures was marked. At the very outset, a committee headed by William Patterson, of Baltimore, invited all persons who possessed any knowledge of cotton or woolen manufactures to aid in turning this to practical account.[67] A considerable demand arose for shares in a company projected for the purpose.[68] The zeal for manufactures extended to shoes.[69] Wool carding also came into its own,[70] and foundations were laid for extensive enterprise.

How the commercial community of Maryland responded to the embargo is illustrated by two letters of William Patterson, written a little more than six months apart, to Wilson

[67] *Republican Watch Tower.* New York, January 8, 1808. From Baltimore, January 2.
[68] The *Independent Chronicle.* Boston, February 25, 1808.
[69] The *Baltimore Evening Post,* May 7, 1808.
[70] *Federal Gazette* and *Baltimore Daily Advertiser,* August 24, 1808. Inserted August 12, 1808.

Cary Nicholas, a Virginia delegate in Congress. In May he declared that:

> . . . every thinking man in the community be him [sic] Republican or Federalist sees and knows the propriety and necessity of the embargo, yet all will not give it their support and many will try to mislead the ignorant in order to give ground to the Federal party, it is very desirable that it should be continued until the powers at war shall feel the necessity of changing their conduct towards us, but I have my doubts and fears that the people of this country have not sufficient virtue and perseverance to wait this event—all the vessels belonging to my House have completed their voyage and are now in port to the number of twelve in all, most of the vessels in the East India trade have returned so that there is now very little American property at sea.[71]

It thus appears that by May, 1808, Patterson and the great merchants of his class had already experienced whatever benefits the embargo had to offer. What followed was chiefly its burdens. These drew from Patterson in December the complaint that "it is every day becoming more and more unpopular and if continued will bring about a revolution in the government and perhaps a Civil War, at any rate it must throw the government into the hands of the Federalists."[72] For an influential Republican writing to one of his own party in Congress, Patterson makes the rather astonishing admission that "circumstanced as we are it is vain to talk of national honor for that has been sacrificed in too many instances already and it is now too late to regain it. Unanimity and the safety of the country are now the great object to be considered."[73]

Severe as this indictment appears, it is nevertheless the judgment of a friend. The real virus of mercantile opinion found vent in personal flings at Jefferson,[74] while extreme

[71] W. C. Nicholas Papers. Wm. Patterson to W. C. Nicholas, May 11, 1808.

[72] Ibid. Same to same. December 1, 1808.

[73] Ibid.

[74] The North American and Mercantile Daily Advertiser. Baltimore, June 6, 1808. Quoting Jackson's Marine Register for June 3rd in a

Federalists in Baltimore went even so far as to rejoice at threatening secession in New England. The following "communication" to a Baltimore newspaper indicates at least an attempt to feel out the position of Maryland Federalists on such a contingency:

> The political intelligence from the great Atlantic States, if it do not warrant an entire confidence that the golden principles of FEDERALISM have revived in full vigor and health, at least instructs us that the fatal *Embargo law* threatens fearful ruin to the tottering cause of democracy. The good and powerful portion of the people are prepared constitutionally to rise up in their strength against the destructive policy of our rulers. Let *democracy,* and her treacherous hand-maid, *French Influence* stand aghast, brooding over their own iniquities. The guilty may escape retributive vengeance for a while, but Justice will overtake them yet. Though majestic in her mien, and bold in her approach, she will steal anon upon her trembling victim, and point with peculiar emphasis at the faithless friends of their country.[75]

But the most formidable expression of revolt was the declaration of the *Baltimore Federal Republican* concerning "Mr. Giles's Bill," in which the doctrines of the Virginia resolution were invoked to show that by exercising powers never delegated by the states, the federal government had dissolved the civil compact. The Giles Bill was a force bill, according to the *Republican,* and the government would do well to remember that "a law which is to be enforced at the point of the bayonet will bring on a struggle which may terminate in the overthrow of the government. Our rulers are answerable for the issue."[76]

Maryland representatives in Congress were more sensitive to the commercial disadvantages of the embargo than to its manufacturing advantages. This was the more natural

comment upon the failure of a single ship that day to enter or leave New York, Philadelphia, or Baltimore. "We shall be consoled, however, for all this temporal privation, by lectures on the *'Revolt of Nations From the Empire of Morality'* by a PHILOSOPHER who has not violated more than one-half of the Decalogue."

[75] *Ibid.,* May 16, 1808.

[76] The *Connecticut Courant.* January 18, 1809. Quoting from the *Baltimore Federal Republican.*

among men who, living outside of their state, could not witness in person the awakening in cotton, woolen, and other manufactures; while commercially they were well aware that Maryland was in a situation to bear the full brunt of the embargo. For unrestricted commerce her location was advantageous, but when the embargo sealed her front door, she had no back door for escape. Northern New England and New York had a Canadian outlet. Trans-Alleghany and the far South touched the Mississippi and Florida, with their lucrative possibilities for smuggling. It was quite otherwise with Maryland, and her isolation moved her to self-pity.[77] Perhaps, though, a hundred per cent. administration would have left no loop-hole for the one hundred thousand barrels of flour, which John Randolph declared with gusto were smuggled out of Baltimore.[78]

The argument for uniformity would have gained in dignity if clothed in an appeal for uniform self-sacrifice and patriotism. But Key reduced it to an absurdity by basing his opposition to the embargo on the inability of his constituents to evade it.[79] Like Josiah Quincy, Key was an advocate of *laissez-faire*. He would allow the merchants to manage their own business, trusting them to impose a voluntary embargo whenever risks outran profits. If the merchants themselves were not clever enough to determine this, the insurance companies would do it for them. "I would, therefore, confide to them the commerce of our country in the exportation of our produce, unshackled by an embargo law."[80] He anticipated events by a year when, in despair of justice from either France or England, he recommended

[77] *Annals of Congress,* XVIII. 1706. Philip B. Key: "Our laws should be uniform; at present large portions of our country have an outlet for commerce and the embargo law operates as a bounty to that part of the community at the expense of the remainder."

[78] *Ibid.,* XVIII. 2239.

[79] *Ibid.,* XVIII. 2119.

[80] *Ibid.,* XVIII. 2122.

commerce only with the rest of the world.[81]   But, with a
curious inconsistency, though he declared war to be preferable to embargo, he refused his vote to the act enabling
Jefferson during the summer recess of Congress to suspend
the operation of the embargo, subject to certain contingen-
cies.   "I cannot consent," said Key, "that the destinies of my
country, that its laws shall be suspended on the will of any
individual, however preeminent in virtue, dignified in station,
or covered with the mantle of public opinion.   The more his
merit, the greater the danger."[82]

When Congress reconvened, Maryland spoke with more
than one voice.   S. Smith took the cheerful view that Liverpool would soon be clamoring for saner counsels in Britain.
On our side, he declared that border smuggling was less extensive than it was rumored to be.   Altogether, he bade the
Senate be of good heart.[83]   Key, however, continued in the
voice of lamentation.   Picturing the entire Union in a competition of suffering, he demanded the prize for Maryland.
In this he represented commercial sentiment, for in Maryland, unlike Pennsylvania, commerce cast the deciding vote
as against manufactures, which, however promising, were
still immature.   And that vote, whether expressed in the correspondence of William Patterson or the furious diatribes of
the Federalist press, became increasingly hostile to the
embargo.

In reaching this point of view, Maryland was in harmony
with her sisters.   With distinct individual differences as to
the incidence of the embargo, the states of the Middle group
shared in varying degree the stimulus to manufactures and
the demoralization of commerce imposed by the times.
Collectively, the burden of their experience impelled them to
vote out the embargo—and to vote in its emasculated sub-

[81] *Annals of Congress,* XVIII. 2123.
[82] *Ibid.,* XVIII. 2124-2125.
[83] *Ibid.,* XIX. 147, 150, 159.

stitute of non-intercourse with Great Britain and France. In vain did friends of the embargo point to its deadly effect upon Great Britain.[84] In vain were smugglers and traitors held up to the execration of their fellow citizens.[85]   Public opinion, which had sustained the embargo in its initial stages and upheld it with tolerable firmness through nine months of increasing pressure, even to the enforcing act of January, 1809, finally succumbed.   As the embargo grew more intolerable and its success appeared less certain, the pendulum swung from rigid government control to extreme individual freedom, and the readiest means was sought for restoring our commerce without too blatant a confession of defeat.

This drift in opinion the Middle States shared with their neighbors, and in the vote of February 27, 1809, which finally overthrew the embargo and replaced it by a non-intercourse act, the Middle States cast the following ballot: New York, 13 to 3 and 1 not voting; New Jersey, 5 to 0; Delaware, 0 to 1; Pennsylvania, 10 to 6 with 2 not voting; Maryland, 7 to 1.   Ohio cast her single vote in the negative.[86]

The Middle States thus spoke decisively.   Theirs was the balance of power.   Without their suffrance, the embargo could not endure.   One may regret, but not condemn their decision. The embargo was a sublime experiment carried out under impossible conditions.   A stronger nationalism was needed if the country was to give the unanimous support essential to success.   In Congress itself a different type of statesmanship was required from that which passed current in 1809.   The practical politician governed then as now and made sad work of it.   Yet, in so far as the nation did uphold it, the embargo pointed toward a brighter world where wars should be no more.   Viewed as a commercial device for rescuing shipping and humbling a foe, the embargo was sordid

[84] The *Palladium*. Frankfort, Kentucky, October 27, 1808.
[85] *Ibid.*, August 18, 1808. Quoting the *National Intelligencer*.
[86] *Annals of Congress*, XIX. 1541.

enough. Viewed as a substitute for war, it assumes the
dignity of one of the most enlightened plans and consistent
efforts ever directed toward world peace. But amid the
losses and discomforts of the time it was not easy to see or
to keep the vision, and if the Middle States, like their sisters,
failed at last to do so, they deserve more credit for what they
did than censure for what they failed to do.

CHAPTER VIII

THE SOUTH AND THE EMBARGO

There remains to consider in this survey of America under the embargo that section which possibly suffered the most, but which certainly complained the least. It was at the hands of her own favorite son that the South received the well nigh fatal thrust. Yet so confiding was she in his wisdom and goodness that the truth was slow in dawning that the section and its hero were both sinking in a common ruin. The wound was, in fact, so deep that hemorrhage was internal, and a contemporary observer would have beheld more immediate destitution among the fishermen of New England than among the tobacco planters of the Eastern Shore. But for New England the future held in store a new prosperity, whereas for the Old South such benefits were long deferred.

Generally speaking, the agricultural South suffered less immediate, but greater permanent loss from the commercial restrictions of 1808 than did a region so wholly given over to commerce as was New England. In comparison with the Middle States, moreover, her opportunities to recuperate by manufactures were slight, although this was not at first realized. The South, then, suffered absolutely as much as her neighbors, and relatively more.

That the South paid no mere lip service to the politico-economic program of her hero, Jefferson, is apparent from many sources. Heavy losses were the measure of devotion. They were felt at once. Before the embargo had been in effect two weeks, a Virginian from Charlottesville wrote to a correspondent in Richmond that:

This Embargo will ruin this state if it continues long. they talk of Locking up the Courts of Justice. to save the Country from distruction (*sic*), in 12 hours after the news of the Embargo, flour fell from 5½$ to 2½. at this place, and Tobacco from 5/2 to 3$ and everything in proportion, & god only knows the result.[1]

Imports fell similarly, a writer of the same week noting that, at Norfolk, "Liverpool salt which sold at a Dollar some days since may now be bot. at 85 cents.—Turks Island has also declined."[2]   The downward price trend was general, and the *Charleston Courier* derived a truly Federalist satisfaction from the situation:

What the effects of this act will be abroad we are to learn hereafter, but those which it is producing at home we begin to feel, and pretty sharply· Rice, which some weeks since sold briskly at 5 dolls. 50 cents is now nominally worth but 1 dollar 75 cents; Black seed Cotton has fallen from 34 cents to 22 a 25 and no sale, and Corn is down to 56 cents.

The North Carolina price current says Flour is down to 2 dolls. 25 cents the barrel, and Tobacco to 2 dolls. 56 cents the cwt. In Maryland it has occasioned a resolution being offered for closing the courts of that State. Such is the beginning of the Embargo measure, but what will be the end?[3]

North Carolina, even more dependent upon exports than her neighbors north and south, felt the pinch acutely. A table of prices at which her leading products sold in May sufficiently explains her predicament:

Blessed effects of the Embargo. The sacrifices which are now making of property upon executions are dreadful. The following rate given me during my attendance upon Bladen Court, by gentlemen of undoubted veracity, who were eye-witnesses, will convey some idea of it.

White oak h hd. staves-per M. 3 dollars 33 cents. Uniform price before the Embargo 25 to 30 dollars.

Rice per bushel, 19 cents—before the embargo, 1 dollar.

A moderately good horse, 3 dollars 50 cents.

[1] The William Taylor Papers, Library of Congress. John Kelly to Wm. Taylor, Charlottesville, January 6, 1808.

[2] W. C. Nicholas Papers, Library of Congress. Moses Myers to W. C. Nicholas, Norfolk, January 3, 1808.

[3] The *Connecticut Courant*, February 17, 1808, quoting from the *Charleston Courier*.

Tar per barrel 45 cents—before the embargo, from 1 dollar 75 cts to 2 dolls.

50 acres of land lying on the north east side of the North West river, and bounded by the river, 18 dollars.

Shingles per M 30 cents—before the embargo 2 dollars·

A cow and yearling 11 shillings.

8 head of hogs, 1 dollar 7 cents.[4]

Economic prostration of the sort just indicated underlay a petition from Lincoln County, North Carolina, in December, 1808, praying Congress to repeal the embargo, "or if that should be found to be unsafe or impolitick that you should modify said laws in such a manner as to permit the vessels of all nations without partiality freely to trade and Carry off our produce where they please at their own risque. . . ."[5]

Distress was so general in Virginia that a moratorium on debts was decided upon. Even before a law was enacted, however, creditors were forced to adopt a policy closely bordering upon it. Thus a citizen of Albemarle County wrote in January, 1808:

The times are such that I cannot think of obliging any person to sell produce at this time, to pay me money— However I think I have a right to Interest on the money that I ought now to receive.[6]

Before three months were past action had been taken for

at the last session of the Virginia assembly they revived the old Replevin law in consequence of the Embargo: and if you press a law process the Debtor can replevy on you for 12 months unless you will take property at three-fourths of its value, which would be a bad Business, when we want money.[7]

More radical than moratorium or replevin was the suspension of all legal process in civil suits:

[4] The *Connecticut Courant*, May 11, 1808, quoting from the *North Carolina Minerva*.

[5] *Petition of sundry inhabitants of Lincoln County in the State of North Carolina*, 20th December, 1808.

[6] W. C. Nicholas Papers. R. Lindsay to W. C. Nicholas, Albemarle County, January 21, 1808.

[7] Wm. Taylor Papers. John Kelly to Wm. Taylor, Charlottesville, Virginia, April 15, 1808.

The accounts from the General Government is alarming—as also this State Legislature [Virginia]. I am told they are about to stop all proceedings on Judgments, and the County Courts Since the Embargo, have taken the liberty to make Laws, and not execute those regularly made—for in nearly all counties, a set of the magistrates meet and adjourn the Court Immy. and will not suffer any Business to be done—this is alarming to Creditors and will in all probability from the delay of Justice lessen the Value of there Claims, in some instances—for the Law of this State between Debtors and Creditors is much in favr. of the former, and this delay of Justice gives them time to inger [sic] the latter or Lessen the Value of his Claim by some fraudulent act, which is frequently practiced.[8]

It is apparent to anyone who compares southern conditions such as these with the similar unprosperous conditions in New England that the South bore a burden of loss which would have justified her in recriminations against the government as bitter as any which emanated from New England. Yet, in their attitude toward the Administration, the two sections were poles apart.   On the hypothesis of purely economic motivation, their attitude should have been almost identical.   But in New England a large share of the political intelligence lay with the men of the opposition.   The "best minds" of the South, on the other hand, were by tradition or by association at the service of the Virginia dynasty and its great chief, Jefferson; and their loyalty was proof against the buffets of a world out of joint.

The loyalty of the South as a whole to Jefferson, and to a measure which spelled ruin to its warmest supporters, is really touching, though of course it need not be supposed that either loyalty or losses were uniform throughout so vast a region.   In large sections of the South, in fact, hope and confidence were sustained in the face of evident loss and distress by a belief that rising manufactures would offset declining agriculture and commerce. For the South

[8] Wm. Taylor Papers. Wm. Murray to Wm. Taylor, Fauquier Court House, January 2, 1809.   See also W. C. Nicholas Papers, Joseph C. Cabell to W. C. Nicholas, Richmond, January 31, 1809.

was not beyond the reach of influences which marked the year 1808 as a distinct turning point in the economic history of the United States. In the South, there was less hostility to manufactures than in New England, but, on the other hand, less progress than in either New England or the Middle States. The South did not at once recognize its limitations as a manufacturing section, but entered upon an industrial program with hopes not easily abandoned. Just as New England was not fully converted to a high tariff and the protection of industry at the expense of commerce until the tariff of 1824, so the South was almost equally belated in recognizing that opposition to a tariff must be her steadfast policy in view of the hopelessness of obtaining for herself the peculiar benefits which tariffs were seen to confer upon manufactures.

These early hopes were finally discovered to be vain, but in spite of the fact that nearly a century was to elapse before the South became in any true sense a manufacturing country, it is of interest to examine the basis upon which false hopes were so much earlier reared. For many Southerners believed firmly in 1808 that new sources of prosperity would compensate for those which were forfeited by the embargo. And every indication of manufacturing enterprise was heralded by the press as a happy augury for the South. The *Richmond Enquirer* lost no time in urging that:

Above all things, household manufactures are the most profitable and useful objects for this country. It was computed in the year 1790 that they were worth at least twenty millions of dollars. If so, they are now worth thirty-five millions, for our population was then four, and is now seven millions of persons. Our women should all learn to spin, card, weave, dye, and manufacture, in the various modes for flax, hemp, cotton and wool. We may not have open markets abroad for years, and our planters will want the aid of our manufactures to keep up the price of their produce, and to furnish supplies.[9]

[9] The *Richmond Enquirer*, February 26, 1808.

High hopes were entertained of a company to be established at Petersburg, Virginia, with a capital of fifty thousand dollars. A modern trust could scarcely aspire to a more varied production than was contemplated by this pioneer venture in the

Carding and Spinning of Cotton and Wool; Fulling, Weaving of Cotton Shirtings, Cambricks, Dimities, Ginghams, Nankeens, Kerseymeres, Velvets, Velveteens, Patent Cords, Duroys, Grandurells, Ticking, Hosieries and all other articles of cotton and wool.—And also manufacture of Iron Ware, such as Nails, Hoes, Spades, Scythes, &c. &c. or such of the said enumerated articles as the society shall from time to time find to be the most productive, and as the calls for consumption may demand.[10]

The suggestion of the *Enquirer*, or more probably the example of Petersburg, brought it about that Richmond, conservative and commercial, soon caught the contagion, for

By the last advice from Richmond, the inhabitants are about to hold a meeting for the laudable purpose of promoting the establishment of manufactories, in imitation of Philadelphia, Baltimore, Pittsburg, Petersburg, and other towns in the United States, where the influence of England is rendered harmless by the superior virtue of the citizens.[11]

Constructive effort of the sort involved in these new ventures was the best possible safeguard against melancholy over commercial or agricultural losses. And the *National Intelligencer*, an organ of the administration, congratulated the country on the progress being made. After alluding to the considerable activity in New England and the Middle States, it pays its respect to the infant industries of Virginia:

In Petersburg Twenty-five thousand dollars have been subscribed in a day.

In Richmond, under the most intelligent and patriotic auspices, a capital of half a million is to be engaged in this object.

In short the patriotic flame appears to be fed throughout the whole union by an inexhaustible fuel.

[10] The *Universal Gazette*, Washington, D. C., May 5, 1808.
[11] The *Public Advertiser*, New York, June 3, 1808.

Already it is computed that at least five millions of dollars have been devoted to manufactures in the past six months; a capital competent to the furnishing manufactured articles to the amount of at least ten millions.

Britain, seeing what is already done, will anticipate what will happen if she persist in her injustice; she will see that, five years hence, we shall not need a tenth part of the manufactured goods we now receive from her.[12]

But, for Richmond at least, fact fell short of fancy. The corporation so hopefully launched went no further than the promotion stage, and became an object of derision to unsympathetic Federalists. Thus the *Richmond Virginian*:

Manufacturing! It will be remembered by the people that a committee recommended the subscribing of 300,000 dollars to carry this project into effect.

From this it was natural to expect that they who could foresee so many advantages would certainly have opened their purse most liberally.

They met—they conferred—they subscribed! But how much? Altogether, not as much as one of these distinguished patriots receives yearly for mismanaging affairs at the armory: and what is more, he is a Bell-Wether among them.

This scheme might do to gull the credulous people, but it is not good enough for the knowing ones of Richmond.[13]

More or less incidental testimonials bear witness to a systematic encouragement of manufactures outside of Virginia. Thus an advertisement in the *Charleston Courier* indicates something more than a universal approbation of child labor. It may, in fact, suggest something beyond merely domestic manufactures:

WOOL is wanted for the manufactory at the Orphan-House, which will be purchased in any quantities, by the Steward of that Institution—*Orphan House, Charleston, 5th March 1808.*[14]

[12] The *National Intelligencer*, Washington, D. C., June 27, 1808. "Of a total capital of $500,000, $200,000 are to be reserved for the state. We are glad to find men of all parties warmly interested in the plan."

[13] The *Richmond Virginian*, quoted in the *American Citizen*, New York, August 17, 1808.

[14] The *Charleston Courier*, March 10, 1808.

Also, a Homespun Company in Charleston attained at least the stock selling stage, proving interest if not progress:

. . . Many persons having already subscribed lists for the promotion of a Homespun Company, they may conceive such subscription as entitling them to shares in the above company.—To avoid misunderstanding on this head, they are informed that no person can be considered as a stockholder in the said company, unless they subscribe with the commissioners, and pay down two dollars on each share they subscribe for.[15]

Further information concerning this Homespun corporation reveals that:

The establishment of the South Carolina Homespun Society, has been agreed upon at Charleston, S. C., its capital to consist of 150,-000 dollars, divided into 15,000 shares at 10 dollars each, 1,000 of which is to be reserved for the legislature. A committee has been appointed to receive subscriptions of stock, and an address delivered to the citizens of that state, signed by the venerable and patriotic historian Ramsay. The object of the institution is "domestic manufactures"—*American*.[16]

While South Carolina was promoting her woolens and homespuns, North Carolina also could boast a new industry, inaugurated under high hopes:

We have pleasure in stating that Mr. Gules of Raleigh (North Carolina) has established a paper mill on an extensive scale. It is, we believe, the first which has been erected in that state, and to which we wish the fullest success.[17]

With the Atlantic states concerning themselves chiefly with textiles, notwithstanding the varied program of the Petersburg promoters and the enterprise at Raleigh just cited, the inland state of Kentucky also achieved considerable progress industrially. Here the manufacture of gunpowder held prominent place. A Kentucky correspondent of David Porter wrote in May of 1808:

Gun Powder is already manufactured by small manufacturers in several places of Kentucky which are furnishing a part of the sup-

[15] *Ibid.*, August 10, 1808.
[16] The *Universal Gazette*, Washington, D. C., September 8, 1808.
[17] The *Washington Expositor*, October 8, 1808.

plies necessary to the War Department but for want of Salt Petre and of Capital the manufacturers are working only on a small scale. Nevertheless as—great deal of Salt Petre can be had from the Missouri I have no doubt—great deal more than at present shall be manufactured as soon as Manufacturers shall meet a convenient encouragement.

The Manufacturing of Canvass has been tried at Lexington this 4 or 5 years ago but did not succeed. I did never inquire on the causes of that ill success but I am daring to attribute it to several causes: want of a good and well-understood plan previous to the execution; want of Economy in the execution want of sufficient capital and want of proper hands but I have no doubt that should an industrious Man be sure of a generous price from the Government for every good piece he could make that sort of Manufactory would be soon up, and would give rise to many others. Our hemp is as good as any other in the world and good Spinners and Weavers could be procured now great deal more easy than 4 or 5 years ago.[18]

Promising or unpromising as southern manufactures appeared to contemporaries—and it depended on the optimism or conservatism with which men viewed the commercial situation and the possibilities for its relief—the net gain to manufactures in the accepted sense of the word was slight, although this was not fully apparent until after 1816, as we know from southern sentiment toward a protective tariff. But, in one respect at least, southern industry was enormously stimulated by the stern necessities of the times. The slaves, not to mention their masters, must be clothed, and household manufactures in spinning and weaving, crude but sufficient, arose to the emergency. Thus Ellis and Allan, leading merchants of Richmond, wrote to one of their business correspondents in November, 1808, that " . . . the Sales of Goods is very much curtailed this fall, people are Struggling to manufacture at home, and it is astonishing what quantities have been fabricated. . . ."[19]

The *Enquirer* elaborated the same thought:

[18] David Porter Letter Book, 1807-1808, September 7-June 15. MS. in the Library of Congress, J. A. Tarascon to David Porter, May 11, 1808.

[19] Ellis and Allan Papers, Library of Congress. Ellis & Allan to J. Heathcote & Company, November 5, 1808.

We have been favored by a gentleman of Amelia with a variety of beautiful specimens of Virginia Manufacture.—Every day's experience convinces us, that the looms of our households are adequate to the supply of many cheaper and excellent substitutes for the Manufactures of Europe.

Among these specimens, is a piece of Carpeting, of cotton warp and yarn filling, whose figure, texture and dyes, are worthy of imitation—one of cotton bed-ticking, much cheaper than those for sale in our stores—some specimens of negro cloathing [sic] for the winter, one of which is cotton warp, filled in with doubled and twisted threads of wool, much warmer and cheaper than the negro cottons of our stores—and some beautiful specimens of dimitty.

To bring these and other articles to great maturity, it is only necessary to turn the *Public Spirit* of Virginia a little more in this direction. We have a plenty of labor and a superabundance of some of the raw materials. The present political state of this country is eminently propitious to these manufacturing improvements.[20]

Though household manufactures do not fully qualify a section to rank as manufacturing in the accepted sense; even more, possibly, than the factory system, they enlisted the workers in a constructive movement for economic independence. The spinners and weavers of the plantation houses might feel a livelier sense of contest with a power whose imports were forsworn than would the mill worker or the capitalist under a more impersonal regime. And it is within the bounds of probability that the intensive development of household industry, marking the period of the embargo, contributed in no small degree to the firmness and stability which characterized southern sentiment throughout the crisis.

For the South, then, the chief result of the manufacturing impetus of 1808 was not the speculative and only partial development of capitalistic production, but rather the large extension of a system of household manufactures, familiar since colonial times. Nevertheless, even the hope of success had important consequences. Politically, the South was encouraged in her immediate loyalty to the embargo and in a harmony of interest with the manufacturing sections of the country which aided the growth of American nationalism

---

[20] The *Richmond Enquirer*, December 27, 1808.

and which did not break down until that harmony was demonstrated to be illusory.

Economically, the failure of her hopes to materialize was a disaster to the South. It meant that many of her older sections were condemned to poverty, until the extreme demand for slaves in the Lower South offered the sickening profits of the inland slave trade. It thrust upon the South an economic isolation which placed her at the mercy of tariff walls erected for the benefit of her neighbors and fostered a feeling that she and her peculiar institution were a land apart. Had it not been for an extraordinary expansion in cotton, destined soon to carry southern energy and industry into the inland empire, the entire South would have found herself hopelessly crippled, as indeed the older tidewater sections of Virginia actually were, by the embargo and the subsequent commercial decline in the years between 1808 and the War of 1812.

The preceding synopsis of economic conditions would prove misleading if the South of 1808 were regarded as entirely homogeneous. For such, in fact, was not the case. Individual interest and preference divided men upon the embargo, much as they had once been divided concerning the Revolution, and were yet to be over Civil War. There were, it is true, few broad factors of division. Commerce was limited to a few ports like Charleston and Savannah, and manufactures, other than household, as we have seen, scarcely existed. But agriculture was a unifier, and, industrially, a region of staples such as cotton, tobacco, and rice, which relied for labor upon so distinctive an institution as slavery, possessed an outward appearance of unity, an appearance which was to a considerable extent reality, in as much as economic interests and political view-points are first cousins. But historically the South had never consented to unity. Tidewater itself had seen many a battle between the ins and the outs. And the up-country could always be relied upon to fight the shore, whether in Pennsylvania or the Carolinas.

Class distinction divided where economic solidarity should have unified. In Richmond and Charleston the old aristocracy was impotently intrenched behind the barricades of Federalism. Everywhere the real political game was fought for control of the Republican party. Here Jefferson and his henchmen had ruled almost without dispute since the great election of 1800, which brought the party into power. A flag of rebellion had, it is true, been raised over the Mississippi question and the Yazoo claims.[21] And the "Quids," as the disaffected Republicans were called, were to seize upon the approaching retirement of Jefferson as occasion for setting up Monroe as a "pretender" in opposition to Madison, the candidate of "legitimacy."[22] But in 1807 Jefferson was unquestionably the master of his party. The embargo which he sponsored went through as a party measure. Its support became an act of faith for all good Republicans, though of course not all southerners could be reckoned among the faithful.

Taking into account the differences between hill country and tidewater, between commercial aristocrat and planter liberal, and keeping in view the battle for party control among Republicans themselves, one appreciates a complexity in the southern attitude which would be incomprehensible if the South were dismissed as simply an agricultural section, with little to lose from commerce destroyed, and able, while letting her crops pile up in their barns, to await with perfect composure such a change in British and French policies as would comport with American dignity.

[21] See A. J. Beveridge, *Life of John Marshall*, II, and Wm. P. Trent, *Southern Statesmen of the Old Regime*, p. 131.

[22] C. H. Ambler, *Sectionalism in Virginia*, 1776-1861, p. 90; also Wm. E. Dodd, *John Taylor*, in the John P. Branch Historical Papers of Randolph Macon College, II. 230.

On the contrary, the South was a battle-ground of contending forces, grouped about patriotism and personal loyalty on the one side and economic self-interest on the other. Here, as elsewhere, individual self-interest was mostly hostile to the embargo, inasmuch as no element in the community, with the possible exception of the lawyers, who were reaping a growing harvest of cases, and the very few manufacturers whose industries it fostered, could be said to derive any profit from the measure. Such gains as the embargo insured were national and political, and even these were hotly denied both in and out of Congress.[23]

Up to this point, I have sketched the economic background of southern attitude with but an occasional glance at the political. Let us now examine the political activity of the South in 1808, with only occasional references to its economic background. But first a word as to the general effect of their losses and misfortunes upon the spirit of the southern people. For political action depends not upon losses and misfortunes as such, but rather upon their effect on the morale of the people. From what has been said, it should be evident that the South had nothing to gain from the embargo. Yet such is human nature that the states, more particularly those at the South, long vied with one another in their courage under losses.[24] The embargo, which was originally advanced as a peaceful substitute for war, stimulated some, at all events, of the virtues most conspicuous on the battlefield. South Carolina, especially, boasted of her willingness to endure all things even unto the end. Planters made the best of straightened circumstances. No other state turned more energetically to household manufactures. Wool

[23] Mrs. St. Julian Ravenel, *Life and Times of William Lowndes*, p. 77.

[24] Jefferson Papers. Governor Pinckney of South Carolina to T. Jefferson, January 2, 1809. ". . . By the average of the sales last year the planters of this State lost one with another fifty per centum and yet you hear of no grumbling among us, but a few very few indeed, violent federalists."

was conserved as never before, and interest awakened in a native sheep supply. Cotton and tobacco vied in protestations of loyalty to a scheme of things as ruinous to the one as to the other, and, as the second crop followed the first into the barns of the planters rather than the warehouses of factors, the merit in patience and long suffering merely grew the greater.[25]

For the unscrupulous, there was some relief, to be sure, in an illicit trade, made doubly profitable by the absence of competition. Considerable quantities of cotton and tobacco did reach England, notwithstanding a general loyalty to the embargo. Thus, between the fervor of self-sacrifice among patriots and the profits of smuggling among traitors, the tidewater section, with the exception of a small party which was frankly commercial and Federalist, supported the embargo.

In the up country and beyond the mountains, different conditions obtained. The "Quids," for example, drew much of their support from the Blue Ridge, among the smaller farmers deprived of their customary market. In Kentucky, also, the embargo encountered some opposition, one of the leaders of which was Matthew Lyon, who, though personally indebted to Jefferson for the greatest favors, had become a Mississippi River magnate since his removal from Vermont and a member of a class that found little to praise in a law which kept shipping at anchor. But just as the "best people" in Virginia upheld the embargo from a distinct *esprit de corps,* so their kindred in the Blue Grass gave the embargo just the support which it had a right to expect from gentlemen, and Kentucky papers like the Frankfort *Palladium* featured as choice tidbits rich morsels of London gossip over British discomfiture at the embargo.[26]

[25] Mrs. St. Julian Ravenel, *op. cit.,* pp. 75-77.
[26] *Palladium,* July 14, 1808.

In some of its larger outlines, southern attitude toward the embargo has now been sketched. But the arena on which these various viewpoints found their liveliest expression was the floor of Congress, and no study of southern sentiment toward the embargo is complete without reference to Congressional debates and votes. The only Southerner among the little group of six "wilful men" in the Senate who dissented to the original passage of the embargo, was Crawford of Georgia.[27] But in the House, southern opposition was more vigorous. In a vote of eighty-two to forty-four, the South furnished its full proportion of negatives.[28] The "Quids" in Virginia mustered four opposing votes, including that of John Randolph. From Kentucky, Matthew Lyon was one of two nonjurors. But the chief stronghold of southern dissent lay in the less developed areas of Georgia and North Carolina. From South Carolina no opposition vote was actually cast, although one absent member afterwards went on record as at first opposed.[29] Her merchants, however, were among the first to petition Congress for relief from the law's effect, on the plea that certain slave ships, which took out clearing papers just after the embargo was passed, should not be detained in port. Their petition, very properly, was ignored. And, human nature being what it is, southern interest never greatly contributed to the success of New England's petitions for special concessions to her fisheries. It lent an equally deaf ear to Philadelphia petitions identical with that of the Charleston merchants.[30]

When loopholes in the embargo became evident, Congress concerned itself with amendments to render it effective. Original opponents now found their opportunity to line up

[27] *Annals of Congress*, XVIII. 51.
[28] *Ibid.*, XVIII. 1222.
[29] *Ibid.*, XVIII. 1651.
[30] *Ibid.*, XVIII. 1243, 1246, 1272, 1274, 1385.

with the party. One of these latter, though announcing officially his conversion, still did what he could to relieve cotton planters from the burden of bonding coastwise cargoes, seemingly unconscious that leniency of this sort would encourage extensive cotton shipments to England at the very time when stricter enforcement was the prime embargo need.[31]   The danger was recognized by Troup, of Georgia, who, for his own state, apprehended disgrace if ships were allowed to sail without bond; for, in that event, "Savannah would be made the depot of the Eastern and Middle States, and thence produce would be conveyed in boats to St. Augustine."[32]   In that way Georgia would be as much the rendezvous for smugglers to Florida as Vermont and New York were for those to Canada.

[31] *Annals of Congress*, XVIII. 1651-52.

[32] *Ibid.*, XVIII. 1652. See also The Madison Papers, Library of Congress. Anonymous to the Governor of East Florida, copy forwarded to the Secretary of State.

To his Excellency the Governor of E. Florida. May it please your Excellency.

The existing embargo in the United States, which has been laid on for great political purposes, of which your excellency has doubtless been apprised, has been evaded in many instances in St. Mary's river.

The method usually pursued to effect this, is to conduct the vessel, employed in this treacherous commerce, into the river in ballast; load her on the Spanish side of the river out of the jurisdiction of the United States; then, under the pretext of clearing out for the Havannah they sail with the cargo for a British port.

The British possessions being supplied from the United States by this legerdemain, the effects of the embargo, which it was hoped might contribute to bring that nation to reason are so far frustrated.

From the recent detection of this procedure it may be presumed that our government is not yet acquainted with it. Your excellency will therefore excuse an individual for recommending the circumstance to your wisdom and patriotism.

Your humble servant

Savannah 10 April, 1808.

To James Madison Esq.

Sir, The person who drafted the original of the within, which is gone on to St. Augustine, thought it might not be amiss to apprise you of the step which he has taken for the public good—his name is unimportant."

[James Madison, Miscellaneous, 1762-1837.]

Much bitterness was injected into the debate by the accusation of Barent Gardenier of New York that the embargo and its enabling acts were dictated by Napoleon. At this the South felt especially affronted. One of her delegates, G. W. Campbell, of Tennessee, paid his respects to Gardenier "as the mere conduit used by those behind the screen to convey these groundless slanders to the public—the common trumpeter, who gives no importance to what he makes public, except what is derived merely from the place he occupies, or the duties assigned him to perform."[33]   One is not surprised that a duel followed. Campbell was an easy victor, returning at once to his seat in the House. Gardenier stayed at home for weeks, nursing serious wounds.

On the whole, the ill temper of Gardenier proved a boomerang to his cause. The reaction was more than the enraged challenge of Campbell. It was rather the conversion of cooler heads, such as Alexander of North Carolina and Bibb of Georgia. Nor was the Gardenier position strengthened by the somewhat incoherent support of Matthew Lyon. On the whole, throughout the first two months of its existence, the embargo was gaining adherents, especially in the South. In a vote of ninety-seven to twenty-two for the March amendment strengthening the embargo, only two southern states contributed to the negative: North Carolina and Kentucky, with two votes each.[34]   Thus, when the long session ended, the South had swung into almost complete unity on the chief measure before the country.

Some southern support could, nevertheless, be enlisted on behalf of a motion now made for an immediate repeal of the embargo, a motion which failed by twenty-four to eighty-four.[35]   But debate focused chiefly upon what policy Congress should authorize the President to pursue during its own

[33] *Annals of Congress*, XVIII. 1672.
[34] *Ibid.*, XVIII. 1712.
[35] *Ibid.*, XVIII. 1853.

recess. The fiery Campbell offered a resolution granting complete freedom of action to the executive in the event that European developments permitted a removal of the embargo.[36] The debate which followed showed that southern Congressmen possessed a considerable knowledge of British conditions, including a fair estimate of John Randolph as a factor in moulding British opinion as to conditions in America. Randolph's proposal of war as a release from embargo was ridiculed, and his opposition to the President's freedom of action during the recess was ascribed quite justly to a petty jealousy, which would load Jefferson with blame for the embarrassments of the embargo and deny him the credit for its relaxation.[37]

There was danger that such a resolution as Campbell's would simply advertise our desire to end the embargo. And, in view of British losses and injuries from the embargo and the new prosperity in American manufactures, this was no time for weakening. Campbell himself saw the force of this consideration and endeavored to combat it by reminding Congress that under no circumstances should the embargo be removed while its provocation remained.[38]

The motion to bestow upon the executive broad powers of initiative during the Congressional recess converted the embargo into a rival of the Louisiana Purchase for the distinction of extending government operations into regions not prescribed by the Constitution. But neither party made strict or loose construction much of an issue in this instance, since each had its own reasons for discarding the embargo. The Republicans were uncomfortably aware of what a party liability the embargo was proving. The Federalists were too eager to escape its rigors to waste much scrutiny upon the means of release. Thus, once again, as in 1803, the South

[36] *Annals of Congress,* XVIII. 2091, also XIX. 588-589.
[37] *Ibid.,* XVIII. 2108, 2132.
[38] *Ibid.,* XVIII. 2139.

was a party to proceedings running counter to its own strict construction theories.

Opinions varied, however, in detail. As usual, there were those who would straddle the issue. Rowan, of Kentucky, for example, warned sententiously against the danger of erecting despotisms by progressive concessions of power, but favored the particular concession in question.[39] Randolph found the debate simply an opportunity for a general tirade against the embargo and all its consequences, present and future. Williams, of South Carolina, on the other hand, urged even more stringent application of the embargo through more severe regulations for revenue inspection. When the vote was finally taken empowering Jefferson to suspend the embargo at discretion if conditions in Europe warranted, the South contributed only five of the twenty-six votes in opposition. To all intents and purposes, Jefferson, in the spring of 1808, was master of a "Solid South."

In the interval of seven months before Congress reassembled the members had abundant opportunity to test the sentiment of their constituencies. And, notwithstanding the increasing irksomeness of the embargo and the failure of negotiations looking toward its abandonment, the speeches of southern Congressmen during November and December confirm the patience with which their section supported the embargo. They recognized that it had not produced all the good effects anticipated, but clung to the hope that perseverance would win. They described their own sufferings as endured for the sake of a New England commerce which could never be of any real concern to themselves. As Pope, of Kentucky, expressed it:

The people I represent are an agricultural people, and I ask the gentlemen of what importance it is to them whether their produce is carried in foreign or American vessels? For what are the agricultural people now suffering, but to maintain our maritime rights:

[39] *Annals of Congress*, XVIII. 2233, 2234.

Sir, we are willing to discard all calculations of profit or loss, and make a common cause with our brethren of other States in defense of our national rights and independence.[40]

A still clearer expression of sectional consciousness, prophetic too of the future, was Crawford's contention that the states which called themselves commercial were in reality manufacturing and would find in the embargo merely a new source of prosperity. For the South, on the other hand, which could not share in the new field of manufactures, the embargo, if long continued, would spell nothing but ruin. "It is impossible for us to find a market for our produce but by foreign commerce; and whenever a change of the kind alluded to is made, that change will operate to the injury of the Southern States more than to the injury of the commercial States so called."[41]

A less extended view of the case enlarged upon the security to property for which the embargo deserved credit, and declared that the only losers by it were merchants who traded on the capital of others and whom it was not a bad idea after all to deprive of a chance to make something out of nothing.[42] The farmer, it was admitted, might seem to be a loser, but former high prices had caused him to overwork his land, to which present stagnation would afford a much needed rest.

While southern politicians were thus attesting their loyalty to the embargo, the iron of discontent was sinking deeper and deeper into the soul of New England. Her leaders proposed the most desperate expedients by way of a substitute, urging the country to renounce the embargo and to determine our commercial and foreign policy solely in accordance with the rates of marine insurance. If risks were too

[40] *Annals of Congress,* XIX. 49-50, 206, 659.
[41] *Ibid.,* XIX. 66. See also Hugh A. Garland, *Life of John Randolph,* p. 268.
[42] *Ibid.,* XIX. 94. Also Edmund Quincy, *op. cit.,* p. 143.

great, insurance would be prohibitive, and an embargo would result automatically. With declining risks, insurance rates would drop and commerce be resumed without awaiting the action of the government. Here was *laissez faire* run riot, and Giles, of Virginia, the administration floor leader in the Senate, punctured it with the query: "Sir, if we repeal the embargo laws without any substitute, and agree to trade under the British Orders in Council, what would be the premium of insurance on our national character and national independence?—Sir, cent per cent. would not insure them."[43]

Not all southerners were so Spartan as their leaders. Stories were rife concerning shipments of flour and tobacco from Virginia to St. Kitts. Innuendoes were even circulated to the effect that Jefferson himself profited by a sudden rise in tobacco prices at the height of the embargo, a charge much easier to make than to refute. Cotton had fallen from an average of twenty cents down to eleven and rice in equal proportion. With two crops now in the barn, even the most resolute would pause before planting a third. But, notwithstanding some discontent and backsliding, it was asserted in Congress that the planters are "unanimously unwilling to place their bales of cotton in one scale and national honor in the other. They are unwilling to put interest, sordid interest in competition with the national independence, which would be sacrificed by payment of the tribute."[44]

To uphold the spirit of the South, reports were circulated of misery in Great Britain far outmatching our own. Indeed, all the comfort to be derived from this supposed weakening of Great Britain was needed in order to reassure the faithful, for, with the new year, the embargo entered upon its last phase, scoring its final victory in January, 1809, when the House by a vote of seventy-one to

[43] *Annals of Congress*, XIX. 226, also p. 791.
[44] *Ibid.*, XIX. 286, 602-604, 598, 658.

thirty-two put through the final enforcement bill.   Once again the South stood by its colors, contributing to the opposition only a sprinkling and scattered vote, and that mostly of the chronic sort, as their earlier ballots had demonstrated.[45]

This was the final effort on behalf of the embargo. Men began to fear that secession, long smouldering in New England, might actually come about.   Within another month, debate was centering no longer upon a strengthening of the law, but upon the proper date for its repeal.   As a symptom of the sudden change of heart, the position of D. R. Williams, of South Carolina, is illuminating.   He had all along manifested toward the embargo a sort of rugged honesty.   He now gave it as his opinion that smuggling, defiance of law, and sectionalism had brought about a condition which admitted of but these alternatives: either a drastic enforcement of the embargo at the cost of civil war, or else its abandonment—"choosing not to enforce the law with the bayonet, I thought it proper to acknowledge to the House that I was ready to abandon the embargo.—I will repeat it—and I could weep over it more than over a lost child."[46]

With a tacit acknowledgment that the embargo was doomed, debate turned gradually to available substitutes. John Randolph, for his part, wanted none.   "Shall a man refuse to be cured of a cancer unless you will provide him with a *substitute?*"[47] Sentiment in New England leaned toward non-intercourse. And more than one southerner declaimed against New England's conversion to the passive obedience of non-intercourse, after thundering for a year past against the embargo as a surrender of our national rights.

[45] *Annals of Congress*, XIX. 1024.
[46] *Ibid.*, XIX. 1236-1238; also *Branch Papers*, II. 297-298.
[47] *Ibid.*, XIX. 1338.

But if embargo was objectionable to many and non-intercourse to some, the real alternative of war was far from popular. Matthew Lyon, for one, was a consistent opponent of the measure. Yet he was staunch against war as a substitute, quoting Falstaff on "What is honor? A word. What is that word? Honor. What is that honor? Air. What hath it? He that died on Wednesday."[48]

The actual facts of near secession in New England and the still unachieved submission of Old England rendered some change of policy essential. The logic of the case called for war, and, if the embargo must be abandoned, war was the preference of the administration. But the country, which would have welcomed war eighteen months earlier when the *Chesapeake* was attacked, had so long been taught to regard the embargo as a substitute for war that its martial spirit had waned. Besides, war against both France and Great Britain was as impracticable now as when the embargo was first adopted.

Aside from war and non-intercourse, there was one alternative; namely, to abolish all restrictions and go on as if British Orders, French Decrees, and American Embargo had never been issued. Outside of a few New Englanders, John Randolph was almost the sole advocate of this policy. His argument was as picturesque as his personality:

We have trusted our most precious interests in this leaky vessel [the embargo] ; and now, by way of amendment, we are going to bore additional holes in this machine, which like a cask, derives all of its value, if it have any, from being water-tight. From some notion of honor or dignity, quite incomprehensible to me, we are to stick to this thing; it is to be hung around our necks, or to be trailed after us like a canister tied to the tail of a miserable persecuted dog.[49]

Randolph could still amuse, but he could no longer influence. The non-intercourse bill defied the shafts of his ridicule

[48] *Annals of Congress,* XIX. 1412.

[49] *Ibid.,* XIX. 1465-1466. See also Edmund Quincy, *op. cit.,* p. 143; also *Branch Papers.* III. p. 55.

and passed the House on February 27, 1809, by a vote of eighty-one to forty, in which the South abandoned the comparative unanimity which had governed her counsels upon the embargo, and split her vote. Some doubtless voted for the new measure because they really desired it; others, as the only obtainable substitute for the embargo, short of complete surrender. On the other hand, some among the nay's may have been proclaiming their loyalty to a lost cause. Others felt non-intercourse itself too severe. Considerations of this sort may serve in part to account for the vote which sealed the final verdict of the South and of the nation upon the embargo.

Nevertheless, when the South embarked with her sister states upon non-intercourse, she was destined to vindicate the foresight of one of her own representatives, G. W. Campbell, who declared that non-intercourse would work only to her disadvantage. The embargo bore with approximate equality upon all the states, said Campbell. Non-intercourse would penalize the southern and western states in favor of the eastern, which would enjoy almost the whole commerce of the country without competition and could develop their manufactures at the expense of the agricultural interest:

Foreign goods being excluded, the manufacturing States would furnish the rest of the Union with their manufactured goods at their own prices. Hence the nonintercourse would operate partially against the Southern and Western, and completely in favor of the Eastern States, and hence the most cogent reasons I have yet discovered why the Eastern gentlemen are almost to a man in favor of it.[50]

Thus a survey of the South in 1808 confirms the impression, which time was only to strengthen, that economic sectionalism, though not universally realized at this period, was already a determining factor in the industrial life of America. The embargo and its emasculated substitute deserve at-

[50] *Annals of Congress,* XIX. 1483-1484.

tention as measures of great influence in intensifying those differences, which from their very nature could only go on increasing. The failure of the embargo to develop a real system of capitalistic manufactures at the South placed her at an economic disadvantage as against first the Middle States and later New England. For the growth of manufactures in the northern states enlisted their interest in a succession of tariffs, which the South came more and more bitterly to oppose. This very opposition increased her isolation and weakened her sense of nationalism, with consequences which were indeed far-reaching. So that it is not too much to say that the developments of 1808 constituted one of the links in the chain finally leading to Civil War.

CHAPTER IX

BRITISH POLITICS AND THE AMERICAN EMBARGO

The personal experiences of Jefferson with the embargo, together with the effect of its enforcement upon the various sections of the United States, have already suggested the influence of the measure upon the powers against which it was aimed. But the extent of this influence and the degree to which it approximated or failed to approximate the hopes of Jefferson, its author, warrant a closer analysis of the effects of the embargo in both England and France. This holds true more especially for England, since England's own blockade of France accomplished more than our embargo alone could have effected. An examination of the results of the embargo upon political thinking and economic activity in England is, therefore, essential to a proper estimate of Jefferson and his policy, whereas the corresponding influence upon France is of rather less significance and may be dismissed with a briefer treatment.

The American policy of Great Britain in 1808 was part of a general system of foreign relations whose philosophy dates from the mercantilism of the early empire and whose manifestations were interwoven with the great war against Napoleon. As yet American independence was recognized only upon land. At sea the overbearing exercise of the right of search, even to the halting of a warship near a home port, and the impressment of sailors, represented an abuse of power not consistent with independence. In fact, limitations upon the freedom of the seas exposed America to the same disadvantages as those under which the colonies had labored when navigation acts could interdict the most profitable routes of trade.[1]

For this shortsighted and ungenerous policy, resentment toward the war for independence was, in part, responsible. Jealousy fanned the flame when America proved herself best qualified of all the neutrals to reap the golden harvest awaiting those who feed while others fight.[2] But the keynote of the times was self-preservation. The great war of 1793 to 1815 was a death grapple of giants, in which measures were passed from immediate necessity and with little reference to the law of nations, to the rights of neutrals, or even to ultimate self-interest.

By 1805, Great Britain was utilizing her sea power to cut off importations from enemy colonies, and American vessels plying between West Indian or other colonies and ports under Napoleon's control were confiscated. A temporary relief came in 1806 with the death of Britain's great war minister, William Pitt. The reins of power descended upon Charles James Fox, a known friend of America, and the brief period of his administration, from January to September, 1806, witnessed a relaxation favorable to neutrals. The coast of Europe from the mouth of the Seine to Ostend remained, nevertheless, under a general blockade, and traders from enemy ports were excluded from Brest clear to the Elbe River.

Meanwhile, on the Continent, the power of Napoleon was reaching its zenith. The battle of Jena had made him master of Prussia. Overtures from Alexander indicated

---

[1] This only semi-independent position of the United States was recognized by British merchants. Cf. a letter from Wm. Murdock, London, July 24, 1808, quoted by the *National Intelligencer* and the Frankfort, Kentucky, *Palladium*, November 3, 1808.

[2] The *Edinburgh Review*, XII. 243, April, 1808. "Neither the government nor the populace of this country have forgiven America for having made herself independent; and the lowest calumnies and grossest absurdities are daily employed by a court faction to keep alive the most vulgar prejudices."

peace in the East, and the tyrant of the land, now free of opposition, confronted the mistress of the seas. Accordingly, in November, 1806, Napoleon issued the Berlin Decree. Intended as retaliation, it quite outstripped the British blockade in its defiance of neutral rights. The blockade by Great Britain was at least partially effective. The actual presence of large British naval forces was the justification for what the law of nations has always recognized, the right of a belligerent actually to exclude the ships of neutrals from ports under blockade. Not so with Napoleon's paper decree. A sweep of the imperial pen was far from being a genuine blockade of the British Isles, capable of rendering all American or other neutral traders with Great Britain legally subject to capture. Warships could alone give legal sanction to so sweeping a measure, and warships Napoleon did not have. His Berlin Decree might have been mere sound and fury, had not Britain herself lent it real effect by her own measures of reprisal.

These were the celebrated Orders in Council of January 7 and November 11, 1807.[3] They were the device of the Duke of Portland's ministry, which succeeded to the helm after a lenient Catholic policy and an injudicious management of the treasury had overthrown the short-lived government of Lord Grenville and his "ministry of all the talents." Under the new administration, the foreign portfolio fell to George Canning, the disciple of Pitt, and the

[3] Hist. MSS Comm., *Fortescue MSS*, p. 143, November 7, 1807. "In mine of yesterday, I omitted to mention that a long proclamation is preparing and will be immediately issued, to put all the coasts and colonies of nations at war with us under a general blockade. This is to be grounded on Buonaparte's proclamation, on the effect which he is giving to it, and on the acquiescence of other countries in that mode of hostilities. It is evident—that it removes the principal motive which the Americans might have had for remaining at peace with us; and it is equally evident that it increases at the moment, the difficulties and distresses of our manufactures". etc.

policy sponsored by him was one of vigor.[4] That this increased as months rolled by appears in the character of the two proclamations. That of January merely forbade neutrals to trade between the ports of France and her allies or dependencies. That of November, in admitted violation of international law,[5] created a paper blockade of all ports under French control. In excuse, it was urged that France had already set the example. But the rigors of this November Order were to be remitted to all neutral vessels which stopped first at English ports and paid a British import duty. Armed with a certificate of this virtuous act, the neutral might proceed whithersoever he would, even into the harbors of France. It only remained for Napoleon to declare that ships submitting to the Orders were lawful prey, and neutral commerce in Europe would cease. This he did by the Milan Decree of December, 1807. It was under these circumstances that the United States enacted the embargo law.[6] In the very complicated situation thus presented, it is of interest to trace the various currents of opinion which contended for mastery in British politics.

Inasmuch as the policy which sponsored the Orders found the support necessary to continue them, it may be assumed that the majority of the nation was committed to their inter-

[4] The opposition lost no opportunity to ridicule this vaunted vigor. Cf. Hist. MSS Comm., *Fortescue MSS*, p. 158. Auckland to Grenville, December 9, 1807. "I am sure that much of the mischief might have been avoided by a system of more sense and less vigour. I really see no reasonable chance of emerging with honor or even with safety from the situation in which we are placed." See also *ibid.*, pp. 143, 155.

[5] For British definition of rights of blockade under international law, cf. *Edinburgh Review*, XII. 229-230, April, 1808. "That a general blockade of ports not actually watched or invested is contrary to the law of nations and totally ineffectual as against neutrals is settled by the uniform decisions of our own courts, even in the present war." The writer then refers to Charles Robinson, *Admiralty Reports*, I. 154. The reference is careless. I. 92-94 is more in point.

[6] Hist. MSS Comm., *Fortescue MSS*, p. 158, December 9, 1807. Auckland to Grenville. "In the present temper of the United States it seems probable that they will enter into the struggle of self privation and will suspend the commerce which we profess to interrupt."

est. Such a view would ignore, however, the opposition, which in Parliament was vigorous, notwithstanding the fact that the proletariat,[7] the class on whom the Orders and Embargo chiefly bore, was not as yet represented at Westminster. Division of opinion, therefore, was presumably more even than parliamentary majorities would indicate. Let us consider first opinion favorable to the government.

As the first aggressive successor to the war ministry of William Pitt, the government was certain of the royal support, on nothing more cheerfully bestowed than upon anti-American measures. And Parliament opened in 1808 particularly warm in its expression of attachment to the sovereign. The moderation of his Majesty's conduct in apologizing for the *Chesapeake* Affair was lauded;[8] the wisdom of his refusal to permit "the question which has arisen out of this Act to be connected with any Pretensions inconsistent with the Maritime Rights of *Great Britain*," was extolled, and his unceasing efforts "to preserve the Relations of Peace and Friendship between the Two Countries" were proclaimed.[9]

Having testified to its loyalty, Parliament proceeded to more serious business. In the debates which followed concerning the merits and wisdom of the Orders in Council, the government insisted upon their retaliatory nature, emphasized French culpability for any infraction of international law, and represented the Orders as the knell of French commerce. Through Lord Hawkesbury, the ministry alleged that the American embargo was decreed prior to any possible knowledge of the Orders in Council,[10] a

[7] Henry Adams, *History of the United States,* IV. 330. "Probably at least five thousand families of working men were reduced to pauperism by the embargo and the decrees of Napoleon, but these sufferers, who possessed not a vote among them and had been in no way party to the acts of either government, were the only real friends whom Jefferson could hope to find among the people of England."

[8] *Journals of the House of Lords,* XLVI. 409, b, January 21, 1808.

[9] *Ibid.*

[10] Hansard, *Parliamentary Debates,* 1st Ser., X. 1241, March 22, 1808.

prime point, to grant which would be to deprive the critics of
their sharpest arrow, since no evils arising from the embargo
could be logically imputed to a measure which it antedated.[11]

This argument, though rung in all its changes by the
speakers for the government, counts for little when the
facts which surrounded the action of the American Congress between December eighteenth and twenty-second are
correctly viewed.[12]   But the ministry had more than a
purely technical basis for action.   Napoleon must be fought
with his own weapons, and, if America suffered, why should
she not?   In its whole attitude, then and afterwards, the
government was typically and stubbornly British.   Disaster
beat vainly against it.   Even the debacle of Sir John Moore
at Corunna served only to temper the national steel.   The
Marquis of Buckingham, a member of the opposition, wrote:

I have no idea that it will produce on the King's mind any one impression save that of increased obstinacy which he will call firmness,
and to his ministers, it will only suggest the increased necessity of
standing by each other.   And this course will succeed to them as
long as the present Parliament lasts, who will most certainly support the King's footman if he should be put at the head of the
Government.[13]

[11] Canning pressed this same point with energy throughout the controversy.   Cf. his letter to Pinkney of November 22, 1808, in *American
State Papers*, Foreign Relations, III. 239.
[12] See Henry Adams (Ed.), *Documents Relating to New England
Federalism*, p. 188.   "The first decision of a French tribunal condemning
an American vessel and cargo under the Berlin decree, and an unofficial
account of the British Order in Council of 11th November, 1807, were
received by Mr. Jefferson on the 17th December, 1807."
See also *The Writings of John Quincy Adams*, III. 186, January 10,
1808; also III. 197; and III. 282-3.   John Quincy Adams III. 186, to
Governor Thomas Sullivan, January 10, 1808.   "There was all, but official intelligence that the British king had issued a retaliatory proclamation to counteract that of France and of equal extent," III. 197.   "It is
indeed true that these orders were not officially communicated with the
President's message recommending the embargo.   They had not been
officially rceived.   But they were announced in several paragraphs from
London and Liverpool papers of the 10th, 11th and 12th of November,
which appeared in the *National Intelligencer* of 18th December."   Also
the *Edinburgh Review*, XIV. 447-448.
Grenville took the same view as John Quincy Adams.   Cf. Hansard,
Parliamentary Debates, 1st Ser., X. 1280, March 29th, 1808.
[13] Hist. MSS Comm., *Fortescue MSS*, p. 273, January 25-31, 1809.

The ministry really was, however, on strong ground. Confident of the temper of the country, and certain of its majority, it was wedded to a policy which it believed to be dictated by necessity, and which it saw no occasion to abandon. The embargo might be working hardship upon the country and creating corresponding ammunition for the opposition. But what the opposition magnified at home, the ministry exploited abroad. It could match poverty and discontent in the cotton districts with similar poverty and more highly organized discontent in New England. Far from repenting, therefore, Mr. Canning indulged in one of his most tantalizing satires, when, in September, 1808, after nine months of the embargo, he assured Mr. Pinkney, the American minister at London, that:

His Majesty would not hesitate to contribute in any manner in his power, to restore to the commerce of the United States, its wanted [*sic*] activity: and if it were possible, to make any sacrifice for the repeal of the embargo, without appearing to deprecate it as a measure of hostility, he would gladly have facilitated its removal as a measure of inconvenient restriction upon the American people.[14]

[14] *American State Papers*, Foreign Relations, III. 231-232, September 23, 1808. For a sober and commonsense verdict on Canning's facetiousness, see Hist. MSS Comm., *Fortescue MSS*, p. 277. Buckingham to Grenville, February 12, 1809. "I enclose to you my proxy on your American question, hoping sincerely that you will grapple to the fullest extent with Mr. Canning's epigrammatic letter to Mr. Pinkney which states distinctly the present course of proceeding towards America, as *necessary* for the purpose of showing that England can do without that branch of commerce! an assertion very questionable in point of fact, and highly indecorous even if true. Her embargo has proved a very important and ruinous measure, and I verily believe her nonintercourse bill will be equally insufficient as a measure of offence to us, or of security to her; but this does not change the question as to the folly of our Orders in Council, or as to the insanity of Canning's refusal to negotiate, which ultimately must bring us to a state of actual war, in which our commercial interests all over the world have everything to lose, and in which we can gain nothing."
  See also *Memoirs of the Court and Cabinets of George III*, IV. 293. Mr. T. Grenville to the Marquis of Buckingham, December 31, 1808. Canning in his reply to Pinkney "rests his objection entirely upon the ground that if we adopt this proposal of conciliation, Bonaparte will say we did it because we could not abide the pressure of the embargo; so that the American and English merchants are gravely told that their ware-houses are shut and their commerce is suspended, not from any

Canning's flippancy, when related to the general situation, is intelligible enough. To him the Orders were but an incident in the war against Napoleon; their American reaction, only a by-product. And a letter written by one of his political enemies, in its subordination of the American situation to other considerations, really sustains the foreign minister. *"Les grands poissons mangent les petits.* The Spanish anxieties have swallowed up all attention to the mad mismanagement respecting Sweden and America; and under this impression, I do not plague you with some long letters from America and from Ireland, which have been transmitted to me from Liverpool respecting the sufferings of the linen, cotton and other trades."[15]   It thus appears that whatever their economic significance, from a political point of view these local discouragements were decidedly secondary.

Irrespective of logic, the Orders existed by the determined will of a powerful government. Yet with a vigorous and intelligent opposition making these same Orders the theme of its constant attack, more than a simple *fiat lex* was needful. The government was obliged to defend its course. The ablest defence of the Orders in Council was put forth in March, 1809, by James Stephen, just after the embargo had been voted out of court. Inasmuch as Orders and Embargo had both been operative for more than a year, the speaker possessed some perspective as to conditions at the time of their imposition as well as information as to their progress and results. Stephen's speech is entitled to consideration as an honest exposition of the point of view held by the British Ministry.

object of interest or hostility between America and England, but for fear that Bonaparte should interpret our reciprocal conciliation into a confession of our being unable to stand against the American embargo. Is not this below par for a sixth form boy?"

[15] Hist. MSS Comm., *Fortescue MSS*, p. 270. Auckland to Grenville January 1, 1809.

BRITISH POLITICS AND EMBARGO   261

Though ready to "do much, very much, to avoid a quarrel with America," Stephen held that it would have been
foolish to "avoid it at the expense of ruin to our manufactures, to our commerce, and our maritime power."[16]
He argued that it was idle to display any sentimental leniency for a power which was so slow to resent the aggressions of France, so swift to retaliate against the measures
of Britain.[17] And the contention that, although the Berlin
Decree preceded the Orders of November in point of time,
its enforcement was delayed until both were practically
synchronous,[18] he refuted by citing the case of the *Horizon.*
This American vessel, seized in a French port in September,
1807, was only one of many proofs that the Berlin Decree
was in actual operation against America, notwithstanding
the evasions of the French Minister of Marine[19] and the
hypocrisies of Talleyrand[20] in affirming that America was
excepted from its incidence. He contended that for at least
two months before the Orders were promulgated the Berlin
Decree was an active menace to the commerce of America as
well as that of Britain, and that it was idle to pretend that
such a condition was unknown in Downing Street when
the Orders were finally determined upon. "It is not, therefore, on the case of the Horizon, or any other particular
captures, that our justification rests. We stand on a much
broader ground, in respect of the actual injury sustained,
if actual precedent injury was necessary to justify our retaliatory Orders."[21]

Moreover, in Stephen's opinion, the retaliation was not
in itself vindictive. "We did not punish neutrals, as has
been alleged, for the Enemy's injustice; we only prevented

[16] *The Speech of James Stephen,* March 6th, 1809, p. 47.
[17] *Ibid.,* p. 78.
[18] Hansard, *Parliamentary Debates,* 1st Ser., X. 1280, March 29, 1808.
[19] *The Speech of James Stephen,* March 6, 1809, p. 62.
[20] *Ibid.,* p. 64.
[21] *Ibid.,* p. 57.

them from trading freely with a power which, in violation
of the rights of their neutrality, prohibited them from trading with us."[22]

In the judgment of its friends, the policy was thus, from
its very inception, amply justified. As time wore on, it
became imperative. Indeed, by an odd turn of reasoning,
Stephen showed that the Orders were a necessary comple-
ment to the embargo itself, equivalent to an overseas enforcement of American law upon vessels which had eluded American port authorities :

> The American government, in resorting to a general Embargo, took
> a measure which was certainly to a great degree efficient. It is
> executed in the ports of America by the municipal authorities on
> shore. But when an Embargo as to France, or as to any particular
> country is spoken of, it is evident that though the term is retained,
> the practical nature of the measure is entirely changed. It becomes
> a law, not against sailing from the ports of America, but against
> proceeding to certain parts of Europe. The violations of it are
> acts not done at home, but abroad : acts not passing under the eye of
> the American port officers, and not capable of being prevented by
> their authority, or by the aid of the civil magistrate.[23]

It may be noted that this sophistry proved equally serviceable
to Napoleon when he undertook to seize the American vessels in his ports.

Having established to his own satisfaction the wisdom
and necessity of the original Orders in Council, Stephen
proceeded to justify their continuance in force after America
had offered to bargain for their removal. He contended that
the overtures of Jefferson looking to a cessation of the embargo in return for a repeal of the Orders were a scheme
to get something for nothing. Remove the embargo, and
non-importation would still remain. Great Britain would
recover those

imports from the United States, which the American people are distressed by withholding, and the want of which is now ascertained

---

[22] *The Speech of James Stephen,* March 6, 1809, p. 59.
[23] *Ibid.,* p. 82.

to be harmless to us and our colonies; but the greater part of our export trade to America would still have remained prohibited. This was too plainly Mr. Jefferson's design, for no offer is made to repeal the Non-importation Act, nor is any power to remove that offensive obstacle to harmony between the two countries, to be found in Mr. Pinckney's instructions.[24]

This being the case, the offer of the Americans to withdraw their embargo only too well merited the satire which Mr. Canning bestowed upon it. Far from sacrificing international good will to the temptation of an epigram, Mr. Canning was playing into the hands of the New England opposition,[25] by giving them a new weapon to use against their misguided government.[26]

The situation demanded strong remedies. The embargo was no light matter. In the opinion of many Britons and of not a few Americans, it amounted to an alliance between Jefferson and Napoleon. In Stephen's synopsis:

If then the neutral rights of America are invaded, as with all due deference for General Armstrong's authority, I maintain they clearly are, by the seizure of her ships in the ports of France, for having merely called at, or being destined to, a port in the British dominions, the effects of the wrong, and of the submission to it by the American Government, are, to us at least, of no trivial kind. They give effect to a plan concerted for our destruction, and which otherwise could not possibly succeed.[27]

Or, to put the matter in even less unmistakable language:

In a word, Sir, the public law maintained by the President of America is this: The sea is the only place of possible offence to

[24] *The Speech of James Stephen*, March 6, 1809, p. 89.

[25] *Ibid.*, p. 78.

[26] William Pinkney, *The Life of William Pinkney*, p. 192. "There is an opinion here, that we are likely to become a divided people, when a rupture with Great Britain is in question; but this opinion is founded upon such American publications as those in a Boston paper, signed 'Pacificus' and upon some pamphlets and private letters of a similar character," January 7, 1808. See also *ibid.*, p. 213, September 7, 1808. "They are so misled in this country as to suppose that the Embargo has already produced very formidable discontent in America, and I am mistaken if the government has not been inclined to calculate upon that discontent in various ways, and at least *to give it a trial.*" Also *ibid.*, p. 241.

[27] *The Speech of James Stephen*, March 6, 1809, p. 97.

neutral powers, because the sea is governed by England; on the Continent everything is lawful, because the Continent is in the hands of Buonaparte.[28]

The speech from which the previous quotations were taken is a model of clear thinking. It is perhaps the most convincing expression of the state of mind which dominated British opinion throughout the period of the embargo. It is not the highest or broadest possible concept of the duties and opportunities of the mistress of sea power in her relations with neutrals in one of the most harassing of naval wars. But it is perfectly intelligible. And, as we trace the more generous and probably more correct views of the opposition, it is needful to remember that the ideas which Stephen grouped together were the ideas which actually shaped the policy of the government.

The opposition, in stating its side of the case, was hampered by the need for caution, because, after all, it was British, and should disaster impend, the safety of the state would compel a united front. Its strength lay chiefly in the ability of its leaders. Though but a qualified success as prime minister, Lord Grenville possessed the wit to discover and the eloquence to proclaim the follies of his successor. Liberal opinion dwelt chiefly with the Whigs, and the ex-minister retained about him a group of gifted men, not unworthy to be called an "opposition of all the talents," so that, when challenged by the legal knowledge of Lord Erskine and Lord Liverpool or confronted by the sound sense of Lord Auckland, with Lord Grey and Lord Holland[29] as weighty reserves, the measures of the government

---

[28] *The Speech of James Stephen*, March 6, 1809, p. 104.

[29] A letter from Lord Holland to Mr. Pinkney deserves reprinting. "London, June 1, 1808. Dear Sir:—From fear that you might have thought what I said to you about your boy a mere matter of form, I write again to you after I have talked it over with Lady Holland, to say that if we are to encounter the misfortune of a war with America, and upon leaving this country, you should wish your son to pursue his education here, Lady Holland and myself beg to assure you, that without the

faced analysis by some of the keenest minds in England. Moreover, the great reviews, the *Edinburgh* and the *Quarterly*, as well as an important section of the press,[30] could be relied upon to keep the opinions of liberals before the public.[31]

The Whigs early foresaw that the Orders in Council offered strategic opportunities as the opening wedge in a general attack. "It branches into all the more important interests external and internal; and we have many advantages in it."[32] They made, therefore, a most lugubrious analysis of the situation. The Orders spelled the decline of British commerce, the prostration of Lancashire manufactures, and war with America,[33] such a war as would thereby complete "the combination of the whole world against our country."[34] The *Edinburgh Review*[35] summed up the case

least inconvenience to us, we can take care of him during the holidays; and between them ascertain, that he is going on properly and give you all the information you would require upon the progress of his studies, state of his health, &c. I only entreat you to adopt this plan, if otherwise agreeable and convenient, without scruple, as I assure you we should not offer it if we did not feel pleasure in the prospect of its being accepted." Pinkney, *The Life of William Pinkney*, p. 60.

[30] Cf. *Bell's Weekly Messenger*, quoted by the Frankfort, Kentucky, *Palladium* for April 29, 1808. See also *Palladium* for October 27, 1808.

[31] Pinkney, *The Life of William Pinkney*, p. 198. ". . . the discussions (through the Liverpool papers and others) by which the vital importance of American connection and intercourse (and even of that American trade which their late orders would injudiciously crush), has been demonstrated to all."

[32] Hist. MSS Comm., *Fortescue MSS*, p. 173, January 18, 1808. Auckland to Grenville.

[33] *Ibid.*, p. 164, January 1, 1808. "It is a silly supposition on the part of those who persuade themselves that a country will not go to war because it is evidently contrary to her interests to go to war." Also *ibid.*, p. 178, February 12. "Private.—Mr. Eden has seen Mr. Pinkney, who privately thinks that the discussions must end in war; and has no account in any of his letters of the instruction which Mr. Monroe is to bring him. You will see in the papers the President's message on the Orders in Council." Also p. 179.

[34] Hansard, *Parliamentary Debates*, 1st Ser., X. 933, March 8, 1808.

[35] The influence of the *Edinburgh Review* upon the thinking public is alluded to by Charles Jared Ingersoll, *A View of the Rights*, etc., p. 46, "To these lights, the Edinburgh reviewers and the evidence of the most respectable merchants before Parliament, and Lord Grenville's speeches,

in a pungent critique of British mistakes.[36]   It acquitted
America of acquiescence in the French usurpations[37] and
defended submission to search by French vessels and the
possession of a certificate of non-British origin of cargo
as innocent.   It warned Britons that the loss of American
trade would bring auxiliary misfortunes not then apparent,
one of which would be the permanent stimulus of American
manufactures.   It forecast that the government would wholly
fail in its main object of inciting revolution against Napoleon
and would succeed only in alienating the sympathies of the
Americans.

Two chief points of attack are here foreshadowed: on
the one hand, commercial and industrial; on the other,
diplomatic.   The commercial interests at stake were in themselves very great, and with them was bound up the question of foreign exchange, which was sure to be complicated
by any interference with the American balance, to disturb
which would mean the outward movement of gold.   Precisely this happened, and, at a time of unprecedented financial
stress, the operations of the exchequer were hampered by
a rise in gold from eight shillings per ounce, in 1807, to
one hundred and ten shillings per ounce in 1813.[38]

A serious rise in the price of gold, besides embarrassing
the treasury, would precipitate discontent among the masses
through the low price for wages and commodities.   Such
discontent did, in fact, arise, for distress among the working classes was widespread, especially in the industrial dis-

gave an effulgence of authenticity that flashed conviction upon the English nation, and was reflected back on their ministers, who have ever
since been more circumspect than they were before in their deportment
towards this country."

[36] The *Edinburgh Review*, April 1808, XII. 230-245, especially article
on "Baring and others on the Orders in Council."

[37] See, also, Hist. MSS Comm., *Fortescue MSS*, p. 151, November
25, 1807.

[38] G. W. Porter, *The Progress of the Nation* (ed. F. W. Hirst), p.
499.

tricts of the north, which depended largely upon American supplies.[39]

In an effort to make political capital out of these embarrassments, the Whigs kept a close eye upon conditions in America. They weighed the relative influence of Anglophiles and Gallophiles; attended the disputes over the slave trade suppression, Yazoo lands, and Spanish policy; and noted the growing opposition within the Democratic-Republican ranks, which culminated in the "Quid" determination to break the Jeffersonian succession in favor of Monroe. In their survey of American political life, they exaggerated the importance of John Randolph and his views. The striking figure of the Virginia eccentric lent a glamour to his utterances out of all proportion to their importance, and the foremost periodical of the day, the *Edinburgh Review*, condescended to analyse his opinions:

The speech of Mr. Randolph is certainly the production of a vigorous mind. It abounds in plain and striking statements, mixed with imagery by no means destitute of merit, though directed by an exceedingly coarse and vulgar taste. But his arguments and opinions are of more importance than his rhetorical pretensions; for he speaks the sentiments of a respectable party in the United States.[40]

Analysis of Randolph's speech revealed his unity with the New England Anglophiles and contributed to that extent in misleading Great Britain as to the actual American point of view. In 1807, Randolph was for avoiding a rupture with England on the ground that American interests were really less endangered in 1806 than in 1793. He held "that the only barrier between France and a universal dominion before which America as well as Europe must fall, is the

---

[39] Pinkney, *The Life of William Pinkney*, p. 224. "The embargo and the loss of our trade are deeply felt here, and will be felt with more severity every day. The wheat harvest is likely to be alarmingly short, and the state of the continent will augment the evil. The discontents among their manufacturers are only quieted for the moment by temporary causes. Cotton is rising and soon will be scarce."

[40] The *Edinburgh Review*, October, 1807, XI. 2, 3.

British navy." He riddled the inconsistency of those who would bluster at England and truckle to Spain. He paid his respects to the clamorous traders of the seaport towns—men "who cannot properly be said to belong to America"—and he dwelt upon the ruin which would follow a war with England, sufficient to make "even the present champions of neutral rights repent of their violence, in six months after they should drive the government into war."[41] For a man who held such views in 1807 to come round to their opposite in 1808[42] was a useful object lesson to Whig politicians in the deplorable effect of the Orders in Council upon American sentiment.

The diplomatic aspect of the Orders was quite as menacing as the industrial. It involved the danger of war with the United States, because to subject American ships to British port duties before allowng them to proceed added just the insult to injury which would and did insure retaliation, and thereby constituted a blunder of the first magnitude. The pressure of the Napoleonic wars was drawing toward a climax. Great Britain stood alone in Europe. Her traditional diplomacy of backing a coalition of weaker nations against the dominant military power of the Continent had been shattered by the humiliation of Austria, the conquest of Prussia, the occupation of Spain and Portugal, and the peace between Napoleon and Russia. The principal weapons still in British hands were an army of observation in Spain, the achievements of which were not as yet conspicuous, and the command of the seas. The latter was scarcely threatened, it is true, by even a naval war with America. But sound statesmanship would conciliate America as a possible ally on the one element promising ultimate victory, rather than force her into a hostility best calculated to pro-

---

[41] The *Edinburgh Review*, October, 1807, XI. 2, 3.
[42] Hist. MSS Comm., *Fortescue MSS*, January, 1808, p. 164.

mote Napoleon's objects. By alienating the last friendly
neutral, Great Britain was multiplying her enemies at a
time when division or subtraction would have yielded better
results.

In addition to the practical argument which has been
already outlined, the Whig opposition possessed a certain
sanction in British constitutional procedure itself. Apart
from their international significance, the Orders in Council
represented a wartime tendency apparent in the politics of
more recent days. War inevitably requires a strengthening
of the executive, which, in England, means its emancipation
from parliamentary control. Even so vital a decision as
that to seize the Danish fleet and bombard Copenhagen was
purely executive. Parliament debated it afterward, and then,
to the credit of the nation, made a vigorous protest. But it
was already a fact accomplished. It was much the same with
the Orders in Council. They were issued in November under
ministerial responsibility, and not debated by Parliament
until January. Facing an accomplished fact, in an hour
of national crisis, Parliament did, as a matter of fact, sustain the government, but the opposition could assume the
approval of conservative believers in government by King,
Lords, and Commons.

Finally, the sadly ignored, but not wholly forgotten,
domain of international law contributed its quota to the
argument of the opposition. It is, in fact, a striking feature
of the debates on the Orders in Council, that among all
the arguments of expediency, at a time when might stalked
abroad with mailed fist, perhaps the most interesting discussion which the whole question elicited was one of abstract
international law. Baron Erskine in this connection deserves the credit for a championship of neutral right which
accords with the best traditions of justice.[43] He maintained

[43] Hansard, *Parliamentary Debates*, 1st Ser., X. 934-964, March 8,
1808.

repeatedly that the law of nations is an integral part of
the law of the land, and declared that no state by its individual action can alter or dispense with the law of nations.
He upheld the right of neutral nations to all the freedom
of commerce granted by the law of nations, though for
belligerents he justified the right of effective blockade, and
defended the visitation of neutrals and the search for contraband. With respect to America in particular, he found
that her neutral position would have been indeed compromised had she acquiesced in French usurpation of her rights,
for this would have rendered her accessory to one belligerent
against another. But the protests of General Armstrong at
Paris had insured American neutrality.

Lord Erskine saw in formal treaties the only legal departure from the law of nations. It was on this point that he
grounded the right of search. Following Lord Liverpool,
he placed the British doctrine that free bottoms do not make
free goods, upon the strict basis of international law. Americans and other neutrals had sought to subvert these by
treaties. Well and good for those participating. But so
long as England refused to enter into such an agreement,
she stood rock strong upon international law. He erected
a telling argument upon this foundation. Since England
derived such immense advantages from the law of nations,
her cherished right of search being solely dependent thereon,
self-interest urged a respect for the law in its entirety. "For
if we take upon ourselves to alter the public law to suit our
own convenience without the consent of other nations, what
is to prevent other nations standing upon our own example,
from returning back the new principle upon us?"[44]

Once more quoting Liverpool, he deprecated the growing
disrespect towards Grotius, Puffendorf, Bynkershoek, Vattel,
and other codifiers of international principles, and defending

[44] Hansard, *Parliamentary Debates*, 1st Ser., X. 955, March 8, 1808.

the sacredness of the law, he denied the right of King or even Parliament to amend it. Only an emergency could justify the King in an embargo, or in similar acts, for the rights of neutrals had been sacred since their recognition by Magna Carta[45] and by the statutes of early kings.[46] Therefore, he moved resolutions against the violation of these ancient rights by the recent Orders in Council.

The economic, diplomatic, constitutional, and legal arguments which have just been indicated as the arsenal of the opposition, were called into active play, and though it is matter of history that the ministry stood its ground, the people gritted their teeth, and the Orders were enforced, yet the very stubbornness of the British forms an interesting study in national psychology, one that, on the whole, is more flattering to the resolution than to the intelligence of John Bull.

To one Englishman, at least, Lord Holland, the contest demonstrated that Great Britain learned nothing and forgot nothing. He condemned British policy as an ill-omened survival of the spirit which had caused the Revolution. He lamented that there were any "persons determined to revive that principle of American revenue which lost that country forever to Great Britain."[47] He regarded it as beyond measure deplorable that England was forfeiting American good will at the very time when it was most needed as a counterpoise to Napoleonic aggression. He suggested the desirability of America as an ally "whilst G. Britain held the balance between the new and the old world and enjoyed all those immense advantages which must result from such a commanding situation. The measures of ministers, how-

[45] Thirtieth chapter.
[46] Edward III and Richard II.
[47] Hansard, *Parliamentary Debates*, 1st Ser., X. 1272, March 29, 1808. Holland also blamed Canning for the failure of the earlier Monroe-Pinkney negotiations which resulted in a treaty so unsatisfactory that Jefferson refused to present it to Congress. See *ibid.*, p. 1273.

ever, forbad [sic] this pleasing prospect, and threatened us with a war with those, from whose increasing prosperity we might otherwise derive the most solid advantages."[48]

Notwithstanding its failure to win Parliament by these melancholy considerations, the opposition received from the British public a livelier response than it had anticipated. Discontent became, in fact, too rampant for the opposition to sponsor. Moreover, the growing tension with America threatened political isolation to those who doubted British wisdom. The political scene shifted, too, with unexpected opportunities for British advantage in Spain and her colonies. So that, by May of 1808, the leaders of his Majesty's opposition showed marked symptoms of hedging. They were seeking to extricate themselves with whatever they might preserve of dignity, consistency, and due regard for the witnesses whom it had formerly served their purpose to summon before Parliament.

An interesting file of correspondence illumines this strategic retreat. The confidential adviser of Lord Grenville wrote on May third that:

from a due regard to the merchants and manufacturers who came so handsomely forward on the subject of the Orders in Council, we ought to have a solemn and efficient debate. We are on excellent grounds in that business, and I know that the Ministers are embarrassed by it. They would have got rid of it if America had gone to war, at present they are in a dilemma; they must either retract an absurd measure in the maintenance of which they are committed; or they must risk operation with increasing distresses to the trade, manufactures, and revenue, to a degree which will at last awaken the whole empire from a stupid apathy.[49]

The same counsellor reiterated his conviction that:

. . . we cannot, with due regard to our own consistency, suffer the session to close, without exhibiting so strong a case as the merchants have established. More especially as I have reason (from the best authority) to believe, that the hope of any early

[48] Hansard, loc. cit., pp. 1275-1276, March 29, 1808.
[49] Hist. MSS Comm., Fortescue MSS, p. 198, Auckland to Grenville, May 3, 1808.

accommodation with the United States, which was for a moment entertained, has quite disappeared.[50]

Consistency never appears so dear as when her flight is imminent, and the solicitude which Lord Auckland here manifested prepares us for his next admission:

Still I quite agree with you that, under the apparent circumstances of the two countries, we cannot debate the subject [Orders in Council] to advantage; and yet, having had so many preliminary discussions with confessed advantage in argument and in truth, and having called to our bar so many respectable individuals who have established a case of great strength against the Orders in Council, I certainly feel that we ought to avoid every possible imputation of *deserting* so good a cause. If you can suggest any decorous and consistent mode of getting out of this dilemma, I shall personally be most glad to take my final leave of the session next Friday.[51]

He went on to say that the ministry was equally desirous of avoiding debate, some of its members being disposed even to withdraw the Orders. He thought he found in the delay of the quarterly reports from the treasury a loophole of excuse for action postponed:

Might not our object be attained with due decorum before the debate on Friday next by my taking notice that the accounts of the *5th April,* for which I heretofore moved, have not yet been given; I could then move them again in a form to obviate the pretended cause of delay; and I could throw out a few remarks which might lead you to postpone for the present, the intended motion for an address, on the fair presumption that the Ministers are endeavouring by negotiation or otherwise to get rid of measures so obviously ruinous to trade and revenue.[52]

The above citations are a revelation. Superficially, they denote a flabby and pusillanimous vacillation on the part of the best minds in the country. But at heart they are the incarnation of nationalism. British policy might be unjust, but British pride demanded that it be enforced. And the Whigs, like Pilate, felt inclined to wash their hands of

[50] Hist. MSS Comm., *Fortescue MSS,* p. 200, May 18, 1808.
[51] *Ibid.,* p. 201. Auckland to Grenville, May 25, 1808.
[52] *Ibid.,* May 25, 1808, Auckland to Grenville.

all responsibility. "The prosperity of the whole kingdom is likely to be destroyed by that mad measure of the Orders in Council; but nobody cares about it, and we have performed a thankless duty."[53]

So long, however, as they continued in force, the Orders remained a natural target for the opposition. The attack was accordingly renewed the following year. Parliament debated the wisdom of renewing American intercourse, and resolutions were introduced which laid great stress upon America's refusal to submit to the French Decrees, "which acquiescence was the only ground on which any Right could accrue to His Majesty to interrupt the innocent Commerce of a Neutral Power."[54] The commercial losses due to the embargo were represented as "particularly calculated in the present Crisis, to assist the Designs of our Enemies,"[55] and a prayer was offered for a speedy resumption of intercourse. A warm debate failed to pass the resolution, and the nation remained committed to a policy which, in the words of a modern Englishman, "served indeed only to give efficacy to the paper blockade of Napoleon, against which the whole trading community of the world would have been arrayed but for the notable expedient of the British government."[56]

The political life of Great Britain during the American embargo reveals, as the preceding pages have suggested, a rather formidable opposition, at least in theory, to the Orders in Council and their consequences, but an opposition distinguished by clear thinking rather than by resolute action. The explanation for such quiescence is to be found in the peril of the times. The members of the opposition were Englishmen and patriots, and their country was shadowed by

[53] Hist. MSS Comm., *Fortescue MSS*, p. 206, June 20, 1808.
[54] *Journals of the House of Lords*, XLVII., 50, a, February 17, 1809.
[55] *Ibid*.
[56] G. W. Porter, *The Progress of the Nation* (ed. by F. W. Hirst), 1912.

the greatest danger since the Armada. With the empire at stake, minor issues counted little. The menace of Napoleon united the nation. Differences of opinion were subordinated to unity of action. When Great Britain made it a point of honor to uphold the Orders in Council as long as the Berlin and Milan Decrees remained in force, calculations of prudence, the wisdom of making friends rather than enemies, the moral impetus of international law, were all sacrificed to an imaginary retaliation against Napoleon. Add to national policy the personal animus of a ministry unwilling to see its pet measure discredited,[57] and only the direst economic distress could be expected to turn the scale. But distress of such magnitude would scarcely develop within one year. Only an equal doggedness in America could put the issue to a fair test, and signs were multiplying that America suffered from divided counsels. With these considerations in mind, the repeated defeat of resolutions aimed against the Orders in Council is not surprising.

[57] *The Life and Correspondence of Rufus King*, V. 99. F. Baring to Rufus King, June 3, 1808. . . . "Unfortunately there is a degree of false shame which induces many to persist in error, rather than to acknowledge it, and if the late administration with 'all the talents' did not succeed, it must be admitted that their successors did not posses [sic] that superior intellect which enables great men to overcome prejudices."

CHAPTER X

BRITISH INDUSTRY AND THE AMERICAN EMBARGO

When Congress voted the embargo, recalled our ships, and forbade them to leave port, it forged a two-edged weapon. Its ostensible purpose was protective. The Berlin Decree and the Orders in Council made neutral sailing precarious. The Milan Decree, soon to be published, made it wellnigh impossible. Prudence demanded the recall of our shipping before it fell into French or British hands. And, as a prudential measure, the embargo met with little opposition, even in New England, where it was soon to drive men to the brink of secession. As a measure of caution, however, its limitations were obvious. The losses from ships at anchor, docks abandoned, and sailors dispersed, might soon equal the risks of enemy capture. In face of economic disaster, the embargo could be justified only as a weapon of offense, and this latter object came, as time wore on, to be more fully recognized.

Strangely enough, the efficiency of the embargo as a weapon of offense has received little attention. Its political and economic reactions on America have been studied, but these concern its defensive aspect. The real clew to the success of the embargo as a substitute for war lies overseas. How did it affect the nations against which it was aimed? France one may dismiss with a word. The British blockade needed no embargo to aid its operations against Napoleon. But for Great Britain the situation is more complex. True, the embargo did not secure the concessions which it sought. Nevertheless, it exerted a decided pressure upon industrial life in Great Britain. The measure of British distress is, accordingly, one measure of American political wisdom in 1808. On the other hand, to ascribe all the misfortunes of British industry in 1808 to American causes would be fallacious. The Berlin and Milan Decrees were in operation throughout the year, and the former of these was already producing an effect[1] before the non-intercourse law was revived by America, and the embargo enacted.[2]

British trade gave signs of disorder as early as August, 1807.[3] Nor did conditions improve as autumn advanced. Writing in October, Lord Auckland, an opponent of the government's policies, drew a lugubrious picture of commerce in decay:

> I am told by the best Custom house and mercantile authorities that our exports are almost totally suspended, and that our imports are gradually contracting; that orders for manufactures are revoking; and that not only our European trade is checked, but that the demand of goods for the United States is interrupted. If this account should be in any degree accurate, it will soon affect not only the customs, but the excise, and will also be followed by much individual distress.[4]

Some weeks later, in the same vein, he predicted that unless prosperity revived before spring, the manufacturing towns would be clamoring for peace.[5] When the Orders in Council were published, he renewed his laments.[6] In fact, the more

[1] It may be added that this effect long outlasted the repeal of the embargo. See A. Andréadès, *History of the Bank of England*, p. xviii.

[2] Thomas Tooke, *A History of Prices and of the State of Circulation from 1793 to 1837*, I. 290, attributes the distresses of the time to the combined effects of French and American enactments.

[3] William Smart, *Economic Annals of the Nineteenth Century*, I. 155. See also *The Speech of James Stephens, Esq., in the Debate in the House of Commons, March 6, 1809, on Mr. Whitbread's Motion, Relative to the Late Overtures of the American Government, with Supplementary Remarks on the Recent Orders in Council*, pp. 11, 28, 32, 56.

[4] Hist. MSS Comm., *Fortescue MSS*, p. 140, October 16, 1807. Lord Auckland to Lord Grenville.

[5] *Ibid.*, p. 143, November 6, 1807. Lord Auckland to Lord Grenville.

[6] *Ibid.*, p. 147, November 17, 1807. "My private belief is that, so far as our manufacturers are interested, the whole of this measure will operate to diminish still further the diminished export; and that, so far as our West Indian embarrassments are concerned, they must be aggravated by a system which tends to lessen the consumption and to increase the accumulation of foreign sugars."

he reflected upon the Orders, the more disastrous they appeared. Quoting French authority, he foresaw that the rupture of commerce must automatically create or stimulate manufactures among former customers of Great Britain,[7] while those at home confronted nothing but depression, with distress in Yorkshire,[8] and general discontent among manufacturers and importers.[9]

Since opposition thrives best on discontent, Lord Auckland, as a party man, may have been less melancholy than the picture he paints. Certainly he and his associates set themselves cheerfully to the task of gleaning party advantage from complaints of merchants[10] and the petitions of malcontents.[11] But discounting exaggerations and the limited perspective of merchants, manufacturers, and noblemen of the opposition, it still appears that the industrial situation at the close of 1807 offered a fair trial to the embargo. Debates in Parliament, articles in the reviews, and private correspondence alike testify to the reality of its pressure.

All these sources indicate that centers of manufactures and commerce were first to feel the embargo.[12] The critical period came with the turning of the year. Protests arose from Manchester, Liverpool, and London.[13] In the March debates, Parliament was reminded of the cries of distress on all sides and regaled with a vision of Liverpool

---

[7] Hist. MSS Comm., *Fortescue MSS*, p. 153, November 28, 1807. "The *Moniteur*, September 25, 1806, says, 'La prohibition des marchandises étrangères de cotes que vient d' ordonner le Gouvernement ne contribuera pas peu à nous faire obtenir le resultat si désirable de fabriquer nous memes la totalité des articles dont nous avons besoin." Also *ibid.*, p. 279, February 15, 1809.

[8] Hist. MSS Comm., *Fortescue MSS*, p. 155, December 5, 1807.

[9] *Ibid.*, p. 158, December 9, 1807.

[10] *Ibid.*, p. 181, March 1-6, 1808.

[11] *Ibid.*, p. 182, March 14, 1808.

[12] Hansard, *Parliamentary Debates*, 1st Ser., X. March 8, 1808.

[13] *Journals of the House of Commons*, LXIII. 400, b,. 417, a.

once more a village, its glory departed.[14] No time was lost in conveying to America reports of unparalleled distress in the manufacturing districts.[15] America was told that many laborers at one time accustomed to a guinea a week were now reduced to sweeping the streets or begging their bread.[16] These accounts were probably exaggerated to meet the taste of their hearers, since wages—at least, nominal wages—had been rising for the past six years[17] and for artisans, at any rate, approached their maximum in 1808.[18] But discounting partisan exaggeration and propaganda, the condition of British labor in the face of a present shortage of the harvest, and a prospective shortage of the raw material for industry, was far from enviable. Its protests, nevertheless, went unheeded. When the shipping and commercial classes even welcomed the withdrawal of the last great neutral from competition, the miseries of a disfranchised and inarticulate proletariat could not be expected to sway the policy of the cabinet. Giant petitions from the manufacturing centers against enforcing the Orders in Council accordingly served no real purpose other than to bolster American morale.[19] New Yorkers learned in July of riots in old Yorkshire in which ten thousand weavers cursed the price of bread and demanded higher wages, refusing to disperse until several hundred of their number lay dead in the streets.[20] Sixty thousand looms were said to be idle.

[14] *Journals of the House of Commons,* LXIII. 957.

[15] Frankfort, Kentucky, *Palladium,* June 23, 1808, quoting the *Richmond Enquirer. London News* of March 20.

[16] *Ibid.,* London, March 23.

[17] William Smart, *Economic Annals of the Nineteenth Century,* I. 182.

[18] Thomas Tooke, *A History of Prices and of the State of Circulation from 1793 to 1837,* I. 288.

[19] Frankfort, Kentucky, *Palladium,* May 19, 1808. "Extract from a letter of an American gentleman in London to the Editors of the Boston *Chronicle,* dated March 12, 1808."

[20] *Ibid.,* August 25, 1808. "Latest from England. From the New York *Gazette,* July 29."

Though later reports pointed to some improvement and some pay increases, discontent was slow to subside[21] and ceased to be a factor only when political developments in Spain brought new energy and hope to the entire industrial life of the nation.[22]

The intensity of suffering in the crowded centers throughout the winter of 1807 and 1808 finds testimony more convincing than such rumors and hasty observations as made their way to America, in the statistics of the poor rate. This, in Manchester, rose in the embargo year from an average of four thousand pounds to no less than forty-nine thousand pounds.[23] And the government gave official recognition to the state of the country by a pledge to distinguish the victims of want from mere trouble brewers "in any measures which the excesses of the misguided may compel us to take."[24] It is unnecessary to claim for the embargo the sole sponsorship for all this wretchedness, in order to maintain that it was a factor with which the British system had distinctly to reckon.

The growth of misery and discontent was hastened by industrial concentration and the failure to diversify industry. This was as apparent in the colonies as in the mother country. Specialization in industry accounted for the economic sensitiveness of Lancashire.[25] Specialization in agriculture was responsible for a similar sensitiveness in the

[21] Frankfort, Kentucky, *Palladium*, September 1, 1808, quoting England, June 9.

[22] William Smart, *Economic Annals of the Nineteenth Century*, says: "It is significant of the new hope that the petitions for peace from the manufacturing towns, where there was considerable distress, at once came to an end. After May [1808] England had again a large seaboard open to her commerce."

[23] Hansard, *Parliamentary Debates*, 1st Ser., XII. 1170.

[24] *Speeches of the Rt. Hon. George Canning*, II. 360, 361, June 24, 1808.

[25] Hist. MSS Comm., *Fortescue MSS*, p. 252, December 28, 1808. Lord Auckland to Lord Grenville.

West Indies. Both British and French, these islands were devoted to the growth of sugar. The entire economic life of the colonies centered in a maximum production of one staple, and starvation impended whenever food imports were threatened. The embargo menaced chiefly the French West Indies, because British sea power cut off normal communication from France. It was believed that they must surrender to Great Britain or starve.[26] But the prospect of having more islands to feed was a doubtful blessing. The requirements of feeding her own impelled Britain to a royal proclamation[27] exempting from interruption neutral carriers of lumber and provisions bound for the colonies in the West Indies or South America, even where the absense of clearance papers indicated a defiance of the embargo.

This official bid to American lawlessness was followed by an act of Parliament opening the door to that free trade between America and the West Indies which was not to come in its fullness until Van Buren's time. For the present, the route was to be circuitous. A free importation of rice, grain, and flour was invited direct "from any Foreign Colonies on the Continent of *America.*"[28] Florida, of course, was meant. But the United States were privileged to send goods "into the British Provinces in *North America*" for reëxport to the islands.

Such allurements did double service. They opened ports to needed goods and rallied American renegades to a violation of their country's laws. Among these, Aaron Burr appears in a characteristic rôle. The peregrinations of Burr had brought him, in 1808, to Nova Scotia, and his name

[26] *Bell's Weekly Messenger,* quoted in the Frankfort, Kentucky, *Palladium,* April 29, 1808.

[27] Dated Windsor, April 11, 1808. See *American State Papers,* Foreign Relations, III. 281.

[28] *Journals of the House of Commons,* LXIII. 466, b, June 17, 1808. See p. 464 for royal assent, June 23, 1808.

was associated with an especially alluring bait for New Englanders chafing under commercial fetters. The items listed by official proclamation as welcome in the ports of Nova Scotia are, at any rate, worthy of Burr's capacity as a tempter—"staves, plank and square timber, boards and scantling, bread, biscuit, flour, peas, beans, wheat, barley, oats, Indian corn, grain, seeds, and meal of all kinds; also tobacco, pitch, tar, turpentine, salted beef and pork, bacon, hog's lard, butter, onions, fruit, etc., from the United States of America and from the Azores, or western islands."[29]

Commercial inducements like those offered in the West Indies and Nova Scotia proceeded from no friendly motive. But with the data at hand it is not easy to determine which of two arguments prevailed, the pinch of necessity or a will to undermine American solidarity. Doubtless it was both. The needs of the West Indies were real. And New England restiveness was well known. Whatever the object, the opportunity of British colonial trade was a distinct concession to the embargo.

The necessity of such a concession was less apparent in the summer than in the early spring of 1808, because events which no one could foresee when the embargo was laid had shaped themselves toward its defeat. These centered about the Spanish struggle for liberty. Great Britain, as the champion of Spanish freedom, was the heir to Spanish commerce.[30] And the possibilities of an El Dorado combined with existing high prices, due to a threatened curtailment of needed supplies,[31] to create a furor of speculation. Credit

[29] Frankfort, Kentucky, *Palladium*, August 4, 1808, quoting from the *Aurora*.

[30] A. Andréadès, *History of the Bank of England*, p. 219.

[31] Thomas Tooke, *A History of Prices and of the State of Circulation from 1793 to 1837*, I. 292.

was greatly expanded,[32] and a huge exportation of goods created the appearance of an economic revival not warranted by the character of the trade, which was highly speculative. Brazil participated in this commercial boom, and a traveler in Rio de Janeiro recorded at the time:

> that more Manchester goods were sent out in the course of a few weeks than had been consumed in the twenty years preceding; and the quantity of English goods of all sorts poured into the city was so very great that warehouses could not be provided sufficient to contain them; and that the most valuable merchandise was actually exposed for weeks on the beach to the weather, and to every sort of depredation. Elegant services of cut glass and china were offered to persons whose most splendid drinking vessels consisted of a horn, or the shell of a cocoanut; tools were sent out, having a hammer on the one side and a hatchet on the other, as if the inhabitants had had nothing more to do than to break the first stone that they met with, and then cut the gold and diamonds from it; and some speculators actually went so far as to send out *skates* to Rio Janeiro.[33]

This sudden activity in new markets communicated itself to the more stabilized routes of commerce. The Baltic, Heligoland, and Malta enjoyed a vast increase in trade, an extension which, according to Tooke, "was probably greater and more sudden within the two years, viz., 1808 and 1809, . . . than had ever before been witnessed, within a similar period."[34]

Home industry also felt the ferment, and new enterprises were launched in excess of actual requirements. The public was invited to subscribe for shares in numerous breweries, distilleries, "fire offices," bridges, and canals.[35] In

[32] A. Andréadès, *History of the Bank of England*, p. 219.

[33] Thomas Tooke, *A History of Prices and of the State of Circulation from 1793 to 1837*, I. 276; quoting M'Culloch, *Principles of Political Economy*, 2d ed., p. 329.

[34] Thomas Tooke, *Thoughts and Details of the High and Low Prices of the Last Thirty Years*, I. 101.

[35] Thomas Tooke, *A History of Prices and of the State of Circulation from 1793 to 1837*, I. 277.

sum, there was, in the sober language of Thomas Tooke, "a great briskness in the general circulation; a rapidity in the interchange between goods and money or credit, which is an invariable attendant on speculative periods."[36]

That the embargo contributed to this era of speculation cannot be doubted. It shared with Napoleon's decrees direct responsibility for a reign of high prices,[37] in view of the fears which Britons entertained that imports could not be relied upon to replace their deficient grain harvest and to meet the requirements of manufactures. It furnished, at the same time, an added incentive to utilize the new Spanish opportunities as an offset for lost markets and even aided the process by withdrawing from all competition. In this way the embargo contributed to its own defeat. Its supposed victims balanced their gains with their losses and discovered at least an imaginary credit. The table of British exports for 1808 shows a loss of £6,604,774 over the 1807 trade to the United States and a gain of £6,152,448 over the 1807 trade to "America, exclusive of the United States."[38] Increased trade with Canada with a view to reëxport to the United States doubtless accounted for a part of this. But the opening of South America manifestly absorbed a large share.

On the whole, however, it would appear that the commercial gains from the embargo were fictitious.[39] The South American trade was not a real substitute for the loss of Great Britain's best customer. Yet it came at the psycholo-

---

[36] Thomas Tooke, *Thoughts and Details on the High and Low Prices of the Last Thirty Years.* I. 103.

[37] *Ibid.*, I. 99, 100.

[38] G. R. Porter, *The Progress of the Nation*, p. 479.

[39] One evidence of this is the increase of bankruptcies. The number rose from 1362 in 1807 to 1433 in 1808, and declined in 1809 to 1382. Thomas Tooke, *Thoughts and Details on the High and Low Prices of the Last Thirty Years*, I. 219.

gical moment to stiffen resistance to Napoleon and Jefferson.
A better index of the effectiveness of the embargo is afforded by manufactures, especially of cotton, the most characteristic development of that industrial revolution on which
British power was founded. Cotton had been singled out for
the most odious provision of the Orders in Council, the nine
pence a pound reëxport tax, and in cotton America might
enjoy her most soul-satisfying retaliation. To achieve this,
however, she must exercise patience, inasmuch as the British
trade faced the crisis with a considerable surplus.[40] Moreover, in the event of its long continuance, fresh supplies were
anticipated from Turkey, by land conveyance through Germany,[41]—an interesting survival of a mediaeval trade route.
Better still, there was a genuine shortage in France, which
would cripple a growing industry.[42] And sound British
policy would discourage any cotton export to fill the gap.[43]
The government even made capital of the well intrenched
position of the cotton trade, boasting that there were more
merchants in favor of than opposed to the Orders in Council.[44] The mustard seed of truth in this Utopia was the rise
in raw cotton, which necessarily accompanied the cessation
of supplies. Dealers and manufacturers who were well stocked
would naturally support any measure which enhanced
prices.[45] Those who now clapped loudest would be the first
to groan when the pinch was real.

If cotton was the real test of the embargo, its solution
would depend, not upon a few rich speculators, but upon

[40] Hansard, *Parliamentary Debates*, 1st Ser., X. 1346, April 8, 1808.
[41] *Ibid.*, X. 1347.
[42] *Ibid.*, X. 1349.
[43] *Ibid.*, X. 1347.
[44] *Ibid.*, X. 1349.
[45] For a biting satire upon this complacency, see the *Edinburgh Review*, XIV. 445, July, 1809.

the prosperity of the rank and file. Here the government boast did not long remain uncontradicted. Lord Grenville, a leader of the opposition forces in Parliament, twitted the optimists with their failure to bring forward witnesses in support of Liverpool trade and Manchester manufactures and the activity of the shipping industry. Free trade, he declared, was the true solution of the cotton manufacture, of raw'material for which British harbors would always insure a supply.[46]

For reasons inherent in the entire industrial and political conditions of America, the most effective enforcement of the embargo was in the southern states. Hence cotton shipments, even discounting a certain leakage by the Amelia Island route, were really small.[47] The consequence was a rapid inroad upon the British surplus of 1807, with a correspondingly enhanced respect for the embargo.[48] By September, the initial supply was mostly consumed, and the expectation of Brazilian and other sources demonstrated to be an illusion. Notwithstanding these adversities, Britons confided in American avarice to break the deadlock. "This country has always considered the Americans so commercial and so avaricious that the people, when two crops are on hand, would force their government to permit the exportation of it on any terms."[49] But American docility under losses, a surprise to the British, premised, if persisted in, "a fair arrangement by the next Spring."[50]

[46] Hansard, *Parliamentary Debates*, 1st Ser., X. 1349-1351, April 8, 1808.

[47] Thomas Tooke, *Thoughts and Details on the High and Low Prices of the Last Thirty Years*, I. 105, gives cotton imports into Great Britain as bales:

        1807—282,667   1808—168,138,   1809—440,382.

[48] Frankfort, Kentucky, *Palladium*, November 17, 1808, quoting Philadelphia, October 27, an "Extract of a letter from an intelligent American gentlemen in London to his friend in this city, dated September 17."

[49] *Ibid.*

[50] *Ibid.*

The diminishing cotton supply was reflected in price changes of moment, proportioned to supply and demand. The accompanying tables are, accordingly, complementary:

TABLE OF IMPORTS OF UNITED STATES COTTON INTO
LIVERPOOL, 1806-14[51]

	Bags		Bags
1806	100,273	1811	97,626
1807	143,756	1812	79,528
1808	25,426	1813	18,640
1809	130,581	1814	40,448
1810	199,220		

AVERAGE ANNUAL COTTON QUOTATIONS FOR THE SAME PERIOD[52]

	Uplands (chiefly American) d. per lb.	Surats (East Indian) d. per lb.
1806	18¼	14½
1807	14½	13
1808	22	19½
1809	20	18½
1810	15¼	15
1811	12½	12
1812	16¾	14
1813	23	17½
1814	29½	21

The importation for 1808 exceeded that of 1813 by only a few thousand bags and is interesting testimony to the comparative efficiency of commercial embargoes and naval wars. The price of 22d., quoted in 1808, is a 50 per cent. rise over 1807, and even this is given only as an average. It was a clear case, too, of the effect of the embargo as distinct from

[51] *American Historical Review*, XXI, No. 2, January, 1916, G. W. Daniels, "Cotton Trade under the Embargo," p. 278. Another estimate of cotton imports into Liverpool gives higher totals, but leaves a similar conclusion. See Hist. MSS. Comm., *Fortescue MSS.*, p. 261, January 6, 1809. Lord Auckland to Lord Grenville, "It appears by an account which I received yesterday from Liverpool that the total import of cotton wool into Great Britain for 1807, was 282,448; 1808, was 168,138, of which from the United States in 1807 was 171,023; 1808, was 37,672." Thomas Tooke, *Thoughts and Details*, etc., I. 105, gives it 168,138 bales, but as a great falling off.

[52] Thomas Ellison, *The Cotton Trade of Great Britain*, p. 245.

the decrees of Napoleon, for British power kept open the sea lanes and insured the arrival of such cotton as came on to the world market.

Speculation ran wild, and, in October, cotton touched three shillings and even three shillings two pence a pound.[53] Manufacturers disposed to keep open their mills were at the mercy of bulls in raw materials and bears in finished products, the market for the latter being overstocked.[54] Over the whole unhealthy structure impended a veritable sword of Damocles, the ever present possibility that the embargo might be removed. Bad now for the entrepreneurs; worse then for the speculators.

The condition of the workingmen was equally distracting. Though their budgets were less imposing, their problem was not less baffling. They were assigned to the well known fourth-dimension formula: "How can half the wages pay twice the prices?" Despairing of a solution, they humbly informed Parliament that they "are brought to great distress by the reduction of their wages, and that they do not obtain, upon a fair average, more than one half the wages for their labour, which they were paid in the year 1792, although since that period, the charges for food, house-rent, firing, and other articles, are nearly doubled, and daily on the increase."[55] To relieve this sad condition, Parliament was urged to fix a higher wage rate for cotton weaving.[56] Tension in the cotton industry diminished with the increasing importations during 1809, and business approached its norm.[57]

[53] "Extract of a letter, dated Liverpool, October 3," given in the Frankfort, Kentucky, *Palladium*, for January 12, 1809.

[54] *Ibid.*

[55] *Journals of the House of Commons*, LXIV. 95, a, February 24, 1809.

[56] *Ibid.*, LXIV. 95, b, February 27, 1809, gives a similar petition from Scotland.

[57] *American Historical Review*, XXI. No. 2, p. 280, January, 1916. Article by G. W. Daniels, "Cotton Trade under the Embargo."

In the linen industry, conditions were more favorable, and Ireland, its headquarters, seems to have enjoyed a prosperity comparable with that which the Great War just terminated has brought her. A contemporary chart shows progress even in the year of embargo:[58]

Year	Yards exported
1805	42,988,621
1806	43,534,971
1807	39,049,727
1808	40,901,442

It is scarcely a measure, however, of embargo efficiency. As regards linen, America possessed no such complete monopoly of raw material as in the case of cotton. The local supply was, nevertheless, inadequate,[59] and "a more general cultivation of flax and hemp was urged."[60]   Holders of linen, like those of cotton, enjoyed a sudden rise in values. Indeed, prosperity in the industry was attributed in part to "the scarcity of flaxseed arising from the embargo, and in part to the exportation of German linens having been checked."[61]   The course of linen, however, exhibited a further difference from that of cotton in that for the latter curtailed supplies meant speculative profits but industrial unrest; while with the former, it was otherwise.   Profits rose, but not their unpleasant corollary.   Does not the American monopoly of cotton suggest the explanation?   Ireland used our flax, but could buy elsewhere; England used our cotton, and could buy little elsewhere.

[58] *Quarterly Review,* I. 427, May, 1809. "An account of the quantity of linen cloth exported from Ireland, from the 25th of March, 1776, to the 5th of January, 1809, inclusive."

[59] *Ibid.,* p. 428. "America, Riga, and the Low Countries furnished flax seed."

[60] *Quarterly Review,* I. 427.

[61] *Edinburgh Review,* July, 1809, XIV. 445, 446. The article is a satire on the supposed prosperity of Irish linens.

The British food situation under the embargo is not easy to determine. Population estimates vary from 11,769,-725 to 17,444,911.[62] Privation for the lower estimate would mean starvation for the higher. The annual importation of wheat for the ten-year average, 1801-10, was reckoned at 600,946 quarters,[63] of which the United States furnished the principal quota. To what extent would the deprivation of this inconvenience the population? Very little, if we accept "a very small fraction above a peck"[64] as the annual import per capita. And this might be more than offset by increased production at home. Land enclosures were progressing at a rapid rate, and the area under cultivation increased by 7,350,577 acres during the reign of George III.[65] Of these, 1,550,010 are credited to the period 1800-09, and in the one year, 1808, ninety-two bills of enclosure became law.[66] Altogether, one would expect Great Britain at this early date to be almost self-sufficing. It is something of a surprise, therefore, to meet with earnest and repeated solicitations to Parliament to stop the whiskey business lest the country be brought to starvation.

There was, nevertheless, sufficient ground to apprehend a food shortage, the more so in view of the difficulty of covering it by importation[67] from either the Continent or

[62] See G. R. Porter, *The Progress of the Nation*, pp. 176, 177. For a third estimate at sixteen and one half millions, see *Annals of Congress, Tenth Congress, Second Session*, p. 877. The lowest estimate best accords with William Smart, *Economic Annals of the Nineteenth Century*, I. 138—who gives 8,870,000 for the year 1803.

[63] For a larger estimate, see *Journals of the House of Commons*, LXIII. 386, a, May 31, 1808—770,000 quarters.

[64] G. R. Porter, *The Progress of the Nation*, p. 177.

[65] *Ibid.*, p. 188.

[66] Thomas Tooke, *Thoughts and Details on the High and Low Prices of the Last Thirty Years*, III. 129.

[67] *Ibid.*, III. 181. To cite the case of wheat and flour only, exports increased from 24,365 quarters in 1807 to 77,567 in 1808, while imports fell from 400,759 quarters to 81,466.

America. The crop of 1807 left no surplus to tide over the wretched harvest of 1808, which was ruined by phenomenal heat followed by wet, stormy weather.[68] If widespread destitution was to be avoided, restrictions upon the distilleries were only a matter of reasonable precaution.[69]

Western Scotland was especially urgent in pointing to restrictions upon distilleries as the one sure relief from distress.[70] Parliament was reminded that Paisley and the neighboring towns of Renfrew depended upon outside supplies the greater part of the year.[71] Similar petitions from Dumbarton and Kilmarnock alleged that grain prices were rising unconscionably from a scarcity of oats and barley, "so that unless the consumption by Distillation ceases for a limited time, the most alarming consequences are to be apprehended."[72]

Temperance was not permitted to cloud the issue, because, in the joint interest of British distillers and West India planters, energy released from grain and malt liquors was to be transferred to rum.[73] The chief opposition to grain economy came, therefore, not from the powerful brewing and distillery barons, but from the landed interest.[74] The quarrel lay between town mouse and country mouse. And the squires brought forth the rather ingenious sophistry that wasteful consumption was the surest stimulus to adequate production. They trembled for their country when

[68] Thomas Tooke, *Thoughts and Details on the High and Low Prices of the Last Thirty Years*, III. 68. Also *ibid.*, I. 105.

[69] *Ibid.*, I. 216; III. 177.

[70] Thomas Tooke, *A History of Prices and of the State of Circulation from 1793 to 1837*, I. 267, shows that the 1807 wheat crop was poorer in Scotland than in England or Wales.

[71] *Journals of the House of Commons*, LXIII. 386, May 31, 1808.

[72] *Ibid.*, LXVIII, 418, b, June 10, 1808, from Dumbarton; and *ibid.*, p. 394.

[73] *Ibid.*, LXIII. 394, b, June 1, 1808. See also Thomas Tooke, *Thoughts and Details, etc.*, III. 68.

[74] *Edinburgh Review*, XIII. 399, January, 1809.

they thought of "the dangerous effect which this measure must have in discouraging the growth of corn; being likewise fully convinced that the best resource against a future scarcity consists in encouraging the distillation of corn."[75]

Wiseacres beheld in the grain restrictions a return to the type of government interference which the philosophy of Adam Smith was supposed to have discredited once and for all. They rose to denounce this flagrant violation of *laissez-faire*. Their argument was simple: If the price of grain rose so little as not to prevent the distiller from using it, there was evidently a very slight degree of scarcity. The moment when the interest of the country required a stoppage of the corn distillery and the moment when the distillers' own interest would have stopped it must coincide very nearly.[76] They condemned as "vague and gratuitous" the assertion that barley was dear, defying any one to know when it was really so. "The price has advanced no doubt; but if the supply is contracted, ought it not to advance?"[77] They admitted that the worst consequences of government action would not develop, because confidence in the power of landowners to repeal the law would encourage farmers to their usual planting.

Permanently to exclude grain from the distilleries would breed disaster, because its production would diminish by precisely, or perhaps even more than, the 470,000 quarters hitherto consumed in spirits.[78] At this point in the argument, China came forward as the horrible example. With naive disingenuousness, Britain's prosperity was attributed to her luxuries; China's indigence, to her short allowance:

[75] *Journals of the House of Commons*, LXIII. 407, a, from petitions submitted by Lincolnshire and Essex.

[76] *Edinburgh Review*, XIII. 398, January, 1809.

[77] *Ibid.*

[78] *Edinburgh Review*, XIII, 399.

The project of substituting sugar for grain in our distilleries is calculated to bring us nearer short allowance—nearer the wretched situation of the Chinese than we hitherto have been, by a quantity equal to the maintenance of 300,000 or 400,000 persons. . . . Hitherto a bad crop might prove inconvenient—henceforth it may be fatal.[79]

While the *Edinburgh Review* was fulminating against this sacrilege to *laissez-faire,* its more youthful rival[80] defended a regulation which inflicted no injury upon British farmers, yet saved the West India planters from ruin.[81] The government itself took the broad view. Though committed to the Orders in Council, it was not blind to their consequences in curtailed supplies of food. It had the good sense to heed the petitions of consumers, and the restrictions advocated finally became law.

When one reflects that the food shortage of 1808 compelled a measure which all the submarines in the World War did not effect, one feels a new respect for an embargo which, in conjunction with Napoleon's measures on the Continent, could diminish British corn, grain, and meal imports from £920,435 in 1807 to £146,119 in 1808,[82] and over the protests of the landed gentry, compel distillers to reorganize the "trade."

[79] *Edinburgh Review,* XIII, 400.

[80] *Quarterly Review,* II. 14-18, August, 1809.   Delay of the article afforded the advantage of a better perspective.

[81] *Edinburgh Review,* XII. 95, shows that the relief of the West Indies was short-lived.

[82] *Journals of the House of Commons,* LXIV. Appendix A1, p. 548. This reduction would seem due almost entirely to the embargo, Napoleon's Berlin Decree having been enforced during much of 1807.

TABLE OF IMPORTS INTO GREAT BRITAIN FROM THE UNITED STATES FOR THE YEARS ENDING JANUARY 5[33]

Article	1807		1808		1809	
	Total	Real Value	Total	Real Value	Total	Real Value
Annotto	£41,277	£71,353	£40,259	£64,402	£4,554	£6,913
Ashes, Pearl and pot	89,726	138,498	94,045	144,326	26,822	38,344
Cochineal	62,253	77,817	7,283	9,104		
Coffee	29,012	25,904	67,191	66,636	124,671	111,313
Corn, grain and meal	233,585	422,429	468,744	922,308	32,855	64,200
Hides	5,708	12,406	9,164	18,590	1,255	2,868
Indigo	6,616	47,297	8,917	69,909	1,564	12,515
Pitch and tar	27,892	34,378	32,729	40,266	9,638	11,792
Seeds, flax and linseed	12,205	11,590	6,759	7,050	1,815	3,139
Skins and furs	32,146	65,062	13,568	26,116	5,565	10,434
Sugar	37,526	51,173	9,555	13,030	74,277	101,218
Tobacco	224,813	417,946	240,224	447,883	62,770	118,261
Turpentine	66,322	100,822	51,308	77,638	14,811	23,349
Wood, deals and fir timber	9,146	64,758	21,962	131,741	4,056	24,534
Wood, mahogany	16,024	29,432	41,512	81,482	2,181	5,306
Wood, masts	12,282	10,121	6,514	5,355	583	466
Wood, staves	59,761	139,203	62,912	146,734	9,377	21,696
Wool, cotton	984,373	2,566,729	1,565,788	4,115,136	425,999	1,144,414
Other articles	49,217	73,825	99,088	143,704	33,737	57,224
Totals	£1,999,884	£4,360,743	£2,847,522	£6,531,410	£836,480	£1,751,986

[33] *Journals of the House of Commons,* LXIV. 648.   Appendix.

TABLE OF EXPORTS FROM GREAT BRITAIN TO THE UNITED STATES FOR THE YEARS ENDING JANUARY 5[84]

Article	1807		1808		1809	
	Total	Real Value	Total	Real Value	Total	Real Value
Brass and copper manufacture	£40,632	£82,142	£84,441	£168,004	£32,947	£69,968
Cotton and linen manufactures and cotton yarn	4,072,840	4,934,783	4,049,209	4,916,032	2,477,819	2,825,564
Glass and earthenware	60,248	175,526	49,733	162,542	11,811	61,850
Haberdashery	21,535	313,764	20,446	310,862	2,851	69,620
Hats	58,305	99,260	39,934	64,620	840	1,851
Iron and steel manufactures	302,681	684,678	325,028	773,188	86,895	220,620
Lead	12,945	44,619	9,390	31,166	8,837	36,661
Salt	84,689	88,989	85,660	89,874	35,460	37,233
Silk manufactures	133,430	425,165	122,144	417,418	885	3,723
Tin and pewter	58,827	79,189	54,650	75,875	40,661	53,916
Woolens	2,949,816	4,866,178	2,509,322	4,239,118	1,139,563	1,642,709
Other articles	483,972	595,195	393,272	597,814	94,963	218,024
British total	£8,279,720	£12,389,488	£7,743,229	£11,846,513	£3,933,532	£5,241,739
Foreign mdse	333,402	476,063	177,891	251,429	58,527	61,127
Total	£8,613,122	£12,865,551	£7,921,120	£12,097,942	£3,992,059	£5,302,866

[84] *Journals of the House of Commons*, LXIV. 648. Appendix.

Cotton and foodstuffs were not the only hostages detained in America for British good behavior. The accompanying tables show beyond peradventure the pinch in Britain, and the self-restraint of America.

As previously indicated, however, this serious loss in the export trade to America was largely compensated for elsewhere, as the following table shows:[85]

Year	Exports to Europe	Exports to Africa	Exports to Asia	Exports to U. S. A.	Exports to America, exclusive of U. S. A.	Total
1806	£11,363,635	£1,163,744	£2,937,895	£12,389,488	£10,877,968	£38,732,730
1807	9,002,237	765,468	3,359,226	11,846,513	10,439,423	35,412,867
1808	9,016,033	633,125	3,524,823	5,241,739	16,591,871	35,007,501

The table of imports, representing a decline of £4,779,-424 (real value) in the year of embargo, is impressive testimony to the determination of the American executive. But gains in other directions enabled the British customs to close the year with a net loss of imports, from Europe, Africa, and America, of only £1,668,633.[86] This slight effect upon British total imports, amounting to less than seven per cent. all told, really explains the failure of the embargo. Couple this with a net loss of only £405,276 in exports out of a total trade amounting to more than £35,000,000, and the stability of British commerce is evident. It is not easy to see how even a total cessation of American exports, an ideal never attainable in a fallen and smuggling world,[87] could

[85] G. R. Porter, *The Progress of the Nation*, p. 479.

[86] *Journals of the House of Commons*, LXIV. 549, and p. 64, for a more general chart of imports from Europe, Africa, and America. The totals for the years 1807, 1808, and 1809 were £25,089,136, £25,453,149, and £23,784,516 respectively. For an interesting chart of timber imports, see G. R. Porter, *The Progress of the Nation*, p. 425.

[87] Hist. MSS Comm., *Fortescue MSS*. N. Vansittart to Lord Auckland, enclosure in a letter to Lord Grenville of June 24, p. 207. "He [Irving] afterwards mentioned that for some weeks past, trade had begun to be more brisk than it had been; and that in particular very large shipments were making to America by old and established houses. He, however, believed they cleared out for Nova Scotia, and not for the

have achieved its object. American products were needed. They were essential to the orderly progress and expansion of British industry. Their absence worked hardship in various industries and raised the price of food to the toiler. Yet Great Britain somehow "carried on." Even the fresh resources of a new continent could not assure to America monopoly control against a power whose flag sailed every sea.[88]

The embargo was, however, a two-edged sword, and if the thrust was slightly weak, the parry proved the master. Vast speculations in South America and huge smuggling operations in Canada but ill concealed the fact that American isolation barred Great Britain from her richest export market and upset the balance of trade in a manner disconcerting. Goods, British and Irish, to the value of £12,389,488, entered America in 1806. A slight falling off was apparent in the following year. But in 1808 the exports shrunk to £5,241,739, appalling tribute to the embargo as an engine of commercial wrath. Nor was the recovery to £7,258,500 in 1809 wholly satisfying,[89] not least among the embarrassments of the period being the dislocation of foreign exchange, a condition for which the embargo, if not wholly, was at least partially responsible.

United States; which circumstance confirms what we have seen in the American papers respecting the great smuggling in the Bay of Fundy." See also the *Life and Correspondence of Rufus King*, V. 144, for the same idea.

[88] Hist. MSS. Comm., *Fortescue MSS.*, p. 223. Lord Auckland to Lord Grenville, October 10, 1808. "The East and West India importations have certainly been very great; but the warehouses are filled to the brim, and the duties, therefore, are not received."

[89] G. R. Porter, *The Progress of the Nation*, p. 479. But see *Journals of the House of Commons*, LXIV. Appendix A, p. 648, for totals of 1807, £12,865,551; 1808, £12,097,942; 1809, £5,302,866; and Hist. MSS Comm., *Fortescue MSS*, February 15, 1809, p. 297, where loss of exports is given as £6,000,000.
Imports,   1,551,000.

£7,551,000.

American commerce had long been the mainstay of British foreign exchange. Under normal conditions, the direct American trade supplied Great Britain with cotton, lumber, flax, and tobacco. But America was still more important as a market, and the balance of trade was high in favor of Great Britain. The contrary was true on the Continent. It, too, looked to America for raw materials and staples, but had never secured the American market in turn. The reasons for this are well known. Colonial America had been a British trade monopoly, and ignorance of the importance of the market, unfamiliarity with American tastes and demands, and preoccupation with a political turmoil ever since 1789, had debarred Continental Europe from any real American foothold. The consequences of this for the balance of trade and foreign exchange were that Great Britain, with a margin of sales to America, drew for payment upon American debtors on the Continent, adjusting the balance by only a slight transfer of gold. To disturb this balance would mean the outward movement of gold. Precisely this happened, and at a time of unprecedented financial stress, the operations of the exchequer were hampered by a rise in gold from a normal of 80s. an ounce in 1807 to 91s. in 1809; 97s. 6d. in 1811; 105s. in 1812; and 110s. in 1813.[90] So serious a rise in the price of gold exercised of necessity a disturbing influence upon wage and commodity prices and brought home to the working man, indirectly it may be admitted, the evils of the embargo and of the abnormal commercial relations which succeeded it.

The export and import tables cited in this chapter were officially printed and therefore common property. Nor was their significance ignored. A modern statistician estimates that, from 1805 to 1807 inclusive, America absorbed nearly one third of British exports.[91] A trade of such magnitude

[90] G. R. Porter, *The Progress of the Nation,* p. 499.

interested the entire nation, and its peril furnished ammunition to the leaders of the opposition, eager to "convince his
majesty's ministers of the ruinous tendency" of the Orders in
Council.[92]   Individual quarters were compared unfavorably
with those of the year preceding;[93] reduced imports were
traced to their source in the Orders in Council;[94] and diminishing exports, bad though their showing, were declared to
be short of the whole truth, since Ireland and Scotland were
omitted—"giving them, therefore, a proportionate share,
the diminution of our commerce may fairly be estimated at
£14,000,000."[95]   By the opposition, at any rate, most evils
of the day were attributed to the Orders, such responsibility
for them as belonged to the Decrees being ignored.   Nor
was it sufficiently consoling that America suffered also,[96]
though the vulgar might find amusement in figure juggling
as to the $48,000,000 supposed American damage.[97]

   With estimates of loss running as high as £14,000,000,
it is apparent that the pressure of the embargo was serious.
Indeed, in the view of some, only a series of fortuitous circumstances averted an actual catastrophe:

We allude to the opening of Spain and Portugal, and our military
expeditions in these countries—the struggle made by Sweden, and
the increased communication with Brazil and Spanish America—
not to mention the fact that the year which gives this amount of loss
comprehends the period when shipments were made on both sides,
before the operation of the embargo, and when hazards were run
by neutral adventurers, upon the presumption that neither of the
regulations would be enforced as they actually were.   Had it not
been for these circumstances, our loss of trade in consequence of
the Orders would probably have been more than double what it

   [91] *Ibid.*, p. 497.
   [92] Hansard, *Parliamentary Debates*, 1st Ser., XI. 708, May 30, 1808.
(See also Hist. MSS Comm., *Fortescue MSS*, p. 302, April 14, 1809.)
   [93] *Ibid.*, p. 707, May 30, 1808.
   [94] *Ibid.*, p. 1129, July 1, 1808.
   [95] *Ibid.*, 1st Ser., XI. 780, February 17, 1809.   (See also *Edinburgh Review*, XIV. 450, July, 1809.)
   [96] *Ibid.*, p. 708.
   [97] *Annual Register*, 1808, pp. 85, 86, quoting from a New York paper.

actually was; and this boasted cure for our commercial embarrassments would, in all probability, have reduced our whole foreign
trade to a little wretched smuggling in Europe and America.[98]

Thus British testimony bears witness to the hardships
imposed by the embargo. The demoralization of the cotton
industry and the desperate measures to conserve the food
supply are themselves sufficient proof that the entire economic
balance was menaced. Yet the embargo wholly failed in
its political purpose, for the Orders in Council, against
which it was aimed, remained in force. How near it
came to achieving its end can never be known. The pre-
cise degree of economic pressure equal to conquering a proud
people defies calculation; and the ability of any single nation
to impose that pressure upon the mistress of the seas might
well be doubted. Certainly no nation should have anticipated
results so gigantic within one year, and the embargo expired in March, 1809. Though conditions in England warranted a continuation of the experiment, America lacked
resolution to pursue it further.

Many factors contributed to its abandonment, not least
of which was the psychological. The embargo was too negative. The British blockade of Europe was, in contrast, positive. Britain's clutch upon Napoleon was not a mere refusal
to ship goods to his coast; it was the will and the power
to prevent others from doing so, either. America in the
nature of things was unprepared to take similar action against
Great Britain. Limited to a passive rôle, she played it with
tolerable efficiency, but gave it too brief a trial. Britain's
more active blockade required five years to produce results.
These came at length with the general uprising of a starving
Europe. The "Battle of the Nations" testified to the groaning of the peoples under an economic yoke almost as galling
as Napoleon's open tyranny.

[98] *Edinburgh Review*, XIV. 450, July, 1809.

Moreover, the British blockade of Europe was openly belligerent. It enlisted the good will of the nation in a fight for existence. For this, no sacrifice would be too great. For America, the contrary held true. Self-denial is heroic, but undramatic. To ruin oneself might starve the enemy, but his injuries were to be imagined; one's own were real. America played blindfold, and the game lacked spirit. Besides, there were none of the prizes of aggressive action, no growing merchant marine to warm the dried veins of rich old merchants, no naval heroes "of Baltic and of Nile" to stir the pulse of youth.

It is pleasant to turn from the more sordid aspects of Orders and embargo to the virtues they called forth. On either side the really noteworthy feature of the embargo is its spiritual contribution. The dogged resolution of England, firm to endure all things, even unto the end; the idealism of America, willing to follow Jefferson in a grand experiment for securing the honor and dignity of his country without the blood cost of war, shine from out the mistakes and miseries of the times as two Anglo-Saxon traits of enduring greatness.

CHAPTER XI

FRANCE AND THE EMBARGO

When Napoleon issued the decrees which drove America into the ranks of his enemies, he could scarcely have harbored any illusions as to the strength of American friendship. Whatever this may have been originally, the neutrality of Washington and the vigor of Adams had shown that American policies were guided by living issues rather than by dead memories, nor was there anything in the record of Jefferson himself to indicate that sentiment for France outweighed the interest of America. The estimate which Adet had transmitted to the department of foreign affairs in 1796, on the occasion of Jefferson's election to the vice-presidency had, indeed, proved singularly prophetic:

I have been brought to the conclusion in this connection, Citizen Minister, that America will have only cause for congratulation for having summoned this man to the second place in the State. I do not know whether, as I am assured, we shall always find in him a man entirely devoted to our interests. Mr. Jefferson loves us, because he detests England; he seeks a rapprochement with us, because he distrusts us less than Great Britain; but he would change perhaps tomorrow from a sentiment favorable to us, if to-morrow Great Britain should cease to inspire him with fears. Jefferson, although a friend of liberty and of science, although an admirer of the efforts which we have put forth to break our chains and dissipate the cloud of ignorance which oppresses the hope of humanity, Jefferson, I say, is an American, and by just so much, he cannot be sincerely our friend. An American is the enemy born of all the European peoples.[1]

The Napoleonic decrees were, in fact, the culmination of a growing resentment at the independent Americanism described by Adet. France, whose original help to the American Revolution rested on dynastic and European aims, expected

---

[1] *American Historical Association, Annual Report,* 1903, II. 983, "Correspondence of French Ministers, 1791-1797."

from the nation she had helped to found a gratitude which nations seldom feel. Experience had demonstrated that America was as fully the slave of self-interest as were the powers of Europe. But truth carried with it the sting of disillusionment.[2] In their term of power, the Federalists had courted mercantile Britain to the neglect of Jacobin France, and the treaty of 1778 had become a dead letter long before its term expired. Even where her own interest seemed to demand action, America had been passive. The principle that free ships make free goods was her most cherished innovation in the law of nations. But she declined to hazard war on its behalf. And the Directory only complicated matters by its decision to treat neutrals in whatever way they allowed themselves to be treated by England. In 1798, war itself was averted only by the narrowest margin.

On becoming First Consul, Napoleon reversed the policy of the Directory. He hastened to propitiate the Americans. He wished to enlist them as more active champions of neutral rights at sea. He ceased to urge the treaty of 1778, grown illusory in practice. His real solicitude was for certain principles of international law. These he deemed indispensable and in October, 1800, he drafted a treaty to include them.

The treaty affirmed the principle that free ships make free goods. It recognized the possibility of contraband of war, but limited the items to a specified list and exempted food stuffs. One provision asserted the right of neutrals to enter all ports not subject to a real blockade. Neutral merchantmen must recognize the right of search save when in the convoy of warships. In the latter case, the military flag was to be sufficient guarantee against fraud. In becoming a signatory of the treaty, America was to obligate herself to a defence of its principles against their infraction by

---

[2] This is quite elaborately analyzed by M. A. Thiers in *Histoire du Consulat et de l'Empire*, II. 125-127.

England.[3] Thus almost the first act of Napoleon's administration was a move to align America with himself in a future naval war. He based his plan on the identity of maritime interests between the two powers. His terms were those which Americans themselves desired. The treaty was signed, but its terms were never consummated.

The secret lies in the string attached. America was not yet strong enough to fight for any principle less vital than independence. It is true the principles which Napoleon was seeking to engraft upon international law were very dear to America's heart. Her policy was, however, to secure their adoption by treaty with individual powers. In this way they would at last become integral in the law of nations, and America greatly the gainer. But it would be folly to mortgage the future and jeopardize our national existence for a non-essential. To America, the Napoleonic scheme merely pictured an ideal. The vision of the freedom of the seas was attractive to a weak and pacific neutral, but it was scarcely a matter of life and death, and this an ill-judged war with Great Britain might be.

Napoleon's own self-interest was obvious. He had every reason to wish trade unhampered. If Great Britain once recognized the freedom of the seas, the lion's claws were pared, and Napoleon in his conquest of Europe need fear no strangling at his throat. He assumed that peaceful America, for an opposite but equally cogent reason, would crave the same untrammeled commerce. Europe needed the goods; America needed the profits. If America could be induced to fight for these profits under the guise of solicitude for righteous principles in the law of nations, so much the better for Napoleon. He would be more likely to have his imports. And he would add an open enemy to England.

The weak link in the scheme was Napoleon's false estimate of American common sense and his misconception of

[3] M. A. Thiers, *L'Histoire du Consulat et de l'Empire*, II. 217-219.

sectional and political interests within the states. Commercial America might desire to fight for her rights, but prudence forbade too great a risk. Besides, commercial America was Anglophile, and willing to go far in submission to British desires. Much of America, on the other hand, despised commerce altogether. This was especially true at the South. Southern men, notwithstanding sentiments which were Gallophile, perceived no motive of self-interest urging them to espouse the cause of France for the sake of Yankee shippers. Their leader, Jefferson, it might be added, had adopted economy and pacifism as guiding principles. Thus, as the century opened, all the dominant forces in America wrought for peace. To overcome this triple weight of inertia became an important object of Napoleon's diplomacy from 1800 to 1807.

The sale of Louisiana was the outstanding manifestation of Napoleon's desire to conciliate. It solved the western problem by removing a source of endless friction between the United States and France. For the moment, Jefferson was justified in his opinion that "Though clouds may occasionally obscure the foreign horizon between us, yet there is a fund of friendship and attachment between the two nations which will always in time dispel these nebulosities."[4] By removing this source of friction and antagonism, Napoleon averted the possible danger of an Anglo-American alliance, for had not Jefferson said:

The day that France takes possession of New Orleans fixes the sentence which is to restrain her forever within her low water mark. It seals the union of two nations who in conjunction can maintain exclusive possession of the ocean. From that moment we must marry ourselves to the British fleet and nation. We must turn all our attention to a maritime force for which our resources place us on very high grounds.[5]

[4] *The Works of Thomas Jefferson*, IX. 357, March 16, 1802.
[5] *Ibid.*, IX. 364, April 18, 1802. See also IX. 366. Convincing testimony, this, to Adet's description of Jefferson's single-minded Americanism.

Jefferson knew how to use a British alliance as leverage against France, and for nearly a year before the purchase he dangled it as a nightmare before Napoleon.[6]   On the administrative side, he planned to pour such a population into the western country that, in the event of war, Louisiana would fall into our lap, an easy prize.[7]   But thanks to the good sense of Napoleon, Jefferson secured his inland empire without paying the price of war or of European entanglements.[8]

If Jefferson, in 1803, thought that the Louisiana purchase had secured us "the course of a peaceful nation,"[9] which had only to bide its time until the next European conflict should toss Florida into her lap,[10] he was taking into account only our progress landward.   Our outlook seaward was less promising, and, in 1804 and 1805, the chief danger to maritime security seemed to emanate from France.   In 1804, Jefferson was reduced to the melancholy admission that "We cannot be respected by France as a neutral nation, nor by the world ourselves as an independent one, if we do not take effectual measures to support, at every risk, our authority in our own harbors."[11]

Just at the time when American relations with France were suffering this increased strain, the tension with Great Britain appeared to relax.   The brief ministry of Charles James Fox seemed to offer promise of a cordiality long unknown, and the project of an Anglo-American alliance in the event of war between the United States and either France or Spain was agitated once more.[12]   In August, 1805, Jeffer-

[6] *The Works of Thomas Jefferson*, IX. 386, July 13, 1802; IX. 437, February 1, 1803; I. 372, April 8, 1803.
[7] *Ibid.*, IX. 464, April 30, 1803.
[8] For his complacency on this account, see his paean of neutrality, *ibid.*, X. 32, October 4, 1803.
[9] *Ibid.*, X. 28, August 9, 1803.
[10] *Ibid.*, X. 29.
[11] *Ibid.*, X. 95, August 15, 1804, to James Madison.
[12] *Ibid.*, X. 168, August 4, 1805.

son was quite feverish about it. "I am strongly impressed," he wrote the secretary of state, "with a belief of hostile and treacherous intentions against us on the part of France, and that we should lose no time in securing something more than a mutual friendship with England."[13]   Even so, he preferred that the treaty should be provisional, should operate solely for the duration of the existing war in Europe, and then only in the event of hostilities between the United States and France or Spain.[14] He believed that a knowledge of the mere existence of such a treaty would bind France and Spain to keep the peace.

But autumn frosts soon chilled an August ardor. By October, Jefferson was congratulating himself that an Anglo-American entente had not eventuated. "It would have been disagreeable," he conceded, "to have proposed closer connections with England at the moment when so much just clamour exists against her for her new encroachments on neutral rights."[15] It was the fate of America to encounter only rebuffs from either belligerent. Our friendship was valued as little as our hostility was feared. There was nothing in the politics of 1805 to augur American attachment toward either France or Great Britain except as self-interest might later direct.

The rift in the clouds, presaged by the sympathy of Fox and Jefferson, closed again with the death of the former, and, under the Portland ministry, all the old antagonisms revived. Nevertheless, the pendulum had far to swing between projected alliance and actual warfare. The same observers who, in February, 1806, predicted that America would not fight either Great Britain or Spain,[16] declared, in

[13] *The Works of Thomas Jefferson*, X. 171, August 25, 1805.
[14] *Ibid.*, X. 172-173, August 27, 1805.
[15] *Ibid.*, X. 179-180, October 25, 1805. To W. C. Nicholas.
[16] "The Correspondence of J. A. Bayard," in *Annual Report of American Historical Association*, 1913, II. 166. See also pp. 168, 169, February 25, 1806.

March, that war was imminent.[17] But these were not in
the confidence of the administration. At the moment when
they were scenting war, Jefferson was assuring a friend that
the government aspired to nothing beyond a rigid neutrality.
"We were not disposed to join in league with Britain, under
any belief that she is fighting for the liberties of mankind
& to enter into war with Spain, & consequently France.—We
are for a peaceable accommodation with all those nations, if
it can be effected honorably."[18]

Six years had now gone by since Napoleon's bid for
American friendship, and the net result of these six years
was a neutrality surprisingly genuine. America stood alone,
watchful of her own self interest, skeptical of European
schemes. Neither France nor Great Britain could bridge the
gulf between America and herself. Each lacked the wisdom to convert neutrality into friendship. Soon each was
to rival the other in turning honest neutrality into bitterness
and rancor. Neither quite appreciated what Jefferson epito-
mized in a letter to Monroe at London, which, so far as his
words go, might have been addressed with equal propriety
to Armstrong at Paris. Picturing America's importance to
European belligerents, he says:

No two countries upon earth have so many points of common interest & friendship; & their rulers must be great bunglers, indeed,
if, with such disposition, they break them asunder. The only rivalry
that can arise is on the ocean. . . . We have the seamen &
materials for 50. ships of the line, & half that number of frigates;
and were France to give us the money & England the disposition to
equip them, they would give to England serious proofs of the stock
from which they are sprung, & the school in which they have been
taught; and added to the effects of the immensity of sea coast lately
united under one power, would leave the state of the ocean no longer
problematical. Were, on the other hand, England to give the money,
& France the disposition to place us on the sea in all our force, the
whole world, out of the continent of Europe, might be our joint
monopoly. We wish for neither of these scenes. We ask for peace

[17] "The Correspondence of J. A. Bayard," *loc. cit.*, p. 169, March 16,
1806.
[18] *The Works of Thomas Jefferson*, X. 241, March 22, 1806.

& justice from all nations; & we will remain uprightly neutral in fact, tho' leaning in belief to the opinion that an English ascendancy on the ocean is safer for us than that of France.[19]

The vision thus conjured up by Jefferson embraced a more distant future than he realized. But it already possessed enough elements of truth to condemn the judgment of any European who deliberately affronted the American people. And when America was finally driven away from the possibility of alliance with either Great Britain or France[20] and forced back upon a neutrality as painful as it was possibly unnecessary, European statesmanship proved itself inadequate. Certainly the American policy of Napoleon from 1800 to 1807, despite brilliant high lights, failed of its objective, and this failure casts discredit upon his statesmanship as a whole. Toward America herself he came to feel all the bitterness of one who has failed.

It would appear that Napoleon's approach to the Continental System, which so completely alienated America, was "fortuitous rather than designed."[21] He inherited it from the Revolution and the Directory. In renewing its application, his primary objective was England. The American implications were, in Napoleon's estimation, only incidental. Even when Champagny, his minister of foreign affairs, called attention to the growing demand in America for silk and other French manufactures and reminded him of the interest felt by French chambers of commerce in the possibilities of extending the trade, Napoleon overlooked the situation.[22] Certainly his decision in September, 1807, respecting a demand for the release of fifty or sixty Americans taken on English warships and detained at Lorient, was altogether

[19] *Ibid.*, X. 263, May 4, 1806.
[20] Jefferson was so irritated with England following the *Chesapeake* Affair that he almost inclined to a French alliance. *The Works of Thomas Jefferson*, X. 483, August 21, 1807. To T. Leiper.
[21] Frank Edgar Melvin, *Napoleon's Navigation System*, p. 10.
[22] *Ibid.*, pp. 19-21.

arbitrary.[23]   It was apparent that Armstrong's hopes that
the general rigor of the Continental System would be relaxed in favor of America had no basis in fact.   And his declaration to Monroe, in July, 1807, that the treaty of 1800 had
not been violated was unduly optimistic.[24]

America as a neutral had, of course, a vital interest in
the recognition which Napoleon might continue to accord
to neutral flags.   The Emperor's pronouncement on this
question, coming only a week after the decision with reference to the captives, was far from encouraging:

In the actual circumstances, navigation offers all sorts of difficulties.
France is not able to regard flags as neutral without consideration.
That of America exposed though it be to the insults of England,
has a kind of existence, since the English still preserve toward it
some measure of regard and since it imposes somewhat upon them.
That of Portugal and that of Denmark no longer exist.   The flag
of the small cities of Germany (Hanseatic) whose names are
scarcely known, has been subjected by the English to whatever
legislation suits their convenience.   England allows it entry to the
ports of France solely as under her dependence and trading for her
interest.   It is necessary to propose a plan of a decree to declare
that ships which enter flying these flags may not go out again, and
that they should be subjected to all the rigors of a blockade.   For
each a particular instruction and legal procedure must be devised.[25]

It will be noticed that, in projecting this drastic code,
Napoleon made some exception in the case of America.
Something of the same solicitude softened his determination to deny an exequatur to an American consul whose
acceptance of British honors had subjected him to suspicion:

Monsieur de Champagny, my intention is to remove the exequatur
from Mr. —————, American consul at Genoa.   He wears a
Maltese cross which the English have given him, something which
is contrary to the American Constitution, and this is otherwise a

[23] *Correspondance de Napoléon Ier*, XVI. No. 13102, September 2,
1807.

[24] Frank Edgar Melvin, *Napoleon's Navigation System*, p. 37.

[25] *Correspondance de Napoléon Ier*, XVI. 20, No. 13135, September 9,
1807.   These retaliatory schemes were drawn up on September 18th but
were not published until December.   See *American State Papers*, Foreign Relations, III. 261.

bad case. You will forewarn the Minister of the United States of
this intention. I am giving orders to the Minister of Police to remove Mr.————— from Genoa.[26]

And in November, just on the eve of the British Orders in
Council of the eleventh, Napoleon underwent a spasm of
caution. "The English," he informed his chief of police,
Fouché, "are plotting a scheme at Moreau for involving us
with the United States of America. Care is needed that our
newspapers make no mention of this."[27] But ten days more,
and this veil of caution was thrown to the winds, while Napoleon proceeded to berate America with a sarcasm worthy
of Canning:

> Monsieur de Champagny, reply to the American minister that,
> since America allows her ships to be visited, she is adopting the
> principle that the flag does not cover merchandise, that since she
> recognizes the absurd laws of the English blockade, she consents
> that her vessels be constantly halted, returned to England and
> thereby turned aside from their navigation, why do not the Amer-
> icans endure the blockade of France? Certainly France is no more
> blockaded by England than England is by France. Why don't the
> Americans suffer equally the visit of French war-ships? To be
> sure, France recognizes that these measures are unjust, illegal and
> violative of the sovereignty of nations. But it is incumbent upon
> the nations to resort to force and to come out boldly against actions
> which dishonor them and encroach upon their independence.[28]

Napoleon's policy was frankly to force America into
war. But to accomplish this he pursued the wrong tack.
For France to heap insult and injury upon the victim of
British insult and injury was merely to confirm America in
hatred of both antagonists. Her leaders rightly insisted that
the embargo to which America was driven was a protest
not against Britain or France singly, but against "contem-
poraneous aggressions of the belligerent Powers, equally
unprovoked and equally indefensible on the presumed ground
of acquiescence."[29] This being so, "war with one of the

---

[26] *Ibid.*, XVI. 67, October 6, 1807.
[27] *Ibid.*, XVI. 139, November 5, 1807.
[28] *Ibid.*, XVI. 165, November 15, 1807.
[29] *American State Papers*, Foreign Relations, III. 261. Also III. 260.

belligerents, only, would be submission to the edicts and will of the other; and a repeal, in whole or in part, of the embargo, must necessarily be war or submission."[30]   Napoleon was playing too vast a game to view it from all angles, but his American policy, by driving America into her only recourse under the circumstances, played into the hands of England by increasing the effectiveness of the blockade.

The embargo which Napoleon's own edicts invited produced an immediate effect to which even the larger aspect of his policy could not blind the Emperor. And the confidence expressed in his instructions of January 12, 1808, to Champagny, that America would move with docility along the path he marked for her,[31] was converted, by February, to the recognition in a dim sort of way that America could not be bullied into partnership with him.[32]   It was then that he cast about for motives nearer home which might lure America from her isolation. He thought he had found the right bait in Florida, and early in February, 1808, he offered to secure Florida in exchange for an alliance. The instructions to Champagny are sufficiently explicit. "Inform the American minister verbally, that whenever war should be declared between America and England, and when in consequence of this war the Americans should push troops into the Floridas to succour the Spaniards and repel the English, I shall be pleased. You will even give him to understand that in the event of America's desiring to enter upon a treaty of alliance with me and to make common cause, I shall be pleased to intervene with the Court of Spain in order to obtain the cession of the same Floridas in favor of the Americans."[33]

[30] American State Papers, Foreign Relations, III. 261.

[31] Correspondance de Napoléon Ier, XVI. 244, January 12, 1808.

[32] American State Papers, Foreign Relations, III. 249, February 8, 1808. Madison's instructions to Armstrong describe the Napoleonic decree as "an empty menace."

[33] Correspondance de Napoléon Ier, XVI. 301, February 2, 1808.

Finding America deaf to blandishments, Napoleon reverted to threats and insults, a form of communication more native to his genius.   The following instructions to Champagny prove that his hand had lost none of its cunning:

Monsieur de Champagny, it is necessary to write to the American
minister, in reply to his letters of the fourth and the eighth, that
France has contracted engagements with America, has negotiated
with her a treaty based on the principle that the flag covers merchandise, and that even if he had not solemnly proclaimed this principle,
His Majesty would proclaim it again; that His Majesty has dealt
with America independent, not with America in chains; that if she
submits to the decree of the King of England of the eleventh of
November, she thereby renounces the protection of her flag; but
that if the Americans, as His Majesty cannot doubt without impugn-
ing their honor, treat this as an act of war, he is prepared to do
justice to all.   In all the possible wars in which other maritime
powers than France find themselves involved, His Majesty holds
fast to his principle of the independence of the flag, and does not
insist upon the right of visit on any vessel; but His Majesty already possesses the right, and this right is the fundamental principle of his public law, of demanding that every nation maintain
the independence of its flag, all the sovereigns being guardians of
their independence and of their sovereignty.[34]

America was by now the only recognized neutral,[35]
Denmark and the Hansa Towns no longer being accounted
such.   And toward America, Napoleon suffered from divided
counsels.   The Milan Decree of December, 1807, had been
followed by a sequestration of neutral shipping in French
ports.   America had escaped at first, but for a few days only.
When, however, Napoleon changed his tactics from brow-
beating to bribery, he planned a modification of the navigation policy.   A council to consider this was summoned for
February 14, 1808.   But just before it met news arrived
of the American embargo; and Napoleon, in his wrath,
vowed that America should "be compelled to take the positive
character either of allies or of neutrals.[36]   The intercessions

---

[34] *Ibid.,* XVI. 319-320, February 11, 1808.
[35] Frank Edgar Melvin, *Napoleon's Navigation System,* p. 64.
[36] *Ibid.,* p. 71.

of La Fayette, Marbois, Talleyrand, Fouché, Cretet, and Champagny brought Napoleon once more, in March, 1808, to a half promise of relaxation in favor of the United States. But before the month was out he had reverted to a policy of harshness, and, in April, issued the Bayonne Decree, in which he asserted that in seizing American ships he was merely aiding the American government in the overseas enforcement of its own embargo.[37]

The irony of the situation was not lost upon the archconspirator. The embargo had sealed the lips of official protest against any fate meted out to its violators, and Napoleon took advantage of this restraint to boast of his piracies against American shipping as only a friendly assistance to a government unable to punish its own rebels. "Inform the American minister," he commanded Champagny on March 31, "that a large number of American ships laden with colonial products pretend to be coming from America, but are in reality hailing from London. Every ship laden with colonial products ought to be confiscated, because the embargo which the Americans have imposed in their ports gives the assurance that these ships do not come from America."[38]

Napoleon was soon to learn that the embargo which he satirized so mockingly was exposing his own West India possessions to utter ruin. The disastrous effects of the embargo upon the British West Indies have been noted elsewhere, and this notwithstanding British control of the seas. The French West Indies, lacking such an advantage, were even more exposed. Napoleon learned the situation while at Bordeaux in April, 1808. He determined to rescue his colonies by convoys undertaken by private initiative with

[37] Frank Edgar Melvin, op. cit., pp. 71-72.

[38] Correspondance de Napoléon Ier, XVI. 459, March 31, 1808. See also ibid., XVII. 60, May 5, 1808; ibid., XVII. 86, May 10, 1808; ibid., XVII. 205, 329, 364.

government subvention.[39]   A far better hope for their
provisioning lay, of course, in a friendly understanding with
the United States, but Napoleon was reluctant to admit the
necessity.

In the diplomatic duel, Armstrong, for the American
government, parried French attacks by asking in his turn
if France had ever squared either her theory or her practice
with the principles of international law, or had ever sought
any other justification for her conduct than American acquiescence in British measures?[40]   And Madison pointed out
the advantages which France would gain by abandoning
the Decrees.   Great Britain would either have to follow
suit, thus lifting the blockade, or; if she refused to do so,
would stand isolated against the combined power of France
and the United States.[41]   America, in her turn, was baiting
the hook for an alliance.   But her offer to restore commerce
proved as vain as Napoleon's offer to turn over Florida.[42]
Diplomacy, in the spring and summer of 1808, accomplished
little for either France or America.   Napoleon clung to the
idea that Great Britain would ultimately force America into
war.   Meanwhile, until America should see fit to defend herself, he did not propose to recognize her flag.   "We recognize no flag that permits itself to be violated.   These are our
principles!" he announced in May, 1808.[43]

General Armstrong found his position most discouraging.   But in August, as a sort of last effort, he made strong
representations as to the help which American shipping
could render to France herself, if allowed to ply between
French and British ports.[44]   His arguments made a far

[39] Frank Edgar Melvin, *Napoleon's Navigation System,* p. 55.
[40] *American State Papers,* Foreign Relations, III. 252, April 2, 1808.
[41] *Ibid.,* III. 252, May 2, 1808; also III. 222.
[42] He soon repented of this offer.   See a letter to Champagny of
June 21, 1808, in *Correspondance de Napoléon Ier,* XVII. 326-327.
[43] *Correspondance de Napoléon Ier,* XVII. 121, May 14, 1808.   To
Joachim, Grand Duc de Berg.
[44] Frank Edgar Melvin, *op. cit.,* p. 73.

deeper impression than he knew,[45] though, while Napoleon was revolving them thoroughly, Armstrong, with no intimation of any prospective modification in French policy, wrote in great dejection to Madison:

We have somewhat overrated our means of coercing the two great belligerents to a course of justice. The embargo is a measure calculated, above any other, to keep us whole and keep us in peace, but beyond this, you must not count upon it. Here it is not felt, and in England (in the midst of the more recent and interesting events of the day) it is forgotten.

I hope that, unless France shall do us justice, we will raise the embargo, and make in its stead the experiment of an armed commerce. Should she adhere to her wicked and foolish measures, we ought not to content ourselves with doing this; there is much, very much besides that we can do, and we ought not to omit doing all we can, because it is believed here that we cannot do much, and even that we will not do what we have the power of doing.[46]

The recommendation of Armstrong did eventually contribute to the modification of Napoleon's Continental System through the granting of special licenses for ships.[47] Napoleon would have included American ships among those favored in this manner had not Armstrong protested that America could not submit to foreign licenses for the high seas trade.[48] Armstrong's mission thus came nearer to success than either he or his countrymen knew. The same was true of the embargo itself. For, notwithstanding his fundamentally false attitude toward the embargo and the futility of Franco-American diplomacy under the blockade, Napoleon had, after all, enough intellectual detachment to perceive the wisdom of the American position and, where no object was to be gained by insulting the United States, even to praise her conduct. Thus, in a "Report to the Emperor," ostensibly composed by Champagny, but really the

[45] Frank Edgar Melvin, *op. cit.*, pp. 74-76.
[46] *American State Papers*, Foreign Relations, III. 256, August 30, 1808.
[47] Frank Edgar Melvin, *op. cit.*, p. 76.
[48] *Ibid.*, p. 101.

work of Napoleon himself, he admits that "The Americans, that people which intrusts its fortune, its prosperity, and almost its existence to commerce, has given the example of a great and courageous sacrifice. It has forbidden itself, by a general embargo, all commerce, all interchange, rather than submit shamefully to that tribute which the English pretend to impose upon the navigators of all nations."[49] And in a speech from the throne delivered at the opening of the *Corps Legislatif* on October 25, 1808, he actually paid a tribute of homage: "The United States of America have preferred to give up commerce and the sea rather than to recognize a state of slavery upon those elements."[50]

Had Napoleon based his earlier course of action upon these fine sentiments, the United States might possibly have become his ally,[51] with incalculable effect upon the Emperor's own destiny and that of Europe. But the golden opportunity passed unseized. Viewed from the standpoint of France and Continental Europe, the embargo is not a test of endurance between American shippers and European consumers, not even a step in the evolution of a new law of the seas, but rather an episode in the economic and finally the military and political downfall of Napoleon.

[49] *Correspondance de Napoléon Ier*, XVII. 485.
[50] *Ibid.*, XVIII. 21, October 25, 1808.
[51] H. E. Egerton, *British Policy in Europe to the End of the 19th Century*, p. 386, concurs in this opinion.

CHAPTER XII

CONCLUSION

In the light of the preceding chapters, one may evaluate the embargo in terms not necessarily novel, but suggestive perhaps of a fairer estimate of its place in Jeffersonian philosophy and American experience than it has received. It was apparent from the outset of the present study that Jefferson, in spite of various inconsistencies, was essentially pacific in his philosophy, that the vicissitudes of his pre-presidential career did not swerve him from this underlying basis of thought, but rather confirmed him in the idea of finding means to combat war with instruments of peace. So that when, in his second term as president, provocation for war became extreme, the weapon lay ready forged for injuring our foes at no blood cost to ourselves.

The urgency of the crisis and the vast prestige of the President carried through a measure which created its own opposition. And the personal experience of Jefferson in enforcing his favorite legislation is an ever memorable object lesson in the tribulations of those who would lead mankind along untrodden paths. The patriotism and self-denial of men who shared the President's vision, and the disloyalty and selfishness of men who failed to see the possibilities of economic pressure as a substitute for war, form an interesting background against which the harassed Jefferson appears at his unhappiest, yet at his best. The philosopher became perforce an administrator; while the excessive love of popularity, which was a possible blot on the true grandeur of his character, yielded place to a stern adherence to truth as Jefferson saw it, even at the cost of what had long been the dearest prize of his career.

In surveying the economic effects of the embargo in America, it would be rash to claim a new point of view, yet it may not exceed the truth to assert a larger increase in manufacturing than has been generally noted. This was most evident in the Middle States, was apparent also in New England, and was so exultantly anticipated in the South that, temporarily, its effects were as pronounced there as elsewhere and served to hold at least the Middle States and the South in a national solidarity, very wholesome as a counteractive to New England separatism.

The European aspects of the Napoleonic System and its circumvention by Great Britain have been so exhaustively studied that a fresh examination of the case can hardly expect to revolutionize the verdict. Yet a student who approaches the embargo from the viewpoint of Jefferson is pleased to find that, if the American opposition found friends and abettors in the British Government, at any rate the friends of the embargo in America could count for aid upon an opposition in England as highly placed as Pickering and his associates, and more generous and intelligent than they. As in the Revolution American patriots were really fighting the battles of Englsh liberty, so in 1808 the leaders of his Majesty's opposition were in reality better Americans than the misguided followers of Timothy Pickering.

An inquiry into the economic effect of the embargo in Great Britain also serves to show that Jefferson was right in the major premise that the embargo would exert an extreme pressure upon British industry. This pressure was, in fact, so great that Jefferson's mode of calculating is vindicated, notwithstanding the failure of the embargo to produce the political results anticipated. The reluctance of America to give embargo an adequate trial and the introduction of wholly unforeseen elements into the international situation, as, for example, in the British adventure in Spain, vitiated the conclusions of Jefferson, but failed to invalidate his philosophy and method. The combination of present loss of exports to Britain's leading customer and prospective surrender of a permanent market to that customer's own growing manufactures, was at least a minor anxiety, even to a power at death's grapple with Napoleon.

It has been recognized since the last of the old time Federalists entered into rest and the rancors of the period melted into the calm of history that Jefferson entered upon the embargo in the interest not of France, but of America. It was not necessary for the present study to stress a point so generally assumed. Nevertheless, these pages bear incidental testimony in abundance to the independence of the Jeffersonian position, for the more clearly the embargo stands forth as a product of Jefferson's personal experience and philosophy, the more self-evident it is that Jefferson was not the dupe and tool of a man whose whole scheme of existence was antithetical to his own, and whose entire character and position in history he despised.

In conclusion, then, one may claim for Jefferson a philosophical consciousness of his own purposes far beyond the mere opportunism of seizing any means to evade the issue forced by the Orders and Decrees. And one may still avoid the pitfalls of hero-worship while at the same time crediting a sage and a philosopher with a forceful adaptation of theory to practice, and with a plan which came near enough to success to vindicate its sponsor as a practical statesman. If Jefferson is not to rank with Sully and Wilson as an originator of grand designs and leagues of nations to end war, he at any rate deserves high rank as a friend of man, who used the means at hand to avert a primal curse.

BIBLIOGRAPHY

MANUSCRIPT COLLECTIONS IN THE LIBRARY OF CONGRESS

The Jefferson Papers.
The Ellis and Allan Papers.
The Nicholas Biddle Papers.
The Sylvanus Bourne Papers,
Broadsides.
The William Eustis Papers.
The Madison Papers.
The James Kent Papers.
The Diary of Daniel Mulford. Manuscript in the Library of Yale
   University, Transcript in the Library of Congress.
The Wilson Cary Nicholas Papers.
The David Porter Letter Book, MSS.
The William Taylor Papers.
The Van Buren Papers.

BOOKS, PAMPHLETS

ADAMS, HENRY, *Documents Relating to New England Federalism.*
Boston, 1877. *The Life of Albert Gallatin.* Philadelpia, 1879.
History of the United States of America. New York, 1891-1901.
ADAMS, JOHN, *The Life and Works of John Adams.* 10 vols. Boston, 1851-1856.
ADAMS, JOHN QUINCY, *Memoirs of John Quincy Adams.* 12 vols.
Philadelphia, 1874-1877. *The Writings of John Quincy Adams.*
7 vols. New York, 1913. *An Address of Members of the House
of Representatives of the Congress of the United States. To
their Constituents on the subject of the War with Great Britain.*
Hanover. Printed and sold by Charles Spear. (Pamphlet.)
Admiralty Reports, Volume I.
AMBLER, C. H., *Sectionalism in Virginia, 1776-1861.* Chicago, 1910.
American Historical Association, *Annual Report,* 1903. .*Corre-
spondence of French Ministers, 1791-1797.*
Ibid., 1913, Vol. II, *The Correspondence of J. A. Bayard.*
American State Papers, Foreign Relations, Vols. I and III.
ANDRÉADÈS, A., *A History of the Bank of England.* London, 1909.
Annals of Congress.
Annual Register, 1808.
BENTLEY, WILLIAM, *The Diary of William Bentley, D.D.* 4 vols.
Salem, Mass., 1905-1914.
BEVERIDGE, A. J., *Life of John Marshall.* 4 vols. Boston, 1916-1919.

BINNEY, CHARLES CHAUNCEY, *The Life of Horace Binney.* Philadelphia, 1903.

BISHOP, ABRAHAM, *Some Remarks and Extracts in Reply to Mr. Pickering's Letter on the Subject of the Embargo.* New Haven, 1808(?). (Pamphlet.)

BRADFORD, ALDEN, *History of Massachusetts.* Boston, 1835.

BURLAMAQUI, J. J., *The Principles of Natural Law* (5th Ed., Dublin, 1791.)

CANNING, GEORGE, *Speeches of the Rt. Hon. George Canning.* Philadelphia, 1835.

CONWAY, MONCURE D., *Life of Thomas Paine.* 2 vols. New York, 1892.

"The Disclosure"—No. 1. *Documents Relating to Violations and Evasions of the Laws During the Commercial Restrictions and Late War with Great Britain &c. Part First. Bath. Printed for the People. J. G. Torrey, Printer.* 1824. (Pamphlet.)

DODD, WILLIAM E., *John Taylor* in John P. Branch Historical Papers of Randolph Macon College, Vol. II. Richmond, 1901-1903.

DUKE OF BUCKINGHAM AND CHANDOS, *Memoirs of the Court & Cabinets of George III.* 4 vols. London, 1853-55.

EGERTON, H. E., *British Foreign Policy in Europe to the End of the 19th Century.* London, 1817.

ELLISON, THOMAS, *The Cotton Trade of Great Britain.* London, 1886.

GARLAND, HUGH A., *Life of John Randolph.* 2 vols. New York, 1854.

Hansard's *Parliamentary Debates,* 1st Ser., Vol. X.

HIGGINSON, THOMAS WENTWORTH, *Life and Times of Stephen Higginson.* Boston, 1907.

HUMPHREYS, FRANCIS LANDON, *The Life of Daniel Humphreys.* 2 vols. New York, 1917.

INGERSOLL, CHARLES JARED, *A View of the Rights and Wrongs, Power and Policy of the United States of America.* (Pamphlet. Philadelphia, 1808.)

JEFFERSON, THOMAS, *The Works of Thomas Jefferson.* Federal Edition. 12 vols. New York and London, 1904-1905.

JEFFERSON, THOMAS, *Thomas Jefferson Correspondence.* Printed from the Originals in the Collections of Wm. K. Bixby.

Journals of the House of Commons, Vol. 63.

Journals of the House of Lords, Vol. 46.

Journal of the House of Representatives, Vol. VI.

KING, RUFUS, *Life and Correspondence of Rufus King.* 6 vols. New York, 1894-1900.

KING, WILLIAM, *Mr. [William] King's Reply to a Pamphlet published at Bath, Me., 1825.* [Bath?] (Pamphlet.)

LATHROP, JOHN, D.D., *We Rejoice with Trembling.* A Discourse Delivered on the Day of Publick Thanksgiving in the State of Massachusetts, December 1, 1808. Boston, 1808. (Pamphlet Sermon.)

MADISON, JAMES, *The Writings of James Madison*, Hunt Edition. 9 vols. New York, 1900-1910.

McLAUGHLIN, J. FAIRFAX, *Matthew Lyon*. New York, 1900.

MELVIN, FRANK EDGAR, *Napoleon's Navigation System*. New York, 1919.

NAPOLEON, *Correspondance de Napoleon 1er, XVI*. 32 vols. Paris, 1858-1870.

PINKNEY, REV. WM., D.D., *The Life of Wm. Pinkney*. New York, 1853.

PORTER, G. R., *The Progress of the Nation*. Ed. F. W. Hirst. London, 1912.

QUINCY, EDMUND, *Life of Josiah Quincy*. 6th Ed. Boston, 1874.

RAVENEL, MRS. ST. JULIAN, *Life and Times of William Lowndes*. Boston, 1901.

Report of a Committee of the House of Representatives Respecting certain Military Orders issued by His Honor Levi Lincoln, Lieutenant Governor, and Commander in Chief of the Commonwealth of Massachusetts, with the Documents referred to in the same. The Report of the Historical Manuscripts Commission, Fortescue MSS.

RIVES, GEORGE LOCKHART, *Selections from the Correspondence of Thomas Barclay*. New York, 1894.

SHAW, ALBERT, *Jefferson's Doctrines Under New Tests*, in *Representative Phi Beta Kappa Orations*. Boston, 1915.

SMART, WILLIAM, *Economic Annals of the Nineteenth Century, I*. 2 vols. London, 1910-1917.

Special Session of Connecticut General Assembly, Hartford, February 23, 1809. (Pamphlet.)

STEINER, BERNARD C., *Life and Correspondence of James McHenry*. Cleveland, 1907.

STEPHEN, JAMES, *The Speech of James Stephen, March 6, 1809*. London, 1809. (Pamphlet.)

STORY, WM. W., *Life and Letters of Joseph Story*. 2 vols. Boston, 1851.

TAYLOR, JOHN, *Curtius, A Defence of the Measures of the Administration of Thomas Jefferson, 1804*. Washington, 1804.

THIERS, ADOLPHE, *Histoire du Consulat et de l'Empire, II*. 21 vols. Paris, 1845-1874.

TOOKE, THOMAS, *A History of Prices and of the State of Circution from 1793 to 1837*. Vol. I. 6 vols. London, 1838-1857.

TOOKE, THOMAS, *Thoughts and Details on the High and Low Prices of the Last Thirty Years*. 2 vols. in 1. London, 1823.

TRENT, WM. P., *Southern Statesmen of the Old Regime*. New York, 1897.

UPHAM, CHARLES W., *The Life of Timothy Pickering*. 4 vols. Boston, 1867-1873.

VATTEL, M. DE., *Le droit des gens, etc.* Introduction by A. de Lapradelle. Carnegie Institution, Washington, 1916.

WASHINGTON, GEORGE, *The Writings of George Washington* (Ford Edition). 14 vols. New York, 1889-1893.

MAGAZINE REFERENCES

The *Edinburgh Review.*

DANIELS, G. W., "Cotton Trade Under the Embargo," in the *American Historical Review*, Vol. XXI, No. 2.

FENWICK, CHARLES G., "The Authority of Vattel," in the *American Political Science Review*, Vol. VII.

Quarterly Review. "An account of the quantity of linen cloth exported from Ireland, from the 25th of March, 1776, to the 5th of January, 1809, inclusive."

REEVES, J. S., "The Influence of the Law of Nature upon International Law in the United States," in the *American Journal of International Law*, Vol. III.

SEARS, LOUIS MARTIN, "The Puritan and his Anglican Allegiance," in *Bibliotheca Sacra*, October, 1917.

VAN TYNE, C. H., "Influences which determined the French Government to make the Treaty with America, 1778," in *American Historical Review*, XXI, No. 3.

NEWSPAPERS, CHIEFLY FROM THE LIBRARY OF CONGRESS AND THE REUBEN T. DURETT COLLECTION AT THE UNIVERSITY OF CHICAGO

The Aurora, Philadelphia.
The American Citizen, New York.
The Balance, Hudson, N. Y.
The Baltimore Evening Post, Baltimore, Md.
The Boston Gazette, Boston, Mass.
The Connecticut Courant, Hartford, Ct.
The Charleston Courier, Charleston, S. C.
The Essex Register, Salem, Mass.
Federal Gazette and *Baltimore Daily Advertiser*, Baltimore, Md.
The Frankfort Palladium, Frankfort, Ky.
The Independent Chronicle, Boston, Mass.
Massachusetts Spy or *Worcester Gazette*, Worcester, Mass.
The National Intelligencer, Washington, D. C.
New England Palladium, Boston, Mass.
New York Evening Post, New York.
N. Y. Republican Watch Tower, New York.
The North American and *Mercantile Daily Advertiser*, Baltimore, Md.
The Public Advertiser, New York.
The Republican and *Savannah Evening Ledger*, Savannah, Ga.
The Repertory, Boston, Mass·
The Richmond Enquirer, Richmond, Va.
The Richmond Virginian, Richmond, Va.
Salem Gazette, Salem, Mass.
The Trenton True American, Trenton, New Jersey.
The United States' Gazette, Philadelphia, Pa.
The Universal Gazette, Washington, D. C.
The Washington Expositor, Washington, D. C.

INDEX

Adams, Henry, comment on New England and Virginia, 126 n.

Adams, John, expected to pursue strong foreign policy, 23; disappoints Jefferson by pro-British attitude, 23; preserves neutrality, 35; previous record on embargo, 153-154; no friend of Pickering, 154.

Adams, John Quincy, defeated for senate, 102; opponent of Pickering, 153; reasons for stand on the embargo, 154-155; proves knowledge of Orders in Council prior to embargo, 155; proposes non-intercourse, 155, seeks to influence Josiah Quincy, 156; letter to Harrison Gray Otis, 158; sees danger to morale, and war a doubtful good, 183-184; not returned to senate, 187.

Adet, P. A., report on Jefferson, 302.

Albany, State Senate condemns opposition to embargo, 198.

Albemarle, Jefferson's resolution proposing embargo, 47, 48.

Alexander I, of Russia, appeal from Jefferson, 51.

Algerine Question, Jefferson seeks solution, 14.

Amiens, Peace of, ends first phase of European War, 144.

Annapolis, Md., resolution approving of embargo, 134.

Armstrong, General John, asserts embargo is war to finish against France, 119; pessimistic views, 120; unduly optimistic, 310; in diplomatic duel with Napoleon,
315; discouraging position, 315; pessimistic on embargo, 316.

Auckland, Lord, recedes from his position, 272-273; pictures decay of British commerce, 277 and n.

Augusta, Me., papers report disturbance, 167.

Bacon, Ezekiel, influential in repealing the embargo, 140; correspondent of J. Q. Adams, 184.

Baltic, heavy trade in 1808, 283.

Baltimore, Federalist approval of possible secession in New England, 223.

Baptists, moderate attitude toward Jefferson, 180.

Baring, Alexander, denounces Orders in Council, 65.

Barnes, J., Consul at Leghorn, favors the embargo, 55.

Bayard, Senator James A., (Delaware) opposed to strengthening embargo, 209.

Bayonne Decree, pretended enforcement of embargo, 314.

Bentley, William, D. D., friendly to Jefferson, 180.

Berlin Decree, issued 1806, 144, 255; proof of operation, 261.

Biddle, Nicholas, testifies to prosperity in Philadelphia, 218.

Binney, Horace, Philadelphia lawyer, witty as to embargo, 213.

Blockade, of 1805, 144; more injurious to France than embargo, 253; partially effective, 255; of Great Britain against Europe, 300-301.